ETHICAL CHIC

Ethical Chic

The Inside Story of the Companies
We Think We Love

FRAN HAWTHORNE

Beacon Press, Boston

Beacon Press
25 Beacon Street
Boston, Massachusetts 02108-2892
www.beacon.org

Beacon Press books
are published under the auspices of
the Unitarian Universalist Association of Congregations.

16   15   14   13   8   7   6   5   4   3   2   1

This book is printed on acid-free paper that meets the uncoated paper
ANSI/NISO specifications for permanence as revised in 1992.

Text design and composition by Wilsted and Taylor Publishing Services

Library of Congress Cataloging-in-Publication Data

Hawthorne, Fran.
   Ethical chic : the inside story of the companies we think we love /
by Fran Hawthorne.
      p. cm.
   Includes bibliographical references.
   ISBN 978-0-8070-0060-1 (paperback: alk. paper)
      1. Corporations—Moral and ethical aspects—United States—Case studies.
2. Business ethics—United States—Case studies. 3. Social responsibility
of business—United States—Case studies. 4. Corporate image—United States—
Case studies. 5. Brand loyalty—United States—Case studies. I. Title.
   HD2785.H37 2012
   174.4—dc23   2011048739

To my father,
Edward Hawthorne

CONTENTS

Business may thrive on change and innovation, but too many changes sure make it hard to write a book about business. Of the six companies profiled in this book, three announced major and abrupt new developments within the last few months of my research and writing, and a fourth tossed in a small complication:

Three days before I was due to hand in the manuscript of this book to my editor, American Apparel revealed that it might file for bankruptcy.

Two months later, just as I was finishing the edit, Timberland was acquired by VF Corporation.

Two months after that, in the midst of yet another round of reviews, Apple's legendary chief executive, Steve Jobs, stepped down. And barely one month afterward, at the verge of the final edits for this book, Jobs died.

Also, I had known for months that Howard Schultz, Starbucks's chief executive, would be publishing the second volume of his autobiography a couple of weeks before my first deadline, which ultimately required a few updates in my manuscript.

So, who can guess what other surprises these companies may serve up between the day you start reading this book and the day you finish?

The Image

Company X is an ideal progressive company. Its products have dramatically challenged conventional thinking while helping people from cerebral palsy patients to schoolkids in Africa to antigovernment protestors in Iran, Tunisia, and Egypt. Its cofounder, a vegetarian, was married in a Buddhist ceremony in Yosemite National Park. Its website posts detailed information about its carbon emissions; moreover, it was the first in its industry to eliminate the most common toxic ingredients. And it has done all this while competing against one of the biggest, most hated companies on Earth. Cutting-edge, creative people wouldn't think of using anyone else's products.

Company Y, on the other hand, is a terrible company for progressives. Its nonunion employees historically labored long hours at the whim of a micromanaging chief executive who changed his mind at the last minute and made impossible demands. Overseas, it uses Chinese sweatshops so dreadful that a dozen workers have committed suicide. It has been slow on environmental issues, acting only after intense prodding by socially responsible mutual funds and a big public campaign from Greenpeace. Actually, it's hard to know anything about this company because it's so secretive that its press people don't return phone calls.

Of course, Company X and Company Y are the same company. The name: Apple Inc.

———

In this age of consumer activism, pinpoint marketing, and unlimited and immediate information, we want the impossible: products and producers that will assure us that we are fashionable, and that don't pollute, harm animals, or contain weird chemicals, that run on alternative energy, pay their workers good salaries, recycle their scraps, use natural ingredients, buy from local suppliers, donate generously to charity, donate in particular to their neighborhoods, and don't throw their weight around by lobbying. (Or maybe they should lobby for the right causes?) Why should we pay good money for something that will make us look nerdy, or that will poison the Earth? We don't think we're being overly demanding. All we're asking for are the kinds of policies we try to follow in our own daily lives, and if we can manage to recycle and avoid animal products, then certainly big companies, with all their clout, can do likewise.

Hard as it is to be so many things to so many consumers, a handful of companies and products—like Apple, Ben & Jerry's ice cream, Converse sneakers, and the grocery store chain Trader Joe's—seem to have hit that magic bull's-eye, at least for a time. Almost no matter what they do, they maintain an image of being cool, fun, and innovative and, at the same time, an equally strong image as green, politically progressive, and ethical.

As a result, their customers are fiercely loyal. At Macworld, the annual conference for users and vendors of Apple products, held in San Francisco in 2010, I met fans who had traveled at their own expense from as far away as Iowa, Illinois, and Michigan just to meet kindred souls and to ooh and ahh over the newest add-ons. And mind you, this was a gathering without the magical presence of Apple's legendary cofounder, Steve Jobs. Meanwhile, Naomi A. Gardberg, an assistant professor at the City University of New York's Zicklin School of Business, has friends who will drive thirty miles to get to Trader Joe's.

Even during the 2008–2009 downturn and the weak recovery afterward, BusinessWeek magazine noted in amazement that stressed-out, debt-ridden, mortgage-foreclosed consumers still found spare change (or unused credit lines) for Apple iPads and Starbucks lattes. They would forgo a new car, switch from brand-name to generic toiletries, and pick up shampoo at discount outlets, the magazine said in an August 2010 cover story. But Apple and Starbucks were irreplaceable.

Investors, too, are more willing to cut certain firms a little slack. "Some companies have built so much trust that shareholders are less likely to vote against management," explained Laura Berry, executive director of the Interfaith Center on Corporate Responsibility (ICCR), a New York City–based organization that represents about three hundred religious institutions and is one of the pioneers of the movement for socially responsible investing. "In some ways, if shareholders bring a resolution that says, 'We want you to report more about your environmental sustainability,' and Apple says, 'We're making our best efforts—you should just trust us and don't vote against us,' we're going to believe them."

In return, more and more business executives are recognizing that ethical-trendy shoppers are a big and growing market. While the desire to be trendy is nothing new, the other factor—what's often called corporate social responsibility, or CSR—has burgeoned more recently.

When Walmart announced plans to run its trucks more efficiently, switch to solar energy at two dozen sites, promote energy-saving compact fluorescent lightbulbs (CFL), use recyclable cardboard cartons, and maybe even install windmills in its parking lots so customers could recharge their hybrid cars, it was clear that the environmental movement, at least, had gone Main Street. *Institutional Investor*, a trade journal that goes to the upper tier of business and finance, devoted a two-part cover package in November 2010 to socially responsible investing—a *favorable* package. The fortieth anniversary of Earth Day in 2010 "has turned into a premier marketing platform for selling a variety of goods and services, like office products, Greek yogurt, and eco-dentistry," the *New York Times* reported. Even the crusty British weekly the *Economist* reluctantly succumbed, in a special issue about CSR on January 19, 2008, with the cover headline "Just Good Business." It harrumphed, "This newspaper has argued that it is often misguided, or worse. But in practice few big companies can now afford to ignore it."

Thus, consumer-oriented businesses are trying to find the words, logo, and image—and, of course, products—that will indelibly brand themselves as the Apple or Trader Joe's of their industry. Unilever, which markets the chemical-laden Knorr soup mixes, reached out to the organic crowd by acquiring Ben & Jerry's. The Clorox Company—whose chlorine bleach is despised by environmental activists for damaging sewers and aquatic life—made a dual effort: It bought the homespun cosmetics company Burt's Bees, founded by a bearded guy who lived in a converted turkey coop in Maine. Plus, it has a new line of plant-based, "green" household cleaning products that touts an endorsement from the Sierra Club. McDonald's has recast some of its outlets with chocolate-colored seats and muted beige walls to look like Starbucks. (Sort of.)

The more that businesses incorporate the image of socially responsible hipness, however, the harder it is for consumers. How can they tell whether the picture of happy cows grazing in a meadow is a marketing mirage? Did Clorox co-opt Burt's Bees? When Starbucks says it buys fair-trade coffee, what does that mean?

Investigating a firm's ethical credentials would seem to be fairly straightforward, because plenty of organizations monitor and produce rosters of "best" companies in a whole range of categories. On the environmental front, according to a directory called the Ecolabel Index, there are at least 365 seals and certifications in 214 countries. For instance, Greenpeace publishes industry-specific lists, including a "Guide to Greener Electronics" for tech manufacturers and a "Supermarket Seafood Sustainability Scorecard"; the nonprofit coalition Ceres issues awards, reports on the sustainability efforts at particular businesses, and posts a list of the eighty-plus "network companies" that have met its green criteria; and the nonprofit environmental organization Climate Counts analyzes the efforts to reduce and measure carbon emissions at the largest firms in seventeen consumer industries.

Which companies treat their employees well? *Fortune* magazine each year publishes its choice of the "100 Best Companies to Work For," ranking nominees according to their internal communication, training, safety, work-life balance, pay, benefits, nondiscrimination, camaraderie, and so on. *Working Mother* has a different set of 100 companies that focuses on working moms and criteria such as flextime, parental leave, child-care benefits, family health coverage, and adoption reimbursement. Other magazines have offered their own lists centered on their particular specialties, including *Latina Style*'s top 50 companies for Hispanic women and *Black Enterprise*'s "40 Best Companies for Diversity." An arm of the AFL-CIO posts an annual roster called "The Labor Day List: Partnerships That Work" in order "to recognize successful partnerships between employers and their employees' labor unions that are working well in the global economy," as the accompanying report puts it.

In the federal Equal Employment Opportunity Commission's archives, you might find press releases announcing lawsuits alleging racial or sex discrimination at various businesses. Homing in specifically on the treatment of lesbian, gay, bisexual, and transgender workers, the

Human Rights Campaign has a "Corporate Equality Index" that rates companies on factors like whether they have a formal nondiscrimination policy or offer domestic-partner benefits. In addition, a consumer might look at the number of women and minorities on a company's board of directors, at least for symbolic reasons, although Aaron Chatterji, an associate professor at Duke University's Fuqua School of Business, suggests that such percentages "may not reflect the way they treat people throughout the firm."

It's a little tougher to analyze working conditions at factories overseas. A lot of organizations monitor them, and activists disagree on which to trust. The Fair Labor Association? The Worker Rights Consortium? Verité? TransFair USA? Sweatshop Watch? Labour Behind the Label? Students & Scholars Against Corporate Misbehavior? The Global Union Federation? Specialized Technology Resources (better known as STR)? Regardless of the monitor, the brand-name multinational companies that contract out to those factories should have codes of conduct guaranteeing a right to collective bargaining and free association, labor experts say. Even better—but rare—would be a guarantee of a living wage, not merely that country's minimum wage (since the factory should theoretically pay the minimum anyway, with or without a code).

Still more. For ethical corporate behavior in general, there are lists from GoodGuide, *Corporate Responsibility* (or CR) magazine, Business for Social Responsibility (BSR), and Green America (which, despite the name, chooses members of its Green Business Network based on whether they are "values-driven" and "using business as a tool for social change," not greenness), to name only a few. *Consumer Reports* analyzes products' reliability, quality, repair record, price, and customer satisfaction. At People for the Ethical Treatment of Animals (PETA), the "Caring Consumer" database names businesses that do and don't test their products on animals. Concerned shoppers and investors can also check the names approved by the socially responsible mutual funds run by financial managers like the Calvert Group, Domini Social Investments, and Pax World Management Corporation. As a gauge of political leanings, the Center for Responsive Politics has detailed listings, going back more than a decade, of contributions to federal campaigns by companies and individual employees, as well as money spent on lobbying.

And I've left out dozens of others.

All these sources and rankings illustrate one big problem: ethically hip consumers are trying to follow too many—and often conflicting—

criteria. Does the company use organic ingredients? Does it test its ingredients on animals? Does it obtain its ingredients from local suppliers? What if the sole source of organic, animal-safe supplies is imported? What if the organic item looks uglier than the one made with pesticides? What if it's twice as expensive? Furthermore, are its employees unionized? Does it recycle? Does a company have to pass every "test" to be considered ethical?

Since no company can be perfect in every category, consumers who are concerned about ethical business behavior have to set priorities. As with anything in life, they compromise and juggle among the questions raised above, and many more, depending on their personal values. Each person's priorities—and favorite companies—will be different. For instance, consider the following issues:

Can a company be socially responsible if it doesn't treat its employees well?

Assuredly not. Now rephrase the question: Can a company be said to treat its workers well if it has no unions? Or if it actively fights union organizing?

With barely 6.9 percent of the US private-sector labor force represented by a union, and with both corporate and public employee unions under severe attack from Republicans in states like Indiana, Michigan, Ohio, and Wisconsin, labor officials would be pretty unrealistic to insist on a union label. Some of them hedge. Warren Pepicelli, an executive international vice president of the apparel workers' union UNITE HERE, put it this way: "I think people should be in unions. That certainly is a criterion for a company being decent. The only way workers have respect is by having their own organization." Ron Blackwell, chief economist for the AFL-CIO, is more tolerant. If the wages, benefits, and working conditions are good and management seems to listen to the workforce, not having a union could be OK, he said. He draws the line, however, "if the company is using their power as an employer to suppress people's effective rights to form unions," by tactics such as threatening to shut down sites where a union drive is under way.

Well, Trader Joe's and Starbucks offer above-average pay and benefits for their industries, even without unions. But both have been accused of using nasty tactics to fight organizing drives—a particularly egregious issue in the case of Trader Joe's, because the supermarket industry is one of the few in the private sector that still has significant union representation. As if that weren't bad enough, Starbucks has had run-ins with CSR groups about whether it cheated impoverished Ethiopian coffee farmers.

And the labor questions don't end there, since being a decent boss is not simply a matter of pay. "Wages and benefits are the first thing an employer wants to give you. It's easy and meaningless; the employer just takes the money out of something else," said Christian E. Weller, an associate professor of public policy at the University of Massachusetts's McCormack Graduate School of Policy Studies, in Boston, and a senior fellow at the Center for American Progress, a liberal think tank based in Washington, DC.

"A union is also about due process," he went on. "Who gets hired, who gets fired, who gets promoted, under what circumstances. Can you complain about things that go wrong without being fired? Also, there should be a promotion-and-review process that has nothing to do with you being friends with the manager."

Can a company be socially responsible if its products are expensive?

Almost anything manufactured or sold in nonstandard ways charges a higher price than standard stuff. The main reason is that these items typically contain hard-to-find ingredients, are made by people who get above-minimum wages, or can't enjoy the economies of scale that come from mass production. Yet by most definitions, to be socially responsible is to care about the welfare of low-income and working-class people who can't afford $5.92-per-pound grass-fed, pasture-raised, no-antibiotic, no-added-hormones ground beef.

Optimistically, Patricia H. Werhane, a senior fellow at the University of Virginia's Olsson Center for Applied Ethics, predicts that prices will drop over time as public pressure forces more companies to follow CSR practices, creating an ethical version of mass production. Even if she's right, though, cash-strapped consumers need to eat and brush their teeth now.

Another suggestion comes from Jill Kickul, director of the Stewart Satter Program in Social Entrepreneurship at New York University's Stern School of Business. "Some of these companies would say, 'We are giving back to low-income people by some of the community service we do.'" Indeed, the glowing reputations of Timberland and Tom's of Maine are built in large part on exactly that sort of community service, because the two companies let employees take time off with pay to do volunteer work. Thus, rich shoppers, by buying expensive, socially responsible products, are subsidizing socially responsible projects for the poor—an organic Robin Hood arrangement.

Maybe. Still, there's something grating and patronizing about this explanation. The poor can't use Tom's healthful toothpaste, but they should be grateful that Tom's staffers might hand them mashed potatoes at a soup kitchen?

And then, when the juggling stops and the balls come to rest, the results can be meaningless or logically impossible.

Like Shell Oil Company getting a perfect score in both 2010 and 2011 on the Human Rights Campaign's corporate-equality list.

An *oil company*, whose basic function is to encourage the wasteful consumption of limited resources, thereby increasing global levels of dangerous carbon emissions? Even worse, Shell's parent company, Royal Dutch Shell, has been accused of environmental damage, oil spills, and human rights abuses in its operations in the Niger Delta in the 1990s. When Ken Saro-Wiwa, a Nigerian author and human rights advocate, led protests against the oil operations, Shell allegedly asked Nigeria's military rulers to stifle him. Saro-Wiwa and other activists were executed, and in 2009, the oil giant paid $15.5 million to settle some of the charges.

How does the Human Rights Campaign explain celebrating this corporate criminal? "In no way do we want to condone drilling or all the horrible environmental things they may be doing," said Eric Bloem, deputy director of the group's workplace project. Nevertheless, first things first, and for the HRC, diversity issues come first. Besides, the criteria for making the equality list are apparently so lax that almost any personnel office would qualify. Out of 615 large companies the HRC analyzed for 2011, fully 337 got a perfect score, and the average, on a scale of 0 to 100, was 87.

R. J. Reynolds Tobacco Company is another giant in another hated industry. Yet there it was, number 96 on the *Fortune* "Best Companies to Work For" roster in 2002. An independent organization called the Great Place to Work Institute, founded by journalists Milton Moskowitz and Robert Levering, compiles the annual ranking, based on a fifty-seven-question survey sent to at least four hundred employees at each company that applies, plus a survey filled out by corporate management. The questions focus on working conditions, not whether the product itself is socially responsible. "Using our methodology, [RJR employees] thought it was a great workplace," Levering told me.

To find a way through this morass, some socially concerned business managers, experts, and consumers have tried to craft an overarching definition to encompass all the contradictions and possibilities. The results are mind-boggling.

Timberland, for instance, has outlined its CSR mission in a grid with "pillars" and "core values." Gordon Peterson, the company's vice president for corporate social responsibility when I interviewed him in spring 2010, spelled it out: Energy, product, workplace, and service are the four pillars; humanity, humility, integrity, and excellence are the four core values; and transparency and accountability are a kind of combined supervalue connecting all of them. (Peterson later switched out of CSR to become vice president of change management and business transformation, overseeing a reworking of the company's business systems.)

The Geneva-based International Organization for Standardization, or ISO—best known for writing technical specifications for things like fasteners and oil burners—set up committees of consumer, business, government, labor, human rights, and other advocates to craft standards for various social values, such as "sustainability criteria for bioenergy." Its 106-page "Guidance on Social Responsibility" report includes seven "core subjects": community involvement and development, consumer issues, the environment, fair operating practices, human rights, labor practices, and organizational governance. Each of these subjects is then analyzed according to subcategories, like discrimination, health and safety, pollution, corruption, and economic, social, and cultural rights.

Not surprisingly, such formal definitions are rare. The National Consumers League doesn't have one; its annual Trumpeter Award almost always goes to individuals, not companies. "It's multiple-dimensional" is the description from Michael Gusmano, a research scholar at the Hastings Center, a think tank in the exurbs north of New York City that specializes in ethical issues in health and the environment. Patricia Werhane, of the Olsson Center for Applied Ethics, doesn't think the topic can ever be defined, "because you're going to leave something out."

So, if there isn't one single form of CSR, and each person or company has to set priorities, the priority that usually wins out is the environment. In fact, when business professors, ethicists, marketing experts, and company officials are asked about social responsibility, many of them launch immediately into a discussion of green products, as though that were the only kind of CSR.

One reason for the corporate emphasis is that "conservation is a little less politically aligned. In the conservation arena, you have both Republicans and Democrats," posits Christian Weller, the labor economist at the Center for American Progress. Thus, there's less risk of alienating customers. Some activists suggest that trying to be green is easier and cheaper for managers than, say, monitoring sweatshops in China, paying higher wages, or avoiding animal testing. "It's a technical fix," said Jeff Ballinger, a veteran antisweatshop activist. "If you have to replace a certain chemical that's a reproductive toxin, you just find the scientists to give you an alternative."

Consumers, for their part, may gravitate toward eco-activism because it's been part of the public discussion much longer than issues like animal welfare or workplace diversity, dating back at least to Rachel Carson's 1962 book *Silent Spring*. Certainly, the Millennial generation has been hearing about recycling and pollution since kindergarten. It's also easier to measure carbon emissions or water pollution than workplace morale.

When consumer groups do focus on work-related issues, they seem to be a lot more concerned about sweatshops overseas than wages, health insurance, family-friendly policies, discrimination, or union membership in the United States. Nike and the Gap changed their policies after public protests charging dangerous, exploitative working conditions at foreign subcontractors. However, where's the outrage when Starbucks is cited by the National Labor Relations Board for illegally firing American union organizers?

An obvious place where ethics-balancing occurs is in investing, which has morphed from the term "socially responsible investing" to "environmental, social, and governance" investing. If ESG activists like the religious ICCR members were to insist on finding corporations that had absolutely no history of pollution, nuclear power, Pentagon contracts, labor violations, outsourcing, nonunion work, ethnically insensitive product names, *and* animal testing, *plus* no ties to tobacco, alcohol, weapons, and gambling, their cash would still be under their mattresses. "Most companies are big, publicly traded, multinational companies that do some good things and do some bad things," said Adam Kanzer, the general counsel and a managing director at Domini, one of the largest of the ESG mutual fund families. "They're too big to carry a one-blanket reputation." Moreover, these are not charities, so in addition to all the touchy-feely social criteria, firms such as Domini, like any investment manager, have to worry about not losing their clients' money.

Thus, their criteria include wiggle room. Often, the final decision comes down to percentages. Boston's Trillium Asset Management allowed 3M Company onto its approved list, even though the manufacturer sold some weapons-related products, in consideration of its good record on the environment and employment, and the fact that just a tiny portion of its revenue came from weapons. Pax World Management and the Calvert Group took some heat in the early 2000s when they opened up their funds to utilities that owned existing nuclear plants. "If a utility company is doing everything right for alternative energy—it had some wind, some solar, but happened to have a legacy nuclear plant—we wouldn't exclude that company from consideration," Paul Hilton, Calvert's director of advanced equity research, said.

Domini juggles two sets of ethical values, along with standard financial criteria. As Steven D. Lydenberg, the chief investment officer, explained, one ethical set is focused on companies' sense of civic responsibility, whether they see themselves as having a responsibility to so-called stakeholders like employees, customers, and the local community, in addition to shareholders. The second ethical overlay, he added, looks for industries and business lines that are "particularly aligned with [Domini's] global standards." Then comes the juggling. "If the business is aligned with our standards, then the stakeholder relations don't have to be as strong as if it isn't aligned," Lydenberg said. "For instance, in pharmaceuticals, we distinguish between companies that have devoted themselves to vaccines, which we believe is most aligned with our goals of preventing illness, versus companies that make patent-protected lifestyle drugs."

Most ESG funds manage to draw some red lines for their bottom lines. Certain kinds of companies and products can never be ethical. Domini, like most socially responsible funds, will not invest in a company specializing in tobacco, weapons, gambling, or nuclear power. (No R. J. Reynolds dilemmas here.)

If it seems hard to define "socially responsible," try defining "cool."

The problem, for starters, is that the quality has to be mysterious, or by definition (if there were one) it wouldn't be cool, hip, fashionable, funky, trendy, and so on. If everything is cool, then nothing is. And if everyone knows what defines cool, then everyone will be able to imitate it.

"It is a universal complaint that hip ceases being hip the moment it spreads beyond one's own circle," pointed out pop-culture journalist John Leland in his 2004 book Hip: The History. "After all, once people fractionally more clueless than yourself are in the club, what is the value of membership?" Leland has a very narrow definition of hip, essentially tying it to black music, but his basic point applies to anything that claims the mantle of fashion.

Still, there do seem to be some commonly agreed-on indicators. For instance, coolness is more likely to be found among the young. "Teenagers and young adults, who have the least stake in the old order, tend to move fluidly in the uncertainty of the new," Leland wrote. Naomi Klein, in her best seller *No Logo*, said that corporate marketers actually didn't begin to focus on the youth audience until the early 1990s, because "1992 was the first year since 1975 that the number of teenagers in America increased"—that is, the audience was big enough to be worthwhile. Once business discovered the booming wallets of the boomers' kids, there was no turning back to old fogies. "Their parents might have gone bargain-basement, but kids, it turned out, were willing to pay up to fit in."

Historically, it was the upper crust who defined "cachet," and the lower classes strove as best as they could to emulate it (or, like Jay Gatsby and Tom Ripley, pretend they were of it). The post–World War II suburban ideal was a Cadillac and a fur coat like a movie star's. In the modern version, middle-class twentysomethings straight out of college dreamed of Rolexes, Jaguars, a converted loft in SoHo, or a ski house in Vail, then went into debt buying them if they could, or settled for Chinese knock-offs if they had to. In her 1998 book *The Overspent American*, Juliet B. Schor, then a senior lecturer at Harvard University, described how the ideal has been creeping ever higher, ever further from our means, from keeping up with the neighbors to keeping up with the boss at work to desperately trying to reach the exalted ranks of *Beverly Hills, 90210*.

That assumption of upward mobility has to be rethought now, however. As former *Esquire* editor in chief Lee Eisenberg wrote in his 2009 book *Shoptimism*: "Beginning in the sixties, it became apparent that tastes no longer just trickled *down* [emphasis in original], they trickled every which way. They trickled in from bohemians and hippie outer fringes, up from the ghetto and the grunge." Blue jeans began as workingman's garb, and when that was no longer grungy enough, they had to be torn and (intentionally) faded. "By the 1990s, inner-city tastes had become an important driver of middle-class fashion," Schor noted. Timberland certainly discovered that in the early 1990s when its traditional blue-collar boots suddenly became popular with the hip-hop crowd, and that popularity propelled the brand out into the broader fashion market.

And once you think you've defined a hip trend, you're too late. Trends come and go too fast to name. "After about a decade of looking at [a product], people say 'Ugh,'" said Arthur Caplan, chair of the Department of Medical Ethics at the University of Pennsylvania. "Familiarity breeds boredom." Starbucks, launched in its modern version in 1987, breached the ten-year line long ago, he said. Apple, founded in 1976, has managed to defy the time limit so far—partly by constantly inventing new product categories, partly because it almost went out of business in the mid-1990s and thus could be said to have restarted the countdown around the turn of the millennium, and partly because anything Steve Jobs ever did is inherently hip.

Robert Passikoff, founder and president of Brand Keys, a New York City–based consulting firm specializing in brand loyalty, said the timeline has actually speeded up in recent years. If a company brought to market something innovative in the 1960s or 1970s, he said, "it would take a year for rivals to copy you. As technology improved, rivals could copy you within six months, so all the products became the same."

Yet, even while it's impossible to categorize, in-ness is the essence of selling and, therefore, of corporate survival. The short cut to achieving this, whether during a thirty-second commercial or on a drive-by billboard or in a one-word Web banner, is by creating a brand. That doesn't mean merely a corporate logo or slogan. After all, ExxonMobil Corporation and McDonald's have recognizable logos, and no one would call them trendy. A true brand is an instant identity card, signage that separates the members from the outsiders. A community.

Unlike hip, the word community has lots of definitions. Passikoff: "It's people who feel an emotional bond to the product." Klein: "The products that will flourish in the future will be the ones presented not as 'commodities' but as concepts: the brand as experience, as lifestyle." Academics Dan Ariely (a professor of behavior economics at Duke University) and Michael I. Norton (an associate professor of business administration at Harvard Business School), in a paper in the 2009 Annual Review of Psychology: It's a way "to signal to ourselves and others our beliefs, attitudes, and social identities," which they label "conceptual consumption." New York Times Magazine consumer columnist Rob Walker, in his book Buying In, gives brand seekers a bit more power, arguing that manufacturers can no longer manipulate popularity the way they once did. A "brand that catches on in the marketplace does so," he claimed, "because of us: because enough of us decided that it had value or meaning and chose to participate."

Originally, especially when fashion meant emulating the wealthy, brands were affixed only to a few elite categories, like cars, clothes, and whiskey. Now, almost anything is branded—kitchen blenders, sunglasses, sneakers, baby strollers, and, the granddaddy of them all, coffee.

But wait—we're not done delineating yet. If there are ordinary corporate brands, like ExxonMobil, and then an inner circle of cool brands, like Starbucks, there is yet an even-more-inner circle of superelite cool brands. Consultants Matthew W. Ragas and Bolivar J. Bueno call them "cult brands"; Klein tags them "attitude brands." They might be the most expensive in their category, the ones used by big-name celebrities, the ones handmade in limited quantities, or the ones with the newest technology, but if so, those are all secondary traits. More important, superelite brands are trendy yet have stood the test of a certain amount of time. Their users may span a few generations, as long as they include the young. And these users build networks. They buy all the newest add-ons. They love these brands passionately. As Ragas and Bueno put it, in their book *The Power of Cult Branding*, these brands somehow evoke a community of "daring and determination" whose fans are so devoted that they will happily proselytize the unconverted—except not too many unconverted, since then of course the brand would lose its exclusivity.

All this may seem a lot to require of one pair of boots, one cup of coffee, or one company. Is it possible for a product to be both trendy and socially responsible? To be trusted and also loved? Yes, a few companies like Apple and Trader Joe's seem to have earned that double halo, but are they the rare exceptions?

This book set out to analyze six candidates, although they're hardly the sole companies in the world that might fit the dual definition. For that matter, the lessons here could be useful to any business. The driving idea is to understand how these privileged companies operate, what customers and activists say about them, why they are viewed as ethical and cool, what they do to try to achieve those images—and whether, in the end, they deserve their reputations.

To pull together a workable collection of names, I started writing down just about every company I could think of that could possibly claim both of the defining characteristics. I pored through notes from my four previous books and from three decades of reporting. I queried consumer, labor, environmental, human rights, and animal-welfare activists I had interviewed before, along with experts in business and ethics, including Steven Lydenberg, of Domini; Karen Ferguson, of the Pension Rights Center; Christian Weller, of the Center for American Progress; and long-time consumer advocate Carol Tucker Foreman. Then I overlaid those nominations against many of the "best" lists mentioned above. A company didn't have to make every ranking; indeed, I never found one that did. Nor did getting a negative vote—or a few—eliminate a company.

Although I tried to set logical ground rules, it had to be an idiosyncratic and subjective process. How else can something as subjective as image be measured? If trendiness is impossible to pin down, how could I grade it?

For instance, I knew instinctively that there was no way a big pharmaceutical, oil, or auto company could ever be accepted; I would be laughed out of bookstores if I suggested that they were either socially responsible or cool. However, small biotechs were possible, depending on the kind of drugs they were researching. One person suggested Zipcar, which rents cars by the hour, on the theory that this system encourages people to consolidate errands and thus drive less, even if its profits are based on carbon-spewing cars.

Coors Brewing Company? "Coors makes it high on almost any socially-responsible-investment list, since they push for environmentally friendly policies," Christian Weller said. "At the same time, they are staunchly antilabor." Unions boycotted the brewer for a decade in the 1970s and 1980s, and an arm of the AFL-CIO still urges customers to shun the beer. Moreover, Peter H. Coors, chairman of the parent company and a scion of the founding family, had run for the Republican nomination for US Senate from Colorado.

Newman's Own? You can't get much more socially responsible than a company that donates all its profits to charity. But is it a "real" company if it does that?

There's always a lot of back-and-forth on Whole Foods. Certainly, it has a hip image and lots of organic and humanely raised food. In fact, Whole Foods created the mass market for organic food almost single-handedly. But it's expensive and antiunion. Arthur Caplan, the University of Pennsylvania ethicist, offered Wegmans Food Markets instead, arguing that it sells organic food at more reasonable prices and buys from local growers. He also praised UPS, which I have to confess I'd never considered trendy (or environmentally sustainable, considering that the entire business relies on driving). Caplan said the company uses propane gas to "green up their delivery."

From Richard Honack, a marketing professor at Northwestern University's Kellogg School of Management, came JetBlue Airways (for its flextime policies and hip image) and the small restaurant chain Panera Bread ("a comer," with its antibiotic-free chicken salads and a reputation as "a nice place to work").

Even Walmart got a surprising number of nominations. The City University of New York's Naomi Gardberg was one of several eco-advocates who pointed to its efforts to reduce energy use, with actions like promoting compact fluorescent lightbulbs and installing solar panels. Thanks to its reviled size, every ecological step Walmart takes reverberates across the global supply chain. However, what about all the lawsuits alleging sex discrimination and forced overtime, and the price-cutting that drives neighborhood stores out of business?

I'm not sure why so many people brought up Patagonia, North Face, REI, and L. L. Bean, except that maybe they assume that any business selling outdoor gear must be green.

In addition to those conceptual criteria, I had practical considerations. While gigantic multinational conglomerates were shunned almost automatically on the assumption that they are taking over the world, the nominees had to be big enough that people would have heard of them and be interested in what they're really like. I also tried to find companies from a variety of industries, in hopes of showing that corporate virtue isn't limited to just a few sectors of the business world. They had to be based in the United States so that I could feasibly visit their headquarters. (Sorry, Ikea and Ecover.) Similarly, I preferred publicly traded companies, which tend to provide information more readily, although I might let in one or two private firms.

And I looked for a story. Each example should illustrate at least one different and challenging facet of the dual reputations. Did Tom's of Maine and Ben & Jerry's sell their souls when they were bought by Colgate-Palmolive Company and Unilever, respectively? Does American Apparel push sexy hipness into sexual harassment? Did Starbucks get too big to be cool?

After a few weeks of name collecting, my list had nearly two dozen serious contenders: American Apparel, Apple, Ball Corporation, Ben & Jerry's, Burt's Bees, Chipotle Mexican Grill, Costco, Dell, Google, Herman Miller, In-N-Out Burger, Kiss My Face, Newman's Own, Nike, Patagonia, Seventh Generation, Starbucks, Stonyfield Farm, Symantec, Timberland, Tom's of Maine, Trader Joe's, and Whole Foods.

In an attempt to put some scientific order on this undertaking, I made a very careful chart. One checkmark for each positive recommendation, one minus sign for each negative. I tallied up the votes, then massaged the tally, based on the need for diversity plus gut instinct.

Kiss My Face, Burt's Bees, and Tom's of Maine were all too similar—kumbaya-Woodstock-hippie-organic little companies in the personal-care business. Kiss My Face had the disadvantage of being privately held. Tom's and Burt's had the same "story" of being bought by big conglomerates. Choose one.

Then, if I took one of those, should I dump Stonyfield and Seventh Generation, which are also kumbaya-Woodstock-hippie-organic little companies but in different lines of business?

For similar reasons, I couldn't have Whole Foods plus Trader Joe's, or Apple and Dell. Too similar.

Not even Apple plus Google. That was a tough call. They're really not alike at all, but with the entire business world to look at, I couldn't justify two tech companies.

And forget Ben & Jerry's and Whole Foods. They've been written about a zillion times.

By contrast, who ever heard of Ball Corporation? What does it do, anyway?

My editors and I conferred further.

Chipotle was too obscure. Costco was too frumpy. Nike still didn't pass the laugh test, even though there were intriguing arguments that it had vastly improved practices in its foreign sweatshops, and Greenpeace claimed it was actually a leader in protecting the Amazon rain forest.

That left around ten names, still too much for one book. We culled it to a manageable six: American Apparel, Apple, Starbucks, Timberland, Tom's of Maine, and Trader Joe's. As backups, I added Google and Seventh Generation, the maker of environmentally conscious household goods like paper towels and laundry detergent.

There were so many admirable ones left out. I could just as reasonably have had a list consisting of Ben & Jerry's, Google, Kiss My Face, Patagonia, Starbucks, and Whole Foods. (I still have lingering regrets over omitting those first two.)

Of course, compiling the roster wasn't the end of the investigation. Although these candidates had made the first cut, I now had to delve into the reality behind the labels, lists, and marketing. And I didn't want to look only at the usual Big Issues, like energy efficiency, recycling, hiring practices, animal treatment, and so on. I would also bring in topics that don't come up in the typical CSR questionnaire: Are the products priced beyond the reach of working-class consumers? Is the company active in political causes? Does it provide real information beyond advertising hype? Does it connect with the wider community, even with people who may not purchase its stuff? Do customers feel comfortable using the products, asking for help, and hanging out in the stores? To do that, not only would I interview the standard universe of sources, I would also go shopping.

Following those informal guidelines, the next six chapters will analyze the companies in depth, one per chapter, to reach a verdict on each: Do they deserve their haloes?

CHAPTER 1

Tom's of Maine

Woodstock Toothpaste

IT WAS MORE THAN an hour into our conversation—sitting in the eighteenth-century brick-and-wood building in downtown Kennebunk, Maine, that he'd salvaged and converted into offices—before Tom Chappell finally laughed. That came when I quoted a few portions from his 1993 book *The Soul of a Business*, in which he emphatically explained why he would never, ever, ever sell his beloved little natural-toothpaste company Tom's of Maine to a bigger company, and how he scorned the buyout offers that periodically made their way to Kennebunk.

For instance: "Family control gives us the chance to be a new model of a successful business, an inspiration to other corporations who also want to change the face of American business." And: "I wondered what life—and business—would be like if Tom's of Maine were under the tutelage of a large American corporation. . . . What if I asked my corporate parent to let me create a position like vice president of community life and to hire a woman who had no experience in corporate life, but a master's of divinity degree? What if I explained to my new bosses that one of the tasks of the department of community life was to give away $150,000 to community groups?"

What changed? I queried.

"You learn more about yourself—the journey of thirty-six years,"

Chappell replied, after he laughed. (He also demanded to know why I hadn't read his other book, *Managing Upside Down*.)

But he stumbled over the next few sentences, and then he became defensive as I pushed further, asking again in different ways the question that loyal Tom's of Maine customers are asking themselves, and would ask Chappell and his wife, Kate, if they could: *Why did you sell out to Colgate-Palmolive?*

Companies buy and sell each other all the time. In 1996, there were sixteen major pharmaceutical manufacturers; by 2010, half of those were gone as independent entities. Where are Northwest Airlines, America West, Manufacturers Hanover, Washington Mutual, Bethlehem Steel, and LTV? Small firms are especially prone to being acquired. In the global marketplace, they need the resources of a larger parent. And sometimes the founders want to cash out and retire rich.

What made the 2006 sale of Tom's to Colgate different was that Tom's wasn't supposed to be just any company. A mythology had developed around the place during its thirty-six years of independence somewhere up in Maine, whether factual or not: It used natural ingredients. It was founded by two hippies. It donated all its profits to charity. Everything was recycled. Working there was like belonging to a commune in the woods, although now and then the happy commune members presumably took time out from singing "Kumbaya" to make a few tubes of toothpaste.

Carol Holding, who runs a brand-strategies consulting firm, Holding Associates, in Seattle, considers Tom's one of only five brands—in addition to Ben & Jerry's, the yogurt maker Stonyfield Farm, the Body Shop, and Green Mountain Coffee Roasters—"that have that fabulous reputation of being a mission-led brand. Tom's defines the user as someone who is hip, who is a better parent, who cares about the world." In her 1998 book *Green Marketing*, consultant Jacquelyn A. Ottman listed just Tom's and outdoor-gear retailer Patagonia as "Two Companies That Do Everything Right." Citing the working conditions, philanthropy, natural ingredients, recycled and recyclable packaging, and other factors, she wrote, "Tom's of Maine is living proof that it is in fact possible to integrate personal values with managing for all traditional goals of business—making money, expanding market share, increasing profits, and building customer loyalty." Dan Shannon, director of youth outreach and campaigns at People for the Ethical Treatment of Animals (PETA) until April 2011, gushed that "Tom's is one of our favorite companies."

The myth has some truth, especially the all-natural and green part. Start inside the tube (since toothpaste constitutes 85 to 90 percent of the product line; the rest consists of dental floss, mouthwash, deodorant, and soap). According to the company, the items contain no animal-based ingredients, no ingredients tested on animals, and no artificial colors, flavors, fragrances, or preservatives. There are none of those strangely named chemicals found in other toothpaste brands that sound like they belong in lighter fluid—no tetrasodium pyrophosphate, sodium hydroxide, propylene glycol, PVM/MA copolymer, or carbomer 965. Instead, here's a partial listing from Tom's peppermint label: glycerin, water, organic *Aloe barbadensis* leaf juice, carrageenan (a seaweed extract that's a common vegetarian food additive), glycyrrhizic acid (derived from licorice root), and "natural flavor." (We'll get to that natural-flavor part a little later.) In addition, the toothpastes and most of the other goods are certified kosher and halal.

The scents of mint and apricot wafted through the headquarters factory, a short drive from Tom and Kate's office, on the day I visited, and just outside the front door mint, sage, thyme, and fennel grow in a small area labeled "Kate's Herb Garden."

Actually, that's another myth: The herbs used in Tom's products come from professional suppliers, not this garden. Nevertheless, plenty of green procedures are real. In his book, Chappell described eco-practices dating back to the early days, such as installing water-saving nozzles on the hoses that clean the equipment and packing the roll-on deodorant in glass rather than plastic, even though glass was more expensive. When recyclers said Tom's didn't generate enough paper to meet the minimum required for a pickup, the company pooled with other groups.

More modern efforts include motion-sensor lighting, vegetable-based inks, deodorant sticks made of recyclable plastic (replacing the troublesome glass), and recycling of almost every sort of material imaginable, including the backings of labels and shrink wrap. Through these and other steps, the company claims to save 250,000 kilowatt-hours per year of electricity, six thousand trees, and 2.5 million gallons of water, and to cut its garbage pickups in half. The restrooms have toilet paper made from unbleached, recycled paper.

Tom's boast that it buys wind-energy credits for all its energy consumption must be taken with some grains of (natural) salt. This is not the same as actually getting all its energy from wind. It simply means that Tom's is buying credits equal to all the power it gets from gas, oil, or other conventional sources, and the cash value of these credits is financing a wind farm so it will produce that same amount of power in a lower-emitting, renewable method. Offsets are controversial, because green activists question whether they simply shift money and emissions from the right hand to the left. Are offset buyers paying to plant trees or to set up wind farms that would have been planted or established anyway? (Of all the most common types of offsets, tree planting tends to be particularly distrusted, since it can take decades for those trees to grow big enough to absorb the carbon they're supposedly offsetting.)

Unfortunately, being natural can conflict with other important attributes, like product performance, cost controls, or customer appeal. "Nature doesn't always give you the same flexibility that a synthetic does," Tom Chappell pointed out. "You can't get long-lasting flavor or cool flavor." So, what gives? "You sacrifice the flavor," Tom said promptly. "You don't sacrifice your morality."

Or you become creative and change the assumptions. "You create a product that has a different taste," Kate said. For instance, Tom's at one point was trying to use ingredients like vitamin E and rosemary extract instead of the standard chemical antioxidants in its bar soap. So far, so good. When the company tried to limit the amount of packaging by ditching the usual cellophane wrapping, however, it turned out that the cellophane was necessary, even within a cardboard box, "to preserve the fragrance and freshness," Kate said. After a lot of searching, the company devised a wrapping made of natural, biodegradable cellulose.

Some things can't be finessed. Most famously, Tom's of Maine's promise to avoid testing on animals or using animal-derived products bumped up against another highly valued credential, the American Dental Association's seal of acceptance. Just as the federal Food and Drug Administration requires drugs to be tested on animals before humans take the risk, the ADA historically wanted dental products animal-tested before it would certify them. Although it's not illegal to market noncertified toothpaste (unlike the case with medicine), it can really hurt sales if customers think the product isn't safe. For years, Tom's haggled with the ADA and even explored an alternative certification. It also tried to substitute human tests on volunteers—including Kate. (Her teeth looked OK when I met her.)

The ADA seal was finally granted for the original toothpaste formula in 1995, which the company claims is the first for a toothpaste without animal testing. Eight other labels of Tom's toothpaste, mouthwash, and floss—though not the entire product line—have since been added. "They pushed the envelope on that issue," said Michael Markarian, chief operating officer of the Humane Society.

Yes, the primary factory really is located in a small town in Maine, albeit not in the middle of a forest. And while it's not a commune, the working conditions are definitely more easygoing, the benefits more generous, and the whole spirit more community minded than at almost any other company on earth. Tom's was a pioneer in granting parental leave to mothers and fathers, a decade before the federal Family and Medical Leave Act of 1993. There's a fitness center on site with a personal trainer who leads the production crew in stretch breaks every day, plus subsidized yoga classes and massages. Employees don't punch a time clock; they merely move a piece on a magnetic sign-in board to indicate whether they're in the building, and that's for safety reasons in case of fire, not for wage monitoring, my tour guide said. The production room itself is high ceilinged and brightly lit. On the afternoon I visited, when production was halted to check the alignment of the shrink wrap on a six-pack of deodorant, the half dozen workers didn't seem particularly anxious.

Probably the most outstanding aspect of working at Tom's is the community service. The company donates 10 percent of pretax profits to charitable causes, and employees can get full pay for spending 5 percent of their work time—twelve days a year—on volunteer activities. According to Tom Chappell, the corporate part began with a $25,000 donation to the town of Kennebunk for curbside recycling bins. (That wasn't a totally unselfish gesture, since it spurred the town to establish a recycling program, which ultimately benefited the company.) The $25,000 morphed into a policy of corporate "tithing," as Tom put it in his book, to support projects in education, the arts and humanities, environmental research and protection, and humanitarian needs, initially at 5 percent of profits and inching up to the current level.

The one glaring workplace omission is that the company is not unionized. That was also one of the few topics that got Tom angry. "There was no union that could have negotiated for benefits more generous than the ones we had," he asserted, mentioning the four weeks of paid parental leave, bonuses, flextime, and the time off for volunteering. One receptionist's husband was a labor organizer, Tom went on, and rather than try to organize the workers, whenever that man came to a Tom's company picnic, "he would commend us for what we were doing, and he would chuckle."

Tom and Kate seem to feel that a union wasn't necessary in an ostensibly egalitarian workplace where corporate values were discussed regularly in group meetings, time cards were unknown, and Tom himself might stop to chat with a secretary about the cost of their respective children's tuition. "I could see the boss-secretary relationship melt into an understanding between two parents," he wrote in *The Soul of a Business*.

"I don't think that the employees felt that they needed an advocate for them against management," Kate added in our interview. "We did as much as we could for them. The company was more like a web of relationships than a hierarchy." Maybe. But Tom Chappell's tuition payments were chiefly for private boarding school—a luxury available to the CEO and owner of a business—while the secretary's payments were for college, something the middle class is more likely to need.

And customers apparently buy the image, along with the toothpaste, floss, and deodorant. Most people I interviewed initially purchased Tom's products for the natural ingredients or the little-guy reputation, then gradually grew accustomed to the taste. Typically, Kate Bieger, a thirty-four-year-old New York City psychologist, said a friend had recommended the brand a few years ago, so she tried it because "I thought it would have fewer chemicals." She went on, "I didn't like it at first. It wasn't sweet enough." Today, she brushes with Tom's peppermint, her three-year-old son uses the kids' strawberry, and "now I can't stand the sugary taste of Colgate, the toothpaste I grew up with." (The irony of a Tom's user trashing the new corporate owner is, of course, tied up in the whole controversy.)

No one cited price as an ethical issue, which would actually be an argument *against* the brand. Tom's products, like most CSR goods, are more expensive than standard ones. The pricing has to cover ethical "frills" such as the time and resources to find the natural cellulose soap wrapper and the salaries paid to employees while they volunteer at animal shelters instead of churning out toothpaste. At one chain drugstore, a 5.5-ounce tube of Tom's was $5.59, while slightly larger tubes of Colgate, Crest, and Arm & Hammer cost at least $1.20 less. "People will pay for value," Tom argued. "Our customer is not buying a toothpaste. They're buying a toothpaste that meets their set of values."

Of course, even ethical products have to work. The Chappells said that when they ran surveys, respondents' first concerns were always how well the toothpaste cleaned their teeth and whether it made their breath smell fresh. Still, ethical factors like natural ingredients, lack of artificial dyes and sweeteners, recycled packaging, and no animal testing—rather than price or taste—came next, buttressing Tom's claim.

Effectiveness appears to be a particular issue with the deodorant. One twenty-nine-year-old art-gallery administrator I spoke to said he would like to use Tom's deodorant for the natural ingredients, especially the lack of aluminum. Unfortunately, he estimated, it's 25 percent less effective at eliminating odors than standard brands. His compromise: "I use it on the weekends when it doesn't matter as much, when I'm not at work." This is a problem that goes back at least twenty years, when the company had to recall a reformulated, more natural honeysuckle deodorant after angry customers complained that it didn't last as long as the predecessor, a petroleum-based version. Indeed, ineffectiveness is a common criticism of natural laundry detergents and cleansers, too.

Toothpaste may not seem like the kind of product that could be considered trendy, but using a brand famous for all those socially responsible virtues can be a quick and easy way for the purchaser to define himself or herself, as Carol Holding said. When a new girlfriend spends the night in your apartment for the first time, the toothpaste on your bathroom sink sends as much of a message as the brand of coffee in your kitchen and the contents of your refrigerator. If you want to prove your greenness, it's a lot simpler to buy a tube of Tom's than to clean up mountain trails and cheaper than a donation to the Sierra Club. Kate recalled that in the earliest days, when the name was barely known outside of health food stores, "musicians, artists, people who were the thinkers, creative types, bought it. It was very hip. The toothpaste for iconoclasts." Although the label is no longer quite so iconoclastic, Kate—who is a painter and printmaker—said it's still the one she sees in the dorms at art-school workshops.

There are competing natural brands, and some Tom's users do switch around. Others are loyal to particular Tom's flavors. And some stick with it out of convenience, finding it more widely available. That's a key point, because it gets to the heart of why Tom and Kate sold the company.

To gauge whether Tom's of Maine can maintain its personality and values without the namesake who created it, a key question is how important that namesake has been to the ongoing enterprise. Was the company really "Tom's," or was that merely a label?

Tom Chappell was (by his own description in his book) "the hottest young salesman" in what was then Aetna Casualty and Life Insurance Inc.'s Philadelphia office in 1968 when he got fed up with the hat-wearing conformity and tedium of office work and decided that "I had better find a career where I had a little more room for self-expression." His heart yearned for the great outdoors of western Massachusetts, where he grew up, and Maine, where he spent childhood vacations. In a step toward those goals, he moved to southern Maine to join his father's business manufacturing industrial detergents.

A skeptic might wonder how much self-expression there is in detergent, but Tom apparently found it by designing a nonpolluting cleaning agent. That led to environmentally conscious laundry detergent, shampoo, and body lotion. Interestingly, the toothpaste didn't come along until 1975.

From the beginning, it was *Tom's of Maine*, not *Tom and Kate's*. This was another topic that annoyed Tom. "Everybody asks that question," he growled. "Gloria Steinem asked that. We weren't thinking about the rights of women, necessarily. We were just a young couple starting out." By the accounts of both Chappells, the enterprise was Tom's baby. Kate was working as a paralegal plus teaching art and reading at their children's school, "because we really needed two sources of income." By the time she got more involved in the toothpaste business, the brand had been established and it was too late to change.

Whatever the name, it was in any case a personalized outfit. Even the packaging had a little note to "Dear friends," signed by "Kate and Tom," encouraging customers to write to them.

Sure, most entrepreneurs are directly and intimately involved in getting their new firms off the ground. For months or even years, they and their families may be the entire staff; they might sleep literally above the store. They have a hand in everything from designing the products to shipping the orders to making change (or taking debit cards) at the cash register. Tom and Kate's involvement, though, went beyond strategic business decisions and day-to-day operations to exactly what he talked about in his book—the soul.

In 1987, feeling stuck in a rut, fearing that his little antiestablishment venture had become too businesslike, Tom enrolled part-time in Harvard Divinity School. He wasn't aiming to become an ordained clergyman but rather was "on a search for meaning. . . . to recapture what had inspired me to start the business in the first place." Four years later, he returned full-time to his creation, brimming with renewed fervor and a clearer vision of how to elucidate the values he wanted the firm to share. As he wrote, "I persuaded my board of directors and my managers to make it our company's main 'mission' to seek financial success while behaving in a socially responsible and environmentally sensitive way. . . . I began to think about how I could transform Tom's of Maine into a company that could live its values—my values [emphasis in the original]." Out of Tom Chappell's personal transformation came a nine-part corporate mission statement, along with the philanthropic donations, the community service, a push for creative thinking, and lots of companywide meetings where people sat in circles. More than ever, toothpaste making was a manifestation of Tom Chappell's beliefs.

So, no wonder Tom insisted for so many years that, as he wrote in his book, "although our corporate suitors all assured us that they would not want to change Tom's of Maine, my response has been the same: My family will continue to control the company."

And then, in 2006, he sold.

Why did you sell out to Colgate-Palmolive?

The Chappells have given two chief reasons for their decision—lack of obvious heirs and lack of marketing clout.

By 2006, Tom and Kate were in their sixties and looking at those issues of mortality that divinity school may stir up. "I was genuinely tired," Tom said flatly. Kate sought to spend more time on her art. Every fifteen to eighteen months for the past few years, the Chappells and their five adult children had been holding family meetings with a psychologist to discuss issues like "how, as parents, we can empower our kids, and what do we need to know about being in business together," Tom explained. Now, it was time to discuss the future of the company. The parents wanted out, but who would take over?

Although all the offspring had at one time or another worked there, only the youngest, Luke, then age twenty-three, was interested in running the business. "He would have required a ten-year development," Kate said. And she and Tom didn't wish to wait ten years.

"We didn't necessarily want to saddle our children with the burden of carrying on the company," Kate added. By selling, "it released them. That seems to be more fulfilling ultimately than just maintaining a business your parents started."

Kate admitted that Luke was disappointed. However, by the time I

talked with the Chappells, four years after their decision, they said that
Luke had his own company in Northern California, Luke's Local, selling locally grown, minimally packaged, healthy—of course!—prepared
food to commuters.

The other motivation involved commercial strategy. Back in 1993,
when Tom wrote *The Soul of a Business*, annual sales were almost $20 mil-
lion, his goal was $100 million, and in some pages he confessed that he
wasn't sure the company could get there on its own. Thirteen years on,
with sales still below $50 million, Tom said—and here's where he began
to stumble in his answer—he was asking himself questions about "the
role that the company needs. 'Do you have the skills to perform for the
company?' I didn't think I was the right leader to take the company to $100
million in sales. I'm an entrepreneur. I don't rely on undue analytical research. When you are making decisions on a larger and larger scale, they
need to be increasingly grounded in a complex level of objective data."

The industry was changing in contradictory ways that hurt small fry
like Tom's. Mom-and-pop grocery stores were disappearing, even as dozens of new toothpastes were invented each year. That meant too much
product for too few outlets. To get onto the shelves of the big stores that
remained, Tom's of Maine needed more marketing muscle. "Unfortunately," Tom said, "toothpaste is dominated by a handful of retailers. If
you want to be a mainstream player, you can't do it without those stores."

With the strategic decision made, all that really remained were the
details of how to cede control. Since the business was too small to raise
sufficient capital by publicly selling stock, the best route was to find an
acquirer with money and experience in the consumer market. Tom emphasized that "we didn't just put the company up for sale" to the highest
bidder; that wouldn't have allowed enough personal involvement in the
selection. Rather, "we were researching the companies that best fit Tom's
of Maine," Kate said. The couple came up with a list of twelve potential
"strategic partners," narrowed that down to five, met with officials from
those candidates, and finally pared the list to three. They won't reveal the
two non-Colgate finalists, except to say that they were, in Tom's words,
"global brands in consumer goods and personal care." He added that one
of those two eliminated itself, fearing that it would destroy the intrinsic
Tom's of Maine values.

Tom and Kate said they spent a lot of time with Colgate managers to
see how they made their decisions and to gauge the kinds of questions
the managers, in turn, were asking. "Their stated values are caring, com-

mitment, continuous improvement," Kate said. "It's been around two hundred years. You don't hear a lot about it, because it doesn't blow its own horn." She praised Colgate for doing "a tremendous job in reducing waste," while Tom cited its frequent appearances on "Best Companies to Work For" lists. (More on that in a minute.) Finally, the deal was sealed, for $100 million.

Tom insisted that he had no regrets. "We made an incredibly good decision," he declared. "They don't want to do anything that would harm the brand. They are committed to natural."

It's important to remember, however, that he and Kate retain 16 percent ownership of the namesake Colgate subsidiary. If he trash-talks Colgate, its stock—and thus a portion of his personal wealth—will drop. There may be a touch of ego at stake, as well. Is he going to criticize his own business decision? Maybe in ten years he could say that the new Tom's management screwed up, but not yet.

If it really needed to sell out, Tom's of Maine could have done worse. While Colgate isn't as sterling as Tom's in terms of environmental sustainability, animal testing, natural ingredients, or working conditions—and what company is?—it scores moderately well in most indexes and wins solid, if not enthusiastic, praise.

In the rankings of Climate Counts and Ceres—the latter issued a December 2008 report, "Corporate Governance and Climate Change"—Colgate came in second out of six in the category of household and personal-goods products, trailing L'Oréal both times. With Climate Counts, Colgate scored best in measuring its carbon impact and lagged in actually reducing its emissions and in supporting public policy. Meanwhile, it notched a not-bad number 39 on *BusinessWeek* magazine's first annual roster of the five hundred "Greenest Big Companies in America" in 2009, but the purchase of Tom's was one of the three reasons cited, which is somewhat of a circular defense.

Wood Turner, the first executive director of Climate Counts, said Colgate had improved markedly, albeit in a category with a "somewhat low bar." He added, "We're seeing very little policy leadership in this sector, no American companies that have stepped forward and said, 'We support mandatory caps on emissions.'"

How about all those workplace rankings Tom Chappell mentioned? *Working Mother* magazine apparently adores Colgate; the company has made this list every year from 2002 through 2009. The magazine singled out a new mentoring initiative in 2008 plus admirable policies on flex-time, telecommuting, health benefits for part-timers, emergency child-care help, and paid extra maternity leave. And on the Human Rights Campaign's "Corporate Equality Index," which analyzes companies' gay-friendly policies—and which is one of the easiest graders around—Colgate corrected some small deficiencies to attain a perfect score in 2011. Its reputation is less glowing at *Fortune*, where it has qualified for the bellwether list of best companies in the United States only in 2003 and (barely squeezing in at number 100) 2010.

Judged by a much broader set of over three hundred data points in areas such as the environment, employee relations, human rights, philanthropy, governance, and finance, Colgate was an impressive number 18 on *Corporate Responsibility* magazine's 2010 list of the "100 Best Corporate Citizens." That was a big improvement over the prior year, when it dawdled in seventy-third place.

Overall, Colgate's social-responsibility efforts have been good enough to pass the screens of environmental, social, and governance (ESG) investment funds like Domini Social Investments and Trillium Asset Management. Steven D. Lydenberg, the chief investment officer of Domini (which held a little more than $4 million in Colgate stock, or about 0.6 percent of the total portfolio, at the time we talked), praised Colgate for its openness in making detailed information about work-place safety, diversity, emissions, violation notices, and energy and water usage available on its website. He thought that the proportions of women and minorities in management—slightly over one-third and one-fourth, respectively—were "very strong" and that energy use per product, water use, and carbon emissions were all on the right track, going steadily down. (The ESG funds never had occasion to evaluate Tom's on its own, since it wasn't publicly traded.)

None of this praise, however, can turn Colgate-Palmolive into Tom's of Maine. It still puts PVM/MA copolymer, sodium lauryl sulfate, propylene glycol, and other weird-sounding stuff in its toothpaste—precisely the kinds of chemicals that Tom's brags that its products don't contain. Indeed, Tom's has singled out one of those Colgate ingredients, sodium lauryl sulfate, or SLS, for special concern. The packaging of certain Tom's flavors notes that "for some consumers [SLS] may cause irritation in the mouth. Our breakthrough formula uses the gentle ingredient glycyrrhizin (derived from licorice root) for natural low foaming." Even worse, the FDA and the Environmental Protection Agency are investigating another ingredient, triclosan, an antibacterial agent used in Colgate's super-strong "total" formulation—as well as in many manufacturers' liquid soap, scouring pads, toilet cleaners, kitchen cutting boards, and other items that don't normally go in people's mouths. "In 2006 it was found to act as a hormone disrupter in the North American bullfrog and must now be clearly labeled as an ingredient," warns the book *A Good Life: The Guide to Ethical Living*. In fairness, most of the focus has been on triclosan's use in liquid soap, but if it's not safe enough for the outside of the body, it hardly seems safe inside.

When I asked Tom Chappell about the parent company's chemicals, he simply said, "They have reasons why they use them. They also have reasons why they want to keep us the way we are."

Weird ingredients may not even be the worst of Colgate's sins. *The Rough Guide to Shopping with a Conscience*, an ethical guide published in 2007, stated that "when it comes to cosmetics, toiletries, and perfumes, the major worry for most consumers is animal testing." And according to PETA, Colgate-Palmolive conducts tests on animals.

Colgate outdoes Tom's in one area, however: workers at its St. Louis plant are represented by a union, Local 15C of the United Food and Commercial Workers International Union.

"You see a number of the iconic socially responsible brand names from the nineties and early 2000s having been acquired by large companies," Steven Lydenberg said. "There are people who are very concerned about how to preserve the model." Ice-cream maker Ben & Jerry's, perhaps the most famous of the CSR breed, was bought by Unilever in 2000. France's Groupe Danone acquired Stonyfield Farm, the yogurt company (and main financial backer of Climate Counts), in stages in the early 2000s. Burt's Bees, which produces natural lip balm, shampoos, and other personal-care products, fell to Clorox a year and a half after Tom's sale. And later, after Lydenberg and I spoke, Timberland would be sold to VF Corporation.

Sometimes the business strategy itself can provide reassurance. In the case of Tom's, the whole point was to gain access to the health niche. As Colgate said in a press release at the time, sales of "natural" oral and personal-care products were increasing 15 percent annually in the United States, and "Tom's of Maine gives Colgate the opportunity to enter the fast-growing health and specialty trade channel, where Tom's toothpaste is the clear market leader." For tactical reasons, it was better to buy its way in rather than try to create an organic Colgate brand from scratch. "You don't want to cannibalize your original line," explained Naomi A. Gardberg, an assistant professor at the City University of New York's Zicklin School of Business. (Gardberg's three children use Tom's strawberry toothpaste.) "If you make an organic line [with the Colgate name], that suggests the original line is dangerous. The acquisition of Tom's was brilliant, because you have a different name, and you already have a following." And the $100 million purchase price was nothing to Colgate, mere petty cash from its $15 billion in annual revenue. Thus, based on motivation and strategy, it would make no sense for Colgate to start messing around with the very qualities that inspired it to buy Tom's.

Another way to reassure Lydenberg's concerned consumers is to consider the guarantees that came with the purchase. Among them: Tom's of Maine headquarters and the primary factory would stay in Kennebunk, and no one would lose his or her job. Said Susan Dewhirst, the only person Colgate would offer up to comment (and who actually works for Tom's), "The deal was, they wouldn't change the fundamental, core things that made Tom's special."

Another part of the agreement guaranteed that Tom Chappell would continue to run the company during a two-year transition. In 2008, he was replaced by a different longtime Tom of Maine—Tom O'Brien, the chief operating officer. "That was great," Kate said. "We had worked with him for eleven years. He knew all the complexities of managing a socially responsible company." The Chappells remain on an advisory board that meets with the new Tom's management every three or four months. "They defer to Kate and me," Tom Chappell insisted.

Are these promises strong enough to ensure that Tom's stays Tom's? The Chappells didn't seek an official ten-year pledge from Colgate, as Ben & Jerry's supposedly did with Unilever. "That's not something that you can dictate in a formal agreement," Tom explained. "They have spent an enormous amount of time to understand the brand. If it doesn't work for 'Maine' and 'natural' to be at the heart of the identity of the brand, then the brand has lost its way. You have to trust the people you are turning it over to." That's nice for now, but what if different managers take over at Colgate? "It's about the culture that remains," he said. On the other hand, he added, "if they were pulling out of Maine or were making decisions that are strictly bottom-line based, I would be unhappy."

To answer Lydenberg's concerns, it's also crucial to see what is actually happening on the ground. Gardberg pointed to the commitment to keep churning out toothpaste at the Tom's factory and assembly lines, rather than shifting production to Colgate facilities. That can help save all those nice worker benefits—including the all-important paid volunteering time—by maintaining Tom's as a distinct place and culture, she said. "Companies feel pressured to standardize their HR practices across the company after an acquisition, especially to phase in new employees," she explained. "If they're running separate facilities, it's less likely they will be integrated." For his part, Lydenberg was glad to see that Tom's maintains its own website. There isn't even a Tom's sublink on the Colgate site. And Tom Chappell's mission statement is on the site, in an expanded version. Although Tom and Kate supposedly remain as advisers, Tom said he wasn't sure whether the corporate tithing is still in effect; the answer, according to Colgate, is yes.

Susan Dewhirst ticked off more ways that, she claimed, the Tom's values and milieu had been preserved, such as the natural ingredients, the stewardship model of environmental sustainability and sourcing, the wind-power credits—that is, the controversial offsets that many greens disdain—and the products themselves. Turnover had been minimal, she said, although she claimed not to have exact numbers. Press reports at the time of the sale mentioned a payroll of about 170, and in 2010, Dewhirst said, there were about 160 employees, which would mean a small net attrition.

If the Chappells really had to sell to gain marketing muscle, did they accomplish that business goal, at least? The answer can be found in almost any CVS, Target, or even Walmart.

"We've gone from one item to five [available] at Target," Tom boasted. At a convention a couple of weeks after the sale, he added, "one of the vice presidents of Walmart came up to me and he said, 'We will now work with you.'" (That memory evoked another rare laugh.) Moreover, Dewhirst suggested that Colgate's size and experience could help with social networking, global outreach, and negotiating FDA approvals.

Countering those benefits, however, Colgate has brought at least three changes that eat away at good old Tom's.

The most notorious is probably the packaging. Criticism of this factor has to be relative, because Tom's packaging, even post-Colgate, is still more informative than most. For instance, the side of the toothpaste box Crest wastes with its logo and ad copy ("Strengthens Enamel. Whitening. Minty Fresh Striped.") is where Tom's explains how it uses licorice-root extract instead of traditional sodium lauryl sulfate. On another side, where Crest puts yet more meaningless self-promotion ("With cleaning action to help prevent tartar buildup and remove surface stains"), Tom's has its socially responsible version of marketing copy—information about its community service, corporate donations, and policy forbidding animal testing.

However, there used to be a lot more information before Tom's re-designed the classic toothpaste packaging in 2010. No longer does the package spell out the source and purpose of each ingredient. (While the information is available online, that's simply not as convenient as being on the box.) Instead of the old label's specifics about the flavors—"cinnamon and organic clove oil with other natural flavors" derived from cinnamon leaves and bark and clove flowers, with the full scientific names included—the new version might just say "natural flavor." On the box side where the ingredient details previously were listed, there is now a short paragraph with more marketing than real facts. For the Wicked Fresh brand, that cute little paragraph gushes, "Our toothpaste uses powerful natural flavor oils and a patent-pending botanical extract to help neutralize stinky VSCs (volatile sulphur compounds) which can be largely responsible for bad breath." What oils? What extract? And gone—for obvious reasons—is the little note from "Kate and Tom." The only good change is that the bigger print and sharper white background are easier to read. But to read what?

Michael Myers, president of Palio Communications, an ad agency in upstate New York, thought the first-version packaging was merely "OK looking" from a design perspective, but, he added, "if you look at it from what it communicates, I think it's cool. They scream on their packaging that it's all about social responsibility and healthy and good products." The revised boxes, he said, still "communicate green" with symbols like little leaves. Yet he admitted that "it almost seems as if they've lessened their packaging focus here on the green aspect versus their older packaging."

Tom Chappell said that he had agreed with the necessity for new packaging because "it hadn't been redesigned for decades." Corporate management "checked with us to make sure they were going in the right direction," Tom continued. However, he and Kate did not oversee the details or the specific wording and design.

Another big shift came in 2011, when the recyclable aluminum toothpaste tube was replaced with plastic. Plastic! That symbol of everything unecological. Even the company's website confessed that "for many of you [customers] these aluminum tubes became synonymous with Tom's of Maine." In the surveys back in her day, Kate said, having recyclable tubes grew more important to respondents as time went by. Furthermore, the environment isn't the sole reason to prefer aluminum. The AFL-CIO endorses aluminum and steel beverage cans rather than plastic bottles, noting that the former industries are unionized.

The new Tom's said it made the switch after consumers complained that the aluminum tubes cracked and leaked, were hard to squeeze, and usually couldn't be recycled through their local programs anyway. The plastic-laminate tubes weigh only half as much, thus saving energy in manufacturing and shipping, the company claimed. And officials said they're seeking ways to recycle the plastic. All that may be. Nevertheless, it's hard to avoid the symbolism of Tom's of Maine turning plastic.

The third change: Four years after the sale, Tom's got a corporatized, automated phone-answering system. ("If this is a medical emergency, press 1. If you are a consumer with a question, press 2. If you are a health foods store with a question, press 3.") Both Dewhirst and another Tom's spokeswoman insisted that really, this was much nicer and more efficient for customers, and you could always get a human if you wanted.

It's hard to tell whether Tom's brushers have stayed faithful. Although the company still hasn't reached the $100 million goal that prompted the buyout, annual sales are up by about $10 million, to $60 million, and after all, a rather big recession has intervened. Toothpaste users tend to have a particularly strong brand loyalty, going back to what Mom put in the medicine cabinet, which could make it easier for Tom's to retain old customers yet harder to entice new ones. Tom Chappell asserted that the number of new buyers is "substantial" but wouldn't give me statistics.

When I randomly interviewed nearly two dozen people purchasing various brands of natural toothpaste, floss, mouthwash, and deodorant in New York City three years after the acquisition, only one, freelance writer Abby Scher, said she had deliberately dumped Tom's. Another, Melissa White, a public health researcher, said she hadn't been aware of the Colgate deal—but now that she knew, she added, she would try to find an alternative to Tom's. "If there were an equal product with similar price and ingredients, I would prefer to buy from an independent company," she said. At the least, she added, the name should be changed to Tom's of Maine, by Colgate.

Contributors on Tom's *Good Matters* blog have certainly not been happy with the acquisition, but blogs are, like any customer-complaint venue, self-selecting for kvetchers. Bloggers think the toothpaste and other products taste more artificial now; they miss the detailed labeling; their favorite flavors have become harder to find. And many of them blame Colgate. "I can only assume that the massive machine known as Colgate has decided to trim the margins, increase efficiency, and streamline the company," Sean wrote in October 2010.

Ethical activists, meanwhile, seem happy to have Tom's in any flavor. Soon after the takeover, recalled PETA's Dan Shannon, the Chappells "came to us and said they wanted to assure us they're going to remain a fully independent subsidiary and continue to follow all the [animal-free] policies," despite the new corporate owner's animal testing.

"There's a purist argument to be made; you're being bought by a big company that does test on animals," Shannon continued. "But at PETA, we really try to look at it from a practical perspective. Tom's is now more widely available than it was previously, because of the distribution power of Colgate. If you live in the middle of nowhere and Walmart is the only store you can go to, Tom's was probably not there before." Thus, while Tom's may now be helping bolster the profits of a company that causes pain to bunny rabbits, it's saving bunnies by reaching customers who might otherwise have bought toothpaste tested on those animals. Bottom line, are more bunnies saved, or hurt? Who knows?

There's one more twist to this tale: could Tom's change Colgate? Tom Chappell claimed that it already had. "It's very clear that our presence in the Colgate family has impact," he asserted, pointing to two postacquisition examples. A year after the sale, he said, Colgate CEO Ian Cook "introduced a companywide commitment to sustainability," and members of Tom's staff were among the small advisory team that was supposed to explain what this meant. His second example was that Tom's employees were asked to help Colgate people "understand the potential for various herbs or plants, whatever their therapeutic benefit was, so Colgate would have an inventory of knowledge for using that in any of their formulations." Tom claimed that these two ideas came from Colgate, not him. He also said that they "weren't brewing before the acquisition," and thus must have been prompted by the arrival of Tom's, pointing out that Cook hadn't been the CEO prior to then. That's a bit disingenuous, since Cook was president and chief operating officer at the time of the sale, his promotion had already been announced, and he would probably have been involved in any major herb or sustainability initiative regardless of his title at that point. For that matter, the projects could have been "brewing" at lower levels for years. But they're nice ideas anyway.

Outside observers are more cautious. "We hope that it influences companies like Colgate, when they see that being a leader in this sector and being attentive to animal welfare and other issues can make Tom's of Maine a profitable, viable brand," said Michael Markarian of the Humane Society.

However, Wood Turner, the former executive director of Climate Counts, pointed out that big companies like Colgate buy little ones like Tom's precisely to fill a niche, not to replace the entire line—as New York University's Naomi Gardberg put it, not to cannibalize the rest of their products. "What they're inclined to do is to provide just enough availability to the conscientious consumer to satisfy their needs, but continue doing business otherwise," Turner said. Unfortunately, he couldn't compare Colgate's carbon-reduction scores before and after the Tom's purchase to see if Tom's had greened the larger company, because Climate Counts was launched the same year as the acquisition.

It's true that Clorox, since absorbing Burt's Bees, has initiated a brand of plant-based, "natural" cleaning products endorsed by the Sierra Club. Still, it's more likely that both decisions, to buy Burt's and to sell natural products, were spurred by Clorox management's awareness of the potential size of the ethical-consumer market, and not that Burt's founders or top managers—who didn't even stay after the acquisition—somehow persuaded Clorox to create the green brand.

THE QUESTION: Does Tom's of Maine deserve its reputation as an exemplar of ethical chic?

THE VERDICT: A worried yes.

Jill Kickul, director of the Stewart Satter Program in Social Entrepreneurship at New York University's Stern School of Business, said that negative press would be a strong sign that Tom's virtue had been corrupted. It's been five years since the sale. So far, the headlines have been pretty quiet.

So maybe things will be OK.

The good news? The factory in Maine, the corporate tithing, and the workers' benefits all seem solid, and the company keeps finding more ways to recycle and save energy. The ingredients certainly remain a lot less yucky and artificial than those in, well, Colgate toothpaste. On the negative side, the new packaging is a big step backwards, toward conventional marketing blather and away from the real information that the old version had provided about those nice ingredients. With so many strong reasons to prefer aluminum over plastic, the arguments about the switch in tubing are unconvincing. And I wish there had been a more firm ten-year pledge as part of the sale, rather than merely the soothing sentiment of "Trust the Chappells" or "Trust Colgate."

Basically, what Tom and Kate say in response to such complaints is, Suck it up. "If people want to feel the way they feel, there's nothing I can do," Tom snapped. "I know what took place. I don't have any discomfort about the decision."

Anyway, Tom and Kate are busy these days with new ventures. Kate is creating and exhibiting her artwork. Both are running Ramblers Way Farm, a business they founded in 2009 to make and sell wool clothing from humane, organic, environmentally sustainable US sheep farms and factories. Visitors walk into their offices, in that converted eighteenth-century building next to the Kennebunk Town Hall, by stepping on a circle of bricks engraved with sayings like, "Connect with goodness" and "Know thyself, be thyself."

If Tom was largely brusque throughout our long interview, sometimes angry, rarely laughing, there was one point where he got quiet: when I asked if they stayed in touch with Tom's of Maine employees, and if those employees felt the place had changed.

"I think people miss the founders," Tom replied. Then he paused. "I don't spend a lot of time with former Tom's people." Even though the factory is only a half-hour away from his new office, he said that, since the sale, "I don't think I've been in the building."

CHAPTER 2

Timberland

How Green Is My Leather

TIMBERLAND COMPANY'S TWO-STORY BRICK headquarters is almost exactly what you would expect from its public image. It sits in a rustic version of an industrial park in Stratham, New Hampshire, adjoining a pond and enveloped by trees and the nonstop twittering of birds. There's a sculpture in the lobby made of recycled plastic soda bottles (used in some shoe parts), along with a stack of bamboo (crunched into the heels of women's shoes). Its oft-praised child-care center includes a half dozen rooms, an indoor gym, an outdoor playground, and a huge fish tank. In a garden just outside, employees grow organic squash, zucchini, and pumpkins that they sell in the corporate cafeteria, donating the proceeds to a food bank.

Next to the garden is a small array of solar panels. The press person guiding me around smiled a little apologetically. The panels are "symbolic," she admitted, because "New Hampshire doesn't get much sun." A facility in California has a much bigger, more practical array.

Timberland itself has become both a symbol and a working model of what to do right as a socially responsible business, winning all sorts of accolades for its environmental and workplace policies from raters like *Business Ethics*, Climate Counts, Ceres, the Dave Thomas Foundation for Adoption, *Forbes*, *Fortune*, *Outside*, the US Green Building Council, and

Working Mother. Laura Berry, executive director of the New York City–based Interfaith Center on Corporate Responsibility (ICCR), which represents about three hundred religious institutional investors, said that "we have never filed or even put a [shareholder] resolution on the table, they're so darn good." Similarly, Steven Lydenberg, of Domini Social Investments, declared that "Timberland is a truly remarkable company. They've taken risks no one else has taken." The company has crafted a complex CSR matrix of "core values" and "pillars," and Gordon Peterson, Timberland's former vice president for corporate social responsibility, told me that the core values of CSR—humanity, humility, integrity, and excellence—are part of employees' performance review.

It's hard to believe that any company could be that perfect. It's particularly hard to believe such perfection of Timberland, for two reasons.

First, the main raw material for its most important products is leather. That requires killing cows. Even before they're killed, the cows present numerous ethical and environmental problems. To create grazing room and meet the growing demand for this raw material, irreplaceable rain forests may have been chopped down in Brazil. For that matter, deforestation anywhere can lead to soil erosion, which in turn pollutes lakes and rivers. Meanwhile, the methane produced by the cows' waste, and their unique digestive system (aka burping), is a serious factor in greenhouse gas emissions. Then, after they leave the grazing fields, the animals probably go to factory feedlots and slaughterhouses, where they are jammed into pens, forced to stand in their own waste, fed an unnatural diet of corn and animal parts, and injected with antibiotics and hormones to counter the effects of that diet. The chemicals used to grow their food pollute the ground and water, and the overuse of antibiotics is spurring resistance in bacteria to the point where we may run out of antibiotics that work when we actually need them. Finally, the process of tanning the leather from these cows can require vast amounts of energy and produce toxic chromium emissions. Thus, this "remarkable," "darn good" company is hurting rivers, lakes, soil, the rain forest, and the Earth's climate—plus the cows.

So, what should Timberland do—give up the leather boots that have been the foundation of its business for more than five decades?

All that is just the first reason for skepticism. Here's the second: if Timberland really is so wonderful, did it jeopardize that reputation by selling itself to a big conglomerate, VF Corporation, in 2011?

———

When Boston shoemaker Nathan Swartz bought the New Hampshire–based Abington Shoe Company in stages from 1952 to 1955, it was a contract manufacturer that made basic, sturdy, low-price footwear for other firms, which then sold the shoes under their own labels to army-navy surplus shops and discount outlets. In 1965, the company—still called Abington but now run by Nathan's sons Herman and Sidney—pioneered what became its trademark, a manufacturing process that melded soles to leather uppers without stitching, thus rendering the boots waterproof. The Timberland logo first appeared on a line of boots in 1973 and became the official corporate name five years later.

Like any company in the fashion business, Timberland has shifted its product line and image over time. Establishing its own label moved it upscale, from anonymous boots for other retailers to high-caliber, reliable work boots that shoppers could ask for by name. The marketing "was all about quality, materials, five hundred steps in the manufacturing process, ruggedness, long-lasting staff," recalled Carol Holding, the brand-strategies consultant, who worked at an agency that developed ads for Timberland in 1980. Then the Swartzes branched into casual shoes, and as those overtook boots in terms of sales, the company needed to reach a second target customer, "an upscale young man, eighteen to thirty-four, a fashion-conscious, quality-conscious young man," according to John Thorbeck, who was hired in 1983 as Timberland's first vice president of marketing.

And the images kept changing. In 1983, the company decided to emphasize outdoor performance, with ads featuring Timberland products that had been field-tested in the Iditarod, the grueling, 1,150-mile Alaskan sled-dog race. Around that same time, there was also a surge of interest from ultra-fashion-conscious Italians; New York City artist Peter Bornstein said that when he was in Turin in 1985, he was offered $120 for his Timberland boat shoes, right off his feet. (He declined.) A few years further on, the company took a different turn, introducing apparel and accessories in 1988, and children's shoes and more accessories such as watches and daypacks, under license, in 1996.

In the early 1990s, without any marketing push—in fact, without company officials even realizing it at first—the brand suddenly became popular among the urban hip-hop crowd. "We noticed some unusual patterns," Thorbeck recalled. "Why was the Four Dudes, a shop in inner-city Washington, DC, one of the best boot customers?" This client base might seem to be the complete opposite of lumberjacks and Iditarod mushers. However, Jim Davey, Timberland's current vice president for global marketing, outlined a connection: "One of the things that the [urban] market loved about the brand is that it was the toughest, best-made boot you could buy. It was a very authentic, plain-speaking brand that didn't try to put on airs."

Whatever the market, Davey said the company replaces about half of its 1,500 footwear products each year, which he claimed is typical of the industry. He added that the brand has different images in different countries—for "hard-core hikers" in Scandinavia, for instance, and as "a high-quality shoe for everyday life" in Asia. While some lower-cost lines can be found at discount outlets, in general it is unabashedly a "premium price" label, selling at perhaps 10 percent to 20 percent above competitors' prices, especially for boots, Davey said.

Ironically, one image Timberland didn't seek for a long time was to be a socially conscious brand. Then, in 1989, the cofounders of City Year—a Boston-based service organization that's often called a "youth urban Peace Corps"—asked Sidney Swartz's son, Jeffrey, to donate fifty pairs of boots. "I think he did it, saying, 'Yeah, yeah, I'd better do this service thing,'" Gordon Peterson said with a laugh. "But I think it transformed him." Some veteran employees cite another possible motivation, noting that there was gossip at the time that the younger Swartz had political ambitions.

Those boots were the first step on a wide path of corporate and employee community service. Within three years Jeffrey Swartz—who was not yet CEO—had started a program allowing staff to take up to sixteen hours' worth of paid time per year for volunteer work, and over the subsequent years would come efforts in recycling, alternative energy, and emissions reduction. In addition, the company's 1992 "Give Racism the Boot" ad campaign helped kick-start the concept of ethical marketing.

Even after Timberland got CSR religion, however, it didn't market any brand specifically as "environmental" until the Earthkeepers line— which sets strict standards for recycled content and other material—in the early 2000s. That remains a niche, accounting for only $100 million of the company's total $1.3 billion in sales in 2010. Timberland is trying to expand the concept both ways, to include more products as Earthkeepers, and to put higher green requirements on all clothing, accessories, and footwear.

Social responsibility, especially concerning the environment, would seem to be an obvious tie-in with the boots' image and customer base, whether it's Iditarod sledders or, as Davey described the current target market, "men and women in their twenties who have a little bit deeper appreciation for the outdoors." But company officials say CSR is actually not a major motivation for their customers. Anyone shopping for shoes or clothes, said Peterson, is more likely to ask, "What does it look like? How much money is it? Is it comfortable? Does it do what I want it to do?" Added Betsy Blaisdell, Timberland's senior manager for environmental stewardship, "The publicity related to how we look at sustainability is great, and it creates a great feel around our brand, but I think it's the durability, the price point, the look, the marketing, that's selling the most."

The customers I've interviewed bear that out. Graham Gaston, age thirty-two, a New York City television producer, was replacing the Timberland shoes he'd bought for a backpacking trip to Europe seven years ago. He talked about how well they had held up and how they were nice enough to wear to his office, but nary a word about the feel-good volunteer work and recycling. At another store, a twenty-nine-year-old cable television inspector said Timberlands are more stylish and less expensive than the boots he's required to buy for work.

Luckily, it's increasingly hip to be the kind of person who goes backpacking and hiking and who cares about the environment, so Timberland is happy to incorporate this image in its marketing today. Davey cited the "Nature Needs Heroes" TV spot for Earthkeepers in fall 2010: a young man, seeing his friend carelessly toss a plastic water bottle toward a trash can (and miss), chases the escaping bottle as it is carried off by the wind, leaping on top of a moving train, racing alongside a raging river—in his Timberland shoes, of course—until he finally catches and recycles the bottle. "We are really focusing on twentysomethings," Davey said, "and the environmental impact of products is a huge issue for them."

It thus seemed like a trifecta of a marketing strategy when, in October 2009, Timberland joined musician Wyclef Jean and his environmental and social charity Yéle Haiti to sponsor scholarships, tree planting, food distribution, sports, and other community-service initiatives in Jean's native Haiti. In one swoop, Timberland could reach out to those inner-city hip-hop fans, burnish its green and community-service cred, and sell more clothes and boots. Among the marketing plans was a world tour by Jean where specially branded "eco" T-shirts, hats, and other Timberland clothing would be sold. In addition, there would be sixteen new lines of boots made from organic and recycled material, store and website displays, promotions via social media, CDs, and a new album.

Barely three months later, a massive earthquake measuring 7.0 on the

Richter scale hit Haiti. That should have made the partnership with Yéle Haiti even more important, as the shoemaker and the charity switched their focus temporarily to earthquake relief, promising to return to the more long-term environmental projects when the situation stabilized.

Instead, public scrutiny of the charity's messy finances accompanied the donations. News accounts started asking why Yéle Haiti hadn't filed tax returns for four years and was late in filing the next three, and why so much of its income seemed to go to businesses connected with Jean's musical career. For instance, the organization paid $250,000 to a TV station and recording studio controlled by Jean and a cousin. The charity replied that the payments were actually for rent—and discount rent at that—because its offices shared space with the studio, and for expenses relating to a benefit concert where Jean performed in 2006. It also claimed that it didn't need to file returns for years in which the charity wasn't active.

Timberland stood by its partnership, and after a few months, the publicity died down. Jean briefly considered running for president of Haiti; the charity turned its attention back to tree planting. Jim Davey declared that all the bad press hadn't hurt. "That's our primary goal, to reforest Haiti, and nothing changed with that," he said. And don't forget that Jean, he added, "is going to help us reengage with the urban market."

The ultimate social-responsibility quandary, of course, circles back to the cows. Timberland officials have a ready answer to any questions: "Our leather production is not responsible for killing animals," Betsy Blaisdell said promptly. "Meat production drives the killing of cattle. The hide is a waste product" that would get discarded anyway if Timberland didn't, in effect, recycle it for clothing. Problem solved.

Not completely.

The next problem lies in how the hides are processed, or tanned. Although Timberland doesn't do this part itself, it chooses the suppliers that do. And Blaisdell noted that "the tanning process is a beast of its own. It's one of those old dirty industries that's energy-intensive and polluting."

A primary tanner collects the hides, removes the hair and flesh, and soaks, pickles, and preserves them before selling the skins to a retannage facility. That facility then sells the stuff to Timberland and other leather-product manufacturers. The standard method of tanning uses a type of chromium salt, which can produce chromium emissions. While the US

Environmental Protection Agency doesn't consider these emissions dangerous, it states that different kinds of chromium compounds can cause cancer and genetic diseases and can be toxic to wildlife.

To be more ecological, Timberland first switched to organic tanners that utilized vegetable-based dyes and materials such as corn sugar, oil, lime, and sodium bicarbonate. That led to a new concern, according to Blaisdell: "The amount of energy it takes to produce vegetable-based dyes is higher."

So the company decided to consider the matter as a question of process rather than ingredients, to seek out "the tanning that's managed best from an environmental standpoint." Joining other shoe manufacturers like Clarks, New Balance, and Nike, Timberland "met with tanners to establish a very detailed environmental protocol, with hundreds of questions" about the procedures and materials used, Blaisdell said. In 2005, they formally created the Leather Working Group, which now has over five dozen members. A detailed monitoring and rating system was established, and facilities are audited by outside experts every eighteen months. The gold-rated tanners, such as ISA Tan Tec facilities in Vietnam and China, track all the environmental inputs and outputs, treat waste water with top-of-the-line primary and secondary systems, even filter their water once more through reed beds, and are "very creative with how they reuse waste," Blaisdell said. "This is a tannery I would eat off the floor of." While Timberland still doesn't get all its leather from the gold scorers, that's the goal.

Lindsey Allen, a senior forest campaigner at Greenpeace, gave Timberland hefty credit for these efforts. "They led in creating the industry group that has made huge strides in trying to clean up the cattle sector, specifically around the tannery process," she said. "A lot of companies say, 'OK, OK, what do we have to do to make Greenpeace happy?' Timberland is working on a lot of initiatives without having to be pushed."

However, things got dicier when Greenpeace went a step further back in the process, back to where hides are a secondary waste product, to look at where the cows came from—specifically, whether Amazonian rain forests in Brazil were being destroyed to create grazing space for cattle ranches. Timberland wasn't chopping down the forests or running the ranches, of course, and the supply chain from rain forest to shoe is long and complex. Cattle farmers push into the rain forest—and other land—to raise their herds, then sell the cows to "fattening farms," which then sell the animals to slaughterhouses, which then sell the meat to

food processors and the hides to the tanneries, and on through the tanning process to the ultimate shoe (or coat or briefcase) manufacturer. It
can be almost impossible to know where a particular shipment of hides
originally munched grass when it was a herd of cows. So Greenpeace
wasn't demanding that Timberland stop cutting trees. The debate really
revolved around what role Timberland was taking—and should take—in
this convoluted process.

According to Allen, Greenpeace's research revealed that "three-
fourths of the currently deforested areas in the Brazilian Amazon rain
forest are occupied by cattle." While the meat from those cows was going
mainly for local consumption, the leather demand was global, and "the
footwear sector came up as a big player." She named almost the same list
that launched the tanning-reform group, including Adidas, Clarks, the
Italian company Geox, Nike, and Timberland.

Allen said Greenpeace contacted Timberland in early 2009 with what
she called "a courtesy letter" stating that "we have concerns around the
demand for leather"—in other words, a warning that the company was
about to become a target. A questionnaire soon followed. At around that
same time, Greenpeace also issued a report about the destruction of the
Amazonian rain forests and the connection with cattle ranching. According to Allen, Greenpeace wanted Timberland and other shoemakers
"to put pressure on your supplier to commit to a moratorium" on buying
cattle from newly deforested rain forest land and to threaten to stop doing business with any supplier that refused.

Although Timberland first questioned why it was being lassoed in
this whole campaign, both sides now acknowledge that the company
may well have obtained some of its leather from a Brazilian slaughterhouse Greenpeace was targeting. What happened next, basically, is that
Timberland said, "We'll handle this our own way, and you can trust us
because you know we're wonderful." And Greenpeace replied, "That's not
good enough."

Timberland's plan was to work privately with the slaughterhouse
management in hopes of easing that processor out of the rain forest, but
not to set a deadline, demand a moratorium, or say anything publicly. As
Jeffrey Swartz described the situation on the *Huffington Post* website in
March 2010, his company's response to Greenpeace was "not meant as
a kiss-off, not meant to be empty promises—in fact the discovery was
pretty startling and it did lead to some candid conversation with our
supplier."

Greenpeace, however, felt that Timberland was being too cautious in using its clout as a major customer. While Timberland was talking quietly with mid-level managers at the slaughterhouse, moving step by step, other leather-goods manufacturers were being more aggressive and going straight to the executive suite—or the press. "What we were hearing is that if enough companies threaten to cancel contracts, it sends a very clear message all the way to the top" of the supplier, Allen said. "We think public accountability is almost always a good thing immediately." Even Nike was acting faster, apparently having learned a few lessons from the consumer protests over its Asian sweatshops. (As mortifying as it may be to Timberland, it seems to be generally accepted among social-activism types that Nike is often the CSR leader in the shoe industry. Domini's Steven Lydenberg agreed that "Nike these days really sets the standard for environmental initiatives when it comes to footwear and apparel.") So, Greenpeace essentially followed through on its warning letter, urging customers and activists to pressure Timberland, and Swartz felt unfairly singled out.

Eventually, Timberland caved. It joined the other shoemakers in demanding a moratorium on buying cattle from newly deforested rain forest area, as Greenpeace had sought, and that autumn the four largest Brazilian slaughterhouses agreed to phase it in. Swartz grudgingly wrote, "Did Greenpeace 'win' because we've adopted some of the terms and guidelines they proposed in working with our Brazilian supplier on this issue? I guess."

There's no question that it was a shock for Timberland to be seen as one of the bad guys, and Allen is sympathetic. "Their surprise was pretty fair," she acknowledged. "They were not experienced in being targeted publicly by environmental groups."

For her part, Blaisdell said she thinks Greenpeace "did the right thing." Then she added, "I won't say I didn't cry. They're my people!"

If it must rely on a business model that uses animals that burp methane gas, cuts down trees for their pasture, kills them, and tans their hides in ways that can pollute—and if it wants to be environmentally responsible—then Timberland needs to figure out how to compensate for the damage its production methods cause.

Start with the ingredients. One step is relatively easy: Blaisdell pointed out that leather, being so durable, fits right into the environmental mantra of "Reduce, reuse, and recycle." People don't have to waste the

Earth's resources by buying new boots every year. Remember Graham
Gaston, the TV producer, whose Timberland hiking shoes were still going strong after seven years? He was replacing them simply because he'd
gotten tired of them. Moreover—at least, in theory—leather from the upper parts of shoes can be used again. In some of the newest lines of boots,
82 percent of the content is reusable. Of course, people first have to bring
those boots back to the store for recycling, and Blaisdell conceded that
that's not too likely to happen.

Nor do the shoes consist entirely of belching-cow, tanned-hide
leather. Hemp, synthetics, recycled PET plastic (the plastic in beverage
bottles, as seen in Timberland's lobby sculpture), and organic canvas are
utilized in the linings, laces, and uppers. Sneakers are made of polyester
blends and other synthetics, and Timberland is famous for being the first
shoemaker to recycle rubber into soles.

Moreover, 30 percent of sales come from gear other than footwear—
clothing and accessories—which certainly doesn't have to contain
leather. These products, including a special "eco-conscious" line, are
typically made of a combination of wool, organic and nonorganic cotton,
leather, and synthetics. The stated position on the corporate website is
to "increase renewable materials and recycled content in our products."
Over one-third of the cotton is organic, and officials say they avoid cotton from Uzbekistan, because of that country's heavy use of child and
forced labor, and shun fur altogether. Colleen Von Haden, Timberland's
senior manager for code of conduct, said the company was trying to find
sources of fair trade cotton in Africa, although standards for fair trade
fabrics are not well established.

As for wool, animal rights advocates praise the company for steering
clear of Australia and its merino sheep. Merinos are usually prized for
their soft wool, but the problem is that they have extra folds of skin, under
which debris such as blowfly larvae can build up. So the folds are usually
cut away through a painful process known as mulesing. Then, after the
sheep become too old to produce wool efficiently, they are shipped to
the Mideast to satisfy the huge Muslim demand for halal meat. Dan
Shannon of PETA claimed that "tens of thousands of sheep are crowded
onto ships" without adequate food and water on voyages that can take
weeks, and that "a huge percentage will die."

Presumably, Timberland could save a lot of cows and reduce pollution
by using more synthetics like pleather rather than leather, but there are
lines it cannot cross. When I asked Jim Davey, he said bluntly, "Leather is

a huge part of what we do. It's consistent with our New England image. We're an outdoor brand; it always comes back to that."

Beyond the ingredients, the company has a detailed list of goals for shrinking its environmental footprint. In some cases, it's smartly ahead of schedule; in other cases, it's equally far behind.

The most important efforts probably have to do with energy usage. Officially, Timberland aims to get 60 percent of its energy from renewable sources by 2015, increase the number of buildings that are architecturally certified as green, and drastically reduce carbon emissions. It further pledges to work with outside energy auditors and to encourage employees to be more energy-conscious.

It's way past the obvious steps. CFL bulbs? Hah! Timberland is already onto the next generation, having replaced almost all its CFL bulbs with the even more efficient LED kind. There's a reflective white roof on the New Hampshire headquarters that's supposed to keep the building cooler in summer, and *Consumer Reports* cited the solar-panel system at the California distribution center—the real version of the symbolic array at headquarters—as one of the largest in the world. All new US stores are built to the highest green-certified standards, while renewable energy will soon be used in the United Kingdom. To inspire the troops, employees who carpool, drive hybrids, or bike get special parking spots, plus hybrid buyers get a $3,000 credit. Where the company had hoped to reduce emissions from staff travel by 25 percent as of year-end 2010, it actually achieved double that reduction.

The catch is that only about 4 percent of Timberland's climate impact comes from its own facilities worldwide—the New Hampshire headquarters, regional headquarters in the United Kingdom and Singapore, a design center in London, three distribution centers, one footwear factory in the Dominican Republic, and about two hundred stores—which means that those solar panels and LED bulbs aren't doing much. Maybe 5 percent more comes from shipping. Most of the energy usage, emissions, pollution, and other damage, not surprisingly, traces back to those cows, ranches, and tanneries Timberland doesn't directly control. Thus, the efforts to save the Amazon rain forest and find gold-level tanneries should help. The corporate website also promises to "leverage the relationship with our footwear supply chain" in order to pressure suppliers to reduce their own climate impact, a step that activists wish all companies would take. Still, these actions can't disguise the fact that Timberland is fairly powerless to compensate for the cows.

That leaves the energy offsets that ecology advocates deplore. Rolf Skar, a Greenpeace senior campaigner, said that the sole valid offsets are projects to increase efficiency and renewable energy. Timberland agrees, which is why it has amended its approach. The initial policy was to become carbon-neutral—that is, to add a net of zero carbon dioxide and other greenhouse gases to the Earth's climate problems—by the end of 2010. Well, by early that year, it was clear that the company could meet the goal only by buying offsets for at least half of the gases it emitted. Even with its LED lights, solar panels, and all the rest, it just couldn't reduce emissions enough. (In fact, as of the December 31, 2010, deadline, Timberland had cut its actual emissions by 38 percent—impressive, albeit far from the target.)

If it had to rely on offsets, the idea was to buy the "good" kinds and, even better, "use the [offset] fund to develop energy efficiency and renewable energy at the factories we source from," Blaisdell said. For instance, Timberland would cover some of the up-front expense of installing more environmentally sustainable power systems at these factories. Blaisdell claimed that suppliers are "very keen to do it," in hopes that efficiency projects would lower their own operating costs over the long term. So it would be a twofer for Timberland—green credits for itself plus lower costs for suppliers that, presumably, would get passed on to customers like Timberland in the form of lower prices. It would be nice if other shoemakers that source from these same suppliers would chip in to pay the installation expenses. Even if they won't, and they simply ride along on Timberland's dime, so be it, Blaisdell said.

Under its new approach, Timberland is still doing all that, but now it emphasizes how much it is actually reducing its own emissions, rather than the overall neutrality target. As for other eco-issues, the shoemaker fell about a year behind its goal of removing all toxic polyvinyl chlorides (PVCs) from its products by the end of 2010. It is using more water-based adhesives instead of the standard glues and solvents, which are made of volatile organic compounds that can cause irritation, headaches, rashes, nausea, and even cancer. Finally, these efforts are published in unusual detail on the Timberland website.

Timberland's first New York City store might even be considered an example of reusing and recycling. Built in the nineteenth century, it was a jewelry factory and an ice skate shop before taking on the Timberland logo in 2009, sales clerks told me. Its cast iron facade dates from 1860, and much of the wood inside is either 100 percent reclaimed or certified as environmentally sustainable. Scattered around the floor, walls, and ceiling are a pair of century-old skates, two refurbished leather jackets from the 1930s, and stools made with reclaimed leather seats. According to the staff, people come from all over the world to gape at the building (not the boots).

Pick up a cardboard box of Timberland refined chukka shoes, and the underside of the box top might tell you that the box is made of 100 percent postconsumer recycled material and printed with soy- and water-based ink. From other parts of the container, you could learn that

- Timberland uses 3.1 kwH of energy to produce each pair of shoes (or used that much energy to make this particular pair—it's not clear).
- Timberland-owned facilities use 5 percent renewable energy.
- No child labor was involved.
- 119,776 hours were spent (by whom? when?) serving "our" communities.
- 100 percent of facilities have been assessed against the company's code of conduct.

A label on the sole of the shoe itself might reveal (in English and French) that

- The box has 100 percent recycled content (again).
- Timberland, as of 2008, planted 919,524 trees.
- 74 percent of the company's products are free of PVCs.
- This pair of shoes contains 3.4 percent eco-conscious material.
- Producing this pair of shoes used 6.6 percent renewable energy.

You don't see labels like this on too many shoe boxes.

The consumer-information effort began around 2004, according to Blaisdell, because Jeffrey Swartz was constantly saying things like, "Why can't we make environmental reporting as simple as the nutrition label on a cereal box?" An environmental label couldn't really be that simple, of course, with so much of the impact coming from the tanneries Timberland doesn't control and the ranches it can't even name. It would thus be impossible to get exact figures, to trace a pair of refined chukka shoes back to Bessie the cow in Brazil.

To devise rough estimates for those ranches and tanneries, Timberland relies on off-the-shelf life-cycle software that calculates the environmental effects of standard production methods, depending on the type and amount of material—the number of cows, the number of hides, whatever. Then Timberland can take the real statistics from its own and subcontractors' factories and plug those into commonly accepted formulas, such as average emissions per unit of energy from the particular fuel used in that factory. This process produces more-or-less accurate data for the average shoe. These are still not the superindividualized labels Swartz wanted, since different styles of footwear require different material, different amounts of that material, and probably different amounts of time (and thus energy) on the assembly line. Obviously, producing a canvas deck shoe demands fewer cows (read: none) than a six-inch boot. The good news is that Timberland has gradually been narrowing the calculations down to a product-by-product level, although it slipped on its goal of having a "green index" label on all footgear by the end of 2011.

Environmentalists' major complaint is that these figures don't account for the energy and emissions attributable to leather scraps that never become part of a finished shoe. That seems awfully nitpicky, considering how meager the leather waste probably is relative to the amount used, and how little most other manufacturers are doing at all. Blaisdell said the "irregularity between hides and the amount of yield you get from each" makes these numbers hard to calculate, although she said Timberland is seeking a methodology to figure out the average amount of waste per measurement of hide. The only reason the company can even try is that the information gathering doesn't cost much—about ten dollars per product line and part of one employee's workweek.

When a customer finishes adding and multiplying, however, what do all these numbers actually reveal? How much is 3.1 kwH of energy? Is it a lot? It's nice to know that Timberland planted all those trees, and eco-activists and ESG investors praise the company for its openness and leadership. Still, Timberland officials, as well as the activists, wonder if it's too confusing and whether anyone pays attention.

Blaisdell thinks it would be more useful if other companies took on similar efforts and there were an industry standard—something like the government's Energy Star labels for appliances—that could enable buyers to match brands side by side. Greenpeace's Lindsey Allen suggested a scorecard showing red, yellow, and green lights. "What's reasonable with consumers is how the thing they're buying compares with another shoe, not the kilograms of carbon dioxide," Blaisdell said. "Consumers want simple, relative information." Lacking an industry standard, she said, Timberland would try to establish its own companywide comparison, labeling each of its products on a scale of zero to ten in terms of climate impact, resources, and chemicals. The next step: taking the data about the environmental impact of each shoe to the designers to see if they can find greener raw materials.

Remember the 119,776 hours "serving our communities" from the shoe label? That hearkens back to the roots of Timberland's social consciousness, the fifty pairs of boots that Jeffrey Swartz half-grudgingly donated to City Year in 1989.

Today's programs go way beyond boots. The main one, called the Path of Service, lets employees take paid time off for almost any type of community service except religious or political activity—launched at sixteen hours per year in 1992 and boosted to forty hours in 1997. People have spent these hours helping with disaster relief and coaching Little League, volunteering at homeless shelters and tutoring at local schools, and much more. In lauding Timberland as one of its "Best Companies" the year after the September 11, 2001, terrorist attacks, *Fortune* noted, "On Sept. 11, 130 employees of this retailer happened to be in the Bronx refurbishing a school. Two weeks later, in Boston, Timberland built a playground in memory of the victims." Two of the volunteer days are supposed to be allotted for activities organized by the company, called Earth Day and Serv-a-palooza Day. (OK, subtract points for the name being too cute.)

In a typical year, according to Gordon Peterson, 78 percent of the staff participates. He conceded that people could theoretically head to the beach on days they claim to be spooning out soup, but he said it would be hard to lie when coworkers ask about their day at the homeless shelter.

While the volunteer program is the most famous, other employee benefits certainly get kudos. *Working Mother* has repeatedly praised the flextime, job sharing, ability to work from home, paid leave for new moms and dads, and adoption aid, and it raves that part-timers who work as little as sixteen hours a week can get health benefits. The child-care center I saw at headquarters is nationally accredited, even accepting kids whose parents don't work for the company. Employees who want to stay healthy can use the free on-site fitness center, take yoga classes, and borrow outdoor gear like canoes, kayaks, and snowshoes. To appeal to health nuts as well as to traditionalists, the headquarters cafeteria has an odd mix of fair trade coffee and horribly unecological plastic water bottles, veggie burgers and breaded chicken fingers, cartons for recycling cans, bottles, and ink cartridges and unrecyclable clamshell takeout containers. All in all, Milton Moskowitz, one of the cofounders of the *Fortune* "Best Companies" ranking, told me, "I have fond memories of reviewing Timberland applications."

Yet the boots have sometimes stumbled. Timberland failed to respond to the Human Rights Campaign's questionnaires on gay and lesbian issues from 2006 through 2011, even though it seems laughably easy to score high. Moreover, the US facilities have never been unionized. "Why didn't we target that particular company? I don't know," said Warren Pepicelli of UNITE HERE, the apparel workers' union. No doubt one reason was that it wasn't his union's territory, because shoe workers had a separate organization in the 1950s and 1960s. Gordon Peterson's analysis, not surprisingly, is that "I don't think our workers needed or wanted it. I guess they're getting what they need." They may well be getting good benefits, but how about organized labor's other function—worker advocacy? "I think our workers' voices get heard pretty well at Timberland," Peterson said, noting that a "corporate culture" official meets with workers every two weeks.

And why, if it was such a wonderful place to work from 1998 through 2007, did both *Fortune* and *Working Mother* drop Timberland from their rankings in 2008?

The two magazines will not explain why companies don't make their lists or even how common it is for a company to slide off. They only point out that the application process can be time consuming and cumbersome. A prospective "Best Companies" candidate must complete a long questionnaire covering topics like pay, benefits, camaraderie, job satisfaction, and communication. For *Fortune*'s list, four hundred or more randomly selected employees are surveyed, in addition to management. Jennifer Owens, the director of special projects at *Working Mother*, said her magazine's six-hundred-question survey can take one thousand "man-hours" (yes, that's the term this women's-magazine editor used) to fill out. She also said the number of applications has been increasing slightly each year, making it harder, by definition, to win a spot.

Peterson said Timberland stopped applying to get on *Working Mother*'s list because the sole employee handling all the "Best Companies" submissions didn't have the hours and resources to compete everywhere— leaving the unspoken implication that this specific magazine was a low priority. Unable to dismiss the *Fortune* loss so easily, he cited a rough financial stretch, starting in late 2005, that undoubtedly hurt morale and, presumably, employees' responses to the *Fortune* survey. Sales and the stock price went on a three-year slide while the company took a $15 million restructuring hit and closed forty-three underperforming stores. (In interviews with me for a news article I wrote for the website Portfolio .com in January 2010, management blamed the slippage partly on a broad cultural shift toward dressier footwear.) Then came the disastrous 2008–2009 recession. "If your coworker just got laid off, do you think it's a good place to work?" Peterson asked rhetorically. As for *Fortune*, he added, "We want back on."

A year after that conversation, Timberland still hadn't made it back, and no one from the company would comment.

The benefits mentioned above apply only to employees at the facilities owned by Timberland. Which means they don't apply to virtually all the workers who actually make the shoes and other goods. According to Colleen Von Haden, Timberland's senior manager for code of conduct, about 90 percent of the output is manufactured by some 250,000 people in over three hundred factories run by subcontractors in thirty-six countries outside the United States, mainly in Brazil, China, India, Thailand, and Vietnam. (Timberland directly controls one shoemaking plant in the Dominican Republic.)

Forget about flextime or paid leave for community service. Ethical shoppers first have to make sure workers are getting their full wages for the hours they are working and that those hours and conditions aren't too grueling. In overseas sweatshops throughout a range of industries— as many activists, books, and news articles have documented—workers toil sixteen-hour days, six or seven days a week, for paltry wages, without bathroom breaks or overtime pay. Young women—the bulk of the sweatshop labor force—are sometimes sexually abused by their supervisors or watched in humiliating ways when they finally get to the toilet. Talking is forbidden. Then they go "home" to crowded, dark, overpriced, barebones, company-mandated dorms.

To counter these abuses, oversight generally starts with a code of conduct, and Timberland's is better than average. For instance, in forbidding child labor, it defines *child* as "younger than sixteen," whereas many codes put the bar at fifteen. Unlike other companies, Peterson said, Timberland grants no exceptions to its ban on working more than sixty hours a week, not even during peak seasons. The code gets extra credit for including the right not just to form unions—which is rare enough—but also to "an equivalent means of independent representation" in places where "the right to freedom of association is restricted under law."

So Timberland says the proper words. Everyone agrees that the real test is whether a trustworthy proctor is at the facility regularly to make sure the words are followed. Most activists say this proctor should absolutely not be from the big multinational brand whose name is on the merchandise, for reasons of obvious conflict of interest. "If anybody believes that internal monitors are going to blow the whistle on the company, it's naive," said Mark Levinson, chief economist of the Service Employees International Union. "The company pays the monitors."

(The relationship between the SEIU and the clothing union, UNITE HERE, is complex: the two big unions that historically represented textile and apparel workers—the International Ladies' Garment Workers' Union and the Amalgamated Clothing and Textile Workers Union—were stitched together in 1995 to create the Union of Needletrades, Industrial, and Textile Employees, or UNITE. In 2004, UNITE merged with the Hotel Employees and Restaurant Employees International Union, or HERE, becoming UNITE HERE, with some 850,000 workers and retirees. Then, in 2009, that group split, and the erstwhile textile leaders formed Workers United, which affiliated with Levinson's SEIU, representing healthcare, public-sector, building-services, food-service, janitorial, and some textile-manufacturing workers, for a total of about 2 million members. The remaining garment workers, mainly in New England, stayed with UNITE HERE.)

However, Timberland takes the opposite view from Levinson and most activists, arguing that only the monitors it has trained and who answer to it can do the job right. It assigns ten employees full-time and two part-time who visit all the plants at least once a year. There is, in addition, some third-party involvement: two contractors are hired for about 9 percent of the site assessments, and every few years an outside firm audits the code and the inspectors. At the time I met with Timberland officials, in 2010, 22 percent of the plants had the lowest rating for environmental, health, or safety issues, and the company's stated aim was to reduce that to 20 percent by 2015, which seems an awfully easy goal.

If the oversight is a bit too cozy, the saving grace is that toughness may be less necessary here than with other companies. Timberland doesn't have a reputation for using particularly bad subcontractors. Also, Andrea Moffat, Ceres's vice president of corporate programs, cited what she called a "close to unique" project to supplement the official monitoring with local organizations, which is probably the best way to maintain any sort of ongoing supervision. "Audits can be effective, but audits are sporadic," she said. "If you can empower community organizations that are actually living next to these factories on a daily basis to understand what worker rights are, pollution, and these sorts of things, you end up with a more democratic supply-chain situation."

Jeff Ballinger, the antisweatshop activist, said Timberland could still do more by pressuring its subcontractors to lobby their local governments for stronger laws and enforcement. Levi Strauss & Company has publicly endorsed putting rigorous labor standards into international trade agreements, according to Mark Levinson.

In reply, Timberland officials plead their company's small size and inexperience. "Policy is a new area for Timberland," Peterson said, and indeed, it didn't rank among the top twenty companies in either the retail or clothing-manufacturing sectors in terms of political donations and lobbying, according to the records of the Center for Responsive Politics. Both Peterson and Colleen Von Haden said the company was starting to dip its toe into advocacy. If so, it's a pretty shallow dip. Von Haden said, "We are looking to engage in public-private partnerships and advocacy efforts" to make sure that existing minimum-wage levels are enforced in the countries it sources from, which is way below what Levinson and Ballinger call for. The two men would probably want Timberland to advocate to *raise* the minimum. Peterson might do exactly that; he said the company was considering working with local suppliers or perhaps other big brands to increase minimum wages. Still, if he were going to get involved in something like lobbying, he added, "I'd rather work on green issues to make better materials choices and reduce our footprint."

When I asked Peterson whether, in light of all the potential problems with overseas plants, he wishes Timberland made more of its stuff in the United States, he ducked the question. "I can't say I spend a lot of time on that," he said.

THE QUESTION: Does Timberland deserve its reputation
as an exemplar of ethical chic?

THE VERDICT: Yes, but . . .

After more than twenty years of tutoring schoolkids, donating boots, recycling rubber, and other steps, Timberland has earned the trust of activists. They're willing to bend the rules on some touchy points.

Consider, for instance, all the problems associated with cows. Michael Markarian, of the Humane Society, allowed that "it would be a heavy lift for companies to be completely leather free." So, for him, it's more important that Timberland not use fur or ingredients from exotic, endangered, or threatened species. Similarly, Dan Shannon, at the more radical PETA, preferred to emphasize that Timberland avoids fur and doesn't obtain its wool from Australia or its leather from India, where, he claimed, cows are transported in "hideously abusive," hot, crowded conditions.

Even if Timberland abandoned its entire business model and stopped using leather altogether, Andrea Moffat at Ceres noted that almost every raw material has ethical problems. Cotton requires huge amounts of pesticides and water. Synthetics are probably petroleum based, thereby exacerbating all the environmental and political issues associated with oil drilling and emissions. Moffat wouldn't answer directly when I asked if Ceres would prefer for Timberland to use less leather, saying merely that her group had discussed the topic with officials there. "If companies can develop new materials, designs, or different types of products that have less impact, these are an improvement," she said. "I'm not an expert on how you replace leather."

More important, Moffat added, is that "they've really tried to integrate environmental-social issues into their business strategies. You'll hear Jeff Swartz talk about those issues to his shareholders and stakeholders. They're engaging their consumers, putting labeling on boxes." And despite that little business in Brazil, Greenpeace's Rolf Skar set a lot of value on the fact that Timberland is relatively open and willing to work with environmental groups. Indeed, noting how cooperative Nike had also been in the Amazon, Skar wondered whether there wasn't something about the shoe industry, particularly athletic and outdoor shoes, that encouraged eco-consciousness.

Activists thus say they have faith that Timberland's virtue can survive the takeover by VF, a North Carolina–based apparel conglomerate that already owns the Nautica, North Face, and Wrangler lines.

For one thing, VF presumably didn't pay $2 billion just for a bunch of leather. The community service, recycling, and eco-tanneries are "part of the brand image," pointed out Andrew Page, senior director of the Humane Society's fur campaign. "They would lose their customers if they changed that." And Jim Davey, Timberland's marketing director, noted that concern for the environment is an inherent corporate value in the boot business. "Our customers are people who love the outdoors, whether it's a park in Shanghai or a hike in the mountains or a puddly March day in the city," he said. "We are an outdoor company, and we need the outdoors."

Another reason for hope is that VF itself doesn't have a terrible reputation. ICCR records show only one episode—a resolution in approximately 2004 seeking better monitoring of the corporation's supply chain—according to the Reverend David Schilling, the ICCR's director of human rights and resources. PETA noted that "many" VF brands shun fur and merino wool. The official Timberland-VF press release quoted VF chief executive Eric Wiseman praising his new toy's "leadership position in sustainability." Then came a quote from Jeff Swartz: "Timberland is proud of . . . its reputation as a responsible and environmentally conscious global citizen, all of which will be preserved and enhanced by becoming part of the VF family."

Yet there are worrisome signs, too. At the time of the purchase, VF emphasized its plans for "expense management" and "operating disciplines"—in other words, cost cutting. It sure will have to save money somehow to justify that $2 billion purchase price, which most business analysts considered a bit rich. A CSR frill such as paying employees to take time off to build playgrounds is one obvious place for hard-nosed managers to cut. Moreover, some sense of ethics, philanthropy, or camaraderie—maybe noblesse oblige—is often lost when a founding family gives way to corporate control (as remains to be seen, perhaps, at Tom's of Maine). At the independent Timberland, Domini's Steven Lydenberg said, many of the policies were possible only "because they are family controlled and run, and the commitment comes from the very top."

In fairness, Schilling said, give the new company six months to a year—that is, around January to July 2012. Some key indicators of trouble would be a cutback in public reporting, fewer webinars with nongovernmental organizations (NGOs) and investors, reductions or reallocation of staff, and less CSR collaboration with other companies.

So a year from now, let's see if the folks from PETA, the Humane Society, Greenpeace, and elsewhere are still wearing Timberland boots.

CHAPTER 3

Starbucks

Coffee as a Brand Name

Mɪᴄʜᴀᴇʟ Tᴏᴍᴀssᴏ, ᴀ ʀᴇᴛɪʀᴇᴅ telephone company technician, age fifty-nine, stops by the Starbucks outlet about a mile from his Brooklyn apartment several times a week, staying half an hour to do the newspaper's daily crossword puzzle. The rest of the week, he works the puzzle at home, but "sometimes I want the ambience at Starbucks." What does he drink? Bottled mocha, never any of the fresh-made coffee concoctions.

Ann Stein (not her real name) was "just killing some time" at the same Starbucks before picking up her five-year-old daughter from preschool. She made it clear that she doesn't do this often, maybe once every two or three weeks, when she's out on errands and it's not worth going home in between. She drinks the anonymous daily brewed coffee.

At a Starbucks a couple of miles away, high school senior Elizabeth Chavez (not her real name) did homework on her laptop until it was time to start her after-school job at a nearby gym. Chavez said she visited this café, as well as one closer to her school, two or three times a week, because "I like the environment. Nobody bothers me." Her beverages: vanilla lattes and the daily brewed coffee.

Barely three blocks further on, at yet a third Starbucks, Caroline Sausville, a thirty-seven-year-old personal shopper from France, was drinking black coffee. "It's so expensive, the fancy, fancy coffees, and I can do the same thing at home," she scoffed. However, she enjoys Starbucks' pastries, especially the Mallorca Sweet Bread.

About a half-mile down the street from Michael and Ann's Starbucks is a much smaller coffee house, one of three in a local chain called Café Grumpy. Thirty-three-year-old Web designer Jeff Meininger is a big fan of the coffee. "Starbucks is crap," he declared. "It tastes burnt."

Lily Meyers (not her real name), a writer and multimedia artist in her fifties, hangs out at Gorilla Coffee, another independent coffee bar, a half-mile in the opposite direction. "The music is better," she said. "At Starbucks, you hear Christmas music at Christmastime, the same thing over and over. Here, it's local bands and old stuff. You rarely hear the same thing twice." She added that the coffee at Gorilla has more flavor. The fact that it's not part of a big conglomerate appeals to her, too. "I really like supporting local places," she said.

Scott Schroeder, thirty-five, who runs an investment fund, brings his eleven-year-old daughter to Grumpy for the zucchini muffins. He prefers Grumpy's coffee to the Starbucks brand—but really, he added with a laugh, "I frequent just about every coffee establishment." It was around 5 P.M., and this was his third coffee stop that day.

A social anthropologist could no doubt find a thesis's worth of trends in this small survey. However, here's the main point: whether they love Starbucks or hate it, Michael, Ann, Elizabeth, Caroline, Jeff, Lily, and Scott were where they were, drinking what they were drinking, because of Starbucks.

Before Starbucks, people drank a generic beverage called coffee. Today, thanks to Starbucks, coffee is an experience. With gourmet beans, a squirt of foamed milk, and a few foreign-sounding (though sometimes made-up or misused) mix-n-match words, Starbucks claims that it enables anyone to feel as sophisticated as an Italian sipping espresso in Venice. Throw in big, comfortable armchairs, copies of the *New York Times* previous customers left behind, a homey brown-and-green decor, and free WiFi to create a "third place," or "an extension of the front porch," as CEO Howard Schultz described it in his first autobiography, *Pour Your Heart into It.* And if those coffee beans—or at least some of them—are grown in environmentally sustainable ways by farmers paid a bit more than average, and if the part-time employee serving them at the counter has corporate-sponsored health insurance, a Starbucks customer can vicariously be a sophisticated world traveler while sitting on a pseudo–front porch and feel virtuous about helping the environment, impoverished farmers, and struggling American workers. All for only, oh, three times the price of a plain old cup of coffee.

"At Starbucks, our product is not just great coffee but also what we call the 'Starbucks experience': an inviting, enriching environment in our stores that is comfortable and accessible yet also stylish and elegant," Schultz wrote.

The "Italian" product names are unabashedly phony. The coffee is genuine. And what about the rest?

Howard Schultz claims he didn't start his career seeking to create gourmet coffee or a front-porch meeting place. For that matter, he neither founded Starbucks nor imported the first cup of espresso to America. He was a businessman selling various products until, by 1979, he wrote, he'd been named head of US operations for the Hammarplast line of "stylish Swedish-designed kitchen equipment and housewares."

But Schultz says he was dreaming of bigger things, of making the world a better place, inspired by President John Kennedy and the Peace Corps. According to Dori Jones Yang, the veteran journalist who cowrote Schultz's autobiography, he was also driven by memories of how his father, Fred, a truck driver, lost his job when he broke his ankle in 1961, leaving the family with "no income, no health insurance, no workers' compensation, nothing to fall back on." Whatever business specialty Schultz eventually settled on, he wanted to run a company that treated its workforce decently. Yang said that's why the book begins with the story of his father. (Conflict-of-interest alert: I worked with Yang years ago at BusinessWeek, before she met Schultz.)

Coffee simply became the vehicle for Schultz's dreams. Noticing that Hammarplast was selling an unexpectedly large number of drip coffee-makers to a small, four-store retailer in Seattle named Starbucks Coffee, Tea, and Spice, he flew west to investigate. He drank a cup and visited the roasting plant, and soon he was begging for a job. "I felt as though I had discovered a whole new continent," Schultz said of that first cup. It was "stronger than any coffee I had ever tasted," with "full flavors as they slipped over my tongue." Company employees discoursed lovingly about the mountains where the beans were grown, the color of the beans, and the roasting process. After a yearlong courtship, Schultz was hired as head of marketing.

While savvy US consumers could find strong, gourmet, European coffee back then, the shops were usually tucked away near a university campus or in the beatnik fringe. What most Americans considered coffee was "light brown and almost see-through," as Temple University history professor Bryant Simon described it in his 2009 book about Starbucks, *Everything but the Coffee*. Schultz called it "dreadful" and "swill," pointing out that typical American coffee before the advent of his company was made with "inferior type [robusta beans] that the coffee traders of London and Amsterdam treated as a cheap commodity." US coffee consumption had actually been declining since the 1960s, replaced mainly by soft drinks.

Understandably, Schultz treads lightly with the two founders who hired him, Gerald Baldwin and Gordon Bowker—the third founder, Zev Siegl, sold out in 1980—but, reading between the lines, it's obvious he considered them overly cautious old fogies who didn't understand modern business practices, including the need to constantly grow. Schultz was, after all, a marketing man. He was also, like many converts, more enthusiastic than the original gurus.

A crucial fissure opened up after he took a business trip to Italy in 1983. Schultz realized he didn't want merely to sell coffee beans for people to take home like groceries, which was Starbucks's specialty. He wanted to operate cafés, the same as in Italy. "What we had to do was unlock the romance and mystery of coffee, firsthand, in coffee bars," he wrote. "The Italians understood the personal relationship that people could have to coffee, its social aspect." When this turned out to be a push too much for Baldwin and Bowker, Schultz severed ties and in 1985 founded his own pseudo-European gourmet-coffee shop, Il Giornale. (It was named, he said, for the Italian word for "daily," although that was also the title of the well-known Italian newspaper then owned by the man who would one day become that country's controversial right-wing prime minister, Silvio Berlusconi.) No hard feelings; Starbucks actually invested $150,000 in Schultz's new venture.

Everything came full circle in 1987, when Baldwin and Bowker decided to sell the business, and Schultz bought it. Now he had a chance to carry out his vision in full: a widespread chain of cafés with Italian-style ambience, high-quality coffee, and fair treatment of workers.

Schultz's description of his starting goals for Il Giornale works equally well for Starbucks. He wanted, he said, "to reinvent a commodity. We would take something old and tired and common—coffee—and weave a sense of romance and community around it. We would rediscover the mystique and charm that had swirled around coffee throughout the centuries. We would enchant customers with an atmosphere of sophistication and style and knowledge."

In many ways, Schultz succeeded, even beyond his dreams. Certainly, Starbucks today is a brand known worldwide, with outlets located everywhere from the Seattle birthplace to Shanghai, from Switzerland to Seoul. It's an icon of America. Everyone goes there: all ages, ethnicities, races, and clothing styles—business types, teenagers, tourists, backpackers, women in Muslim head scarves, nursing mothers, and much more—even if "latte-drinking" has become a pejorative shorthand for liberal, white-wine-sipping, tree-hugging Democrats who live in San Francisco. Dori Jones Yang, Schultz's coauthor, recalled that when she asked him who he was marketing to, he would say, "Go to Starbucks and look at the people in line. You get the cops and the construction people from nearby sites, as well as upper-income people."

(Almost the only place on Earth lacking a Starbucks latte is Israel, and the exception was a subject of some controversy in the blogosphere when the coffee company ended its joint venture there in 2003. While Starbucks, in a posting on its website, blamed business disagreements with its local partner, the company had come under tremendous pressure from Palestinian activists ever since Schultz spoke in defense of Israel at his synagogue, and supporters of the Jewish state expressed fears that the chain was knuckling under to anti-Israeli pressure.)

Has it built an extended front porch? Heck, it may be an entire house. People know they can stay for hours with their laptops and an empty cup, or stop in just to use the restroom, no questions asked. Bryant Simon, sitting in Starbucks venues ten to fifteen hours a week for nine months for his book, found real estate agents poring over maps with prospective tenants and entrepreneurs interviewing job seekers. In the heart of San Francisco, I saw one man snoring away in an easy chair.

Furthermore, Starbucks has helped provide some of the entertainment people might carry to its tables. In 1995, the chain began compiling and selling CDs of jazz, classical music, and blues. It followed up by acquiring the Hear Music label, producing original CDs and albums, publishing a quarterly magazine called Joe with Time Inc., cosponsoring the MSNBC show Morning Joe, promoting books and movies, and selling DVDs. It also established a private, in-store digital channel to give Starbucks-goers exclusive access to selected book excerpts, news articles, iTunes music, and educational games. (Not all those enterprises lasted.) To publicize the heartwarming 2008 novel For One More Day, the company brought author Mitch Albom to its flagship Manhattan store, and arranged phone chats in twenty-five cities. The ultimate achievement: it bagged eight Grammies in 2005 for *Genius Loves Company*, the final album by Ray Charles, which it coproduced.

However, Starbucks has discovered limits to its front porch. Even Schultz admitted that he hadn't quite created the "third place" he envisioned. That concept, first outlined by Florida sociology professor Ray Oldenburg in 1989, was supposed to mean "informal public places where [people] can gather, put aside the concerns of work and home, relax, and talk," Schultz wrote. In the Italian cafés he so much admired, he added, "you can hear the interplay of people meeting for the first time, as well as people greeting friends they see every day at the bar." It's the image, as well, of the traditional French café, with passionate artists arguing endlessly over strong coffee and stronger cigarettes (without the cigarettes). Thus, in the ideal Starbucks, a customer would sip a cup of cappuccino—or, better still, a few refills—while chatting amiably with whoever was in the next seat. Kind of like calling out to your neighbor while you rock on your real front porch.

Yet, for all the armchairs, Schultz said that when an ad agency did a survey in Los Angeles, "fewer than 10 percent of the people they observed in our stores at any given time actually ever talked to anybody." Making matter worse, barely 20 percent of patrons linger long enough to schmooze even if they wanted to; the vast majority get their caffeine hits to go.

Author Bryant Simon, during his nine months of Starbucks sitting, tried vainly to engage strangers in conversation. "No one talked with anyone they didn't seem to already know or hadn't come there to meet," he wrote in obvious frustration. Similarly, labor organizer Kim Fellner stayed an entire day, from 5 A.M. until 9 P.M., at her local outlet for her 2008 book *Wrestling with Starbucks*, and she reported only two instances where customers "leaped into" an ongoing conversation among strangers or joined in after "eavesdropping." I got the same sort of results every time I stopped by. It would seem that the most common activity at Starbucks is typing on a laptop, solo.

In 2009, the company tried to stir up some family-style dining and conversation by installing long wooden tables in the middle of some of its restaurants, replacing the individual chair-and-table arrangements. However, customers have simply converted those into individual tables,

very carefully leaving an empty seat between themselves and other patrons, and proceeding to converse with their own companions or work
on their laptops.

Whether or not the customers talk to each other, the baristas—
despite the chain's vaunted reputation for friendly staff—don't talk much
with them.

During more than three dozen visits over ten months at Starbucks
venues of all sizes, in all sorts of neighborhoods, at all times of day, from
the heart of San Francisco to suburban Massachusetts, from office-park
Los Angeles to downtown Washington, DC, from a small town in upstate
New York to the hippest niches of Manhattan, and more, I almost never
saw any over-the-counter chitchat. Out of 420 customers at the counter
during those visits, merely 25 talked with baristas. That's actually a far
lower percentage than the amount of interaction I found at other coffee
places like Gorilla, Grumpy, and the granddaddy of the movement, Peet's
Coffee & Tea, where the ratio was 1 out of 10. Fellner's experience was apparently similar, although her book isn't always clear about who is talking with whom.

It's not that Starbucks baristas are terse or unfriendly. Most of them
say, "May I help you?" cheerfully enough—perhaps a tad more cheerfully
than elsewhere, perhaps not. Naturally, some are more outgoing than
others. There was the Latino guy in San Francisco who seemed to find
something warm to say to everyone, and the barista in upstate New York
who sang out "Helloooo!" and the woman in Los Angeles who suggested
another place I might find a bagel one evening when her store had run
out, then remembered me the next morning. I overheard conversations
about the most recent Redskins-Texans game, long hours at work, shopping for a new car, and a son going off to college. But those were the
exceptions. Far more common were the customers who never took their
mouths away from their cell phones and the baristas who were too busy
talking with each other to spare any unnecessary words for their clientele. What about the iconic barista who supposedly knows the favorite
beverage of all the regulars? I saw exactly two examples of that.

On the other hand, Richard Honack, a marketing professor at Northwestern University's Kellogg Graduate School of Management, seems to
have had much more positive encounters. The staff, he claimed, give customers the sense that "you're the most important person, because we're
talking with you." If someone doesn't quite know the name of a particular drink, the barista will try to figure it out, and if that fails, "people

in line help them get it. Someone will say, 'I tried that macchiato—it really is good.'" If a customer wants to invent something, that's OK, too. Honack said that the manager of one nearby outlet makes sure to have a bottle of eggnog on hand every day for a friend of Honack's who likes eggnog latte, even when it's not in season. Of course Schultz, in his second book, *Onward*, offers plenty of examples of dedicated baristas who are BFFs with their customers, including one who donated a kidney to a longtime coffee drinker.

Then there's Michael Gates Gill, a son of the famed *New Yorker* columnist Brendan Gill, who became a barista at age sixty-three and actually titled his 2007 memoir *How Starbucks Saved My Life*. The book is full of examples of Gill and coworkers chattering away with regulars as well as newcomers, memorizing the drinks certain people ordered every day.

Schultz claimed that "we train baristas to make eye contact with customers" and that the staff are supposed to be "romancing" the public. "If we greet customers, exchange a few extra words with them, and then custom make a drink exactly to their taste, they will be eager to come back." In theory, sure. But, Howard, you try buying a latte—incognito.

The problem of depersonalization only worsened as Starbucks kept on growing. From 6 stores when Schultz took charge in 1987, it jumped to over 100 in 1992, when the company went public, to a staggering pace of one new opening per day by the end of 1995, culminating with 13,000 around the globe by 2007. After all, that was why Schultz had broken with the founders to begin with, because he envisioned a nationwide chain. Even after he resigned as CEO in 2000, the drive plowed on, as Schultz remained in the chairman's seat and "turned my attention to expanding Starbucks around the world," according to *Onward*.

It can get tough for any company that grows that fast to maintain its grip on quality and the personal touch. And—perhaps because Schultz was distracted by other interests, like his private equity fund and part ownership of the then Seattle SuperSonics—Starbucks handled matters particularly badly.

Most notoriously, in the name of efficiency, the stores stopped grinding their coffee on site and replaced their old-fashioned, hand-operated espresso machines with a semiautomated version. Customers could literally no longer smell the coffee. Furthermore, the new machines were bigger than their predecessors, blocking the public's view of the baristas at work. "It didn't sound or smell like European coffee shops anymore," pointed out Robert Passikoff, president and founder of Brand Keys, a New York City–based consulting firm that focuses on issues of brand loyalty. "People were paying 40 percent more for coffee they could get down the block, but they didn't see coffee being handcrafted." If any Starbucks workers really had gotten to know their customers, said Ashley Woodruff, a financial analyst at T. Rowe Price specializing in restaurants and grocery stores, the rapid corporate buildup killed the relationship. "One of the problems when you're expanding at the pace Starbucks was, there's constant churn," she said. "You never see the same person in the same store."

With chain size came complaints of big-chain mentality. Bryant Simon, in his book, asserted that the music became more commercial. So did the ambience, with outlets selling toys and tchotchkes that evoked the feel of a souvenir store at a highway rest stop. Some customers protested the corporate move into breakfast foods such as eggs and said the place smelled like McDonald's. Others faulted what they saw as a cookie-cutter sameness to the decor as each new store was slapped down and laid out in one of four official designs and color schemes. The finances felt the hit, from both a decline in customers and the costs of expansion. Starting in late 2006, the stock plunged, and same-store sales for outlets open more than a year (the standard retail yardstick) barely increased after sixteen years of 5 percent annual growth. Of course, the slide got worse during the 2008–2009 recession.

You just cease being the quirky, hip, neighborhood coffeehouse if someone can find three of you within six blocks. Jill Kickul, of New York University's social-entrepreneurship program, said that her undergraduate students "see Starbucks as too corporate now and too standardized and not unique enough, not edgy enough, not grimy enough." Added Carol Holding, the brand-strategies consultant who's based right in the company's hometown, "There's such Starbucks fatigue. The ubiquity reduced the exclusivity."

As the author Naomi Klein—no fan of Starbucks or any well-known chain—pointed out in her classic book No Logo, the key reason select companies like the Gap, Ikea, and Starbucks managed for so long to avoid being seen as another McDonald's or Walmart is that they "don't flash with the garish, cartoonlike plastic yellow shells and golden arches; they are more apt to glow with a healthy New Age sheen." That is, they look more sophisticated and trendy.

It was a shaky balancing act, and the weight of 13,000 stores finally pushed things over. By the 1999 meeting of the World Trade Organization in Seattle, Starbucks had become such a symbol of multinational McDonaldization that antiglobalization protesters hurled rocks through its café windows.

Howard Schultz didn't initially understand the criticism. In his first book—published in 1997, in the still-booming days—he wrote, "When Starbucks started being targeted, it caught us off guard. We were so used to regarding ourselves as the good guys, as the struggling underdogs." Yang, his coauthor, told me that "he was kind of surprised by [the comparisons to big chains], and a little bit hurt by that. He pointed out that it wasn't like Walmart, which goes in and offers lower prices than all the local companies and drives them out of business." (True enough: You can hardly accuse Starbucks of underpricing, as we'll discuss in more detail.)

Nevertheless, by winter 2007, even Schultz couldn't ignore the festering unhappiness. He penned a memo to his successor that quickly became public, conceding that, as a result of growth over the prior decade, "we have had to make a series of decisions that, in retrospect, have lead [sic] to the watering down of the Starbucks experience, and what some might call the commoditization of our brand." Among other issues, he cited the automated espresso machines and loss of fresh coffee beans.

Moreover, dissatisfied patrons had alternatives. Now that Starbucks had proved there's a broad demand for gourmet varieties, a slew of actual neighborhood places had sprung up offering the one-of-a-kind, funky, edgy image that Starbucks used to claim, like Café Grumpy. Gorilla, Think Coffee (favored by Kickul's New York University students), Ozzie's Coffee and Tea, Café Regular, Root Hill Café, Southside Coffee, Oslo, Verb, Mud, Ninth Street Espresso, Gimmel Coffee, Jack's Stir Brew, Abraço Espresso, Everyman Espresso—and those were merely a few of the names in New York City in the fall of 2009. Pushing from the other side, McDonald's and Dunkin' Donuts began offering less-expensive Italianate drinks.

Interestingly, labor activist and author Kim Fellner suggested that their very trendiness makes the little guys actually *less* socially responsible than Starbucks, if their highfalutin airs put off many of Schultz's construction-worker customers. "Neither an artisan shop like Murky [a coffeehouse in her Washington, DC, neighborhood she thinks has the best-tasting brew locally] nor an industrial shop like Dunkin', [Starbucks] broadcasts accessibility to all regardless of race or class, while retaining the music, the lighting, and the ambience that speak to high-end aspirations," she wrote. In addition, Starbucks is a lot more welcoming to laptops and other electronic gizmos than some of the quainter shops.

The world certainly has room for all these venues, Starbucks and small. Yang said that's what Schultz always felt: "His point of view was that the whole pie was growing larger, and Starbucks was just taking a larger portion of a larger pie." By his statistics, US gourmet coffee drinking had zoomed 18 percent annually between 1984 and the time his first book was published. For that matter, Starbucks itself owns the middle-market brand Seattle's Best.

Inevitably, some of the little guys go out of business, but that doesn't mean Starbucks pushed them over. About half of all start-ups fail within the first five years, according to the US Small Business Administration. Schultz in part blames landlords who, he said, "use Starbucks as a bargaining chip, informing another coffee company or another prospective tenant that we are interested in the space and then jacking up the rent." Without any help from Starbucks, Gorilla Coffee managed to shut itself down for more than two weeks in April 2010 in a dispute between staff and the owners.

In any case, apparently Schultz's memo wasn't enough to revive the brand, and Schultz returned in person as CEO in 2008. A whirlwind of changes followed. For starters, he closed all the stores for three hours to retrain the entire staff. Then he brought back in-store bean grinding, installed shorter espresso machines, ordered the baristas to make fresh batches more frequently, brewed a new, milder blend called Pike's Place Roast, acquired the manufacturer of a highly regarded brewing machine, the Clover, revamped the reviled breakfast sandwiches, and—shockingly for this maven of growth—shuttered nearly 1,000 stores, cutting costs by some $580 million. But that was just to get stabilized.

Looking ahead, Schultz introduced innovations such as a loyalty card with discounts, healthier and trendier food choices, a jazzed-up website, and the chain's first big ad campaign. Another surprising flourish was Via instant coffee for people to make at home. (So much for the "third place" and the communal experience of the Italian coffee bar.) Meanwhile, Schultz slightly redrew the logo—which he insists is a siren from Greek mythology but most people call a mermaid—and signed a partnership that paved the way to the biggest untapped market, India. For dessert, he bought Evolution Fresh, a maker of natural fruit and vegetable juices.

Hedging its bets, Starbucks in 2009 opened two outlets in its hometown incognito, under the monikers 15 Ave Coffee and Tea, and Roy Street Coffee and Tea, with nary a mermaid (or siren) in sight. Aficionados of the buy-local movement screamed that Starbucks was tricking coffee drinkers who specifically did not want to buy from a big chain. Starbucks officials retorted that they had to give the new places different names since they sell beer and wine, which classic Starbucks outlets don't. "We were not trying to hide anything," Schultz insisted, rather ridiculously, merely hoping to "experiment with other retail concepts that would further elevate our coffee authority."

Perhaps most important was the sheer fact of his return: even if Howard Schultz is no Steve Jobs, rarely can anyone boost morale like a company founder.

There were stumbles, of course. The sugary, yogurtlike Sorbetto flopped after a year; Starbucks trailed badly behind Green Mountain Coffee Roasters in the realm of take-home packets; and the redrawn logo has attracted criticism, as alterations of any traditional symbol often do. Overall, however, the changes were widely lauded. Via is considered a big success, and same-store sales and the stock perked up in late 2009. Many experts think Starbucks can recapture some of its magic.

But a good chunk is lost forever. It's been too many years, too many look-alike stores, too much fresh competition.

If coffee is Starbucks's key product, where and how it obtains the raw ingredient ought to be key to its social responsibility, or lack thereof. Indeed, coffee sourcing is one of the policies the company particularly likes to brag about, and most people seem to have a vague idea that all its coffee is fair trade, even if they don't quite know what the term means. Carol Holding, the branding consultant, said that "people absolutely support Starbucks for that. It balances out the price."

Well, the image is and isn't true. Starbucks does spell out a lot of policies to help struggling farmers in the poorest parts of the world where coffee is grown. But not all its coffee is fair trade. It's not the only coffee company trying to buy fair trade. And fair trade isn't the sole sourcing issue.

"Fair Trade Certified" is an official label that means a product has been audited by one of several NGOs to ensure that it follows a set of international standards. Among the standards, fair trade goods must be grown in environmentally sustainable ways; the workers must be treated decently and paid a living wage; they are guaranteed freedom of association and a safe workplace; forced child labor is forbidden; growers are promised a minimum payment level; and the producers must invest in long-term planning to improve both growing and social conditions. Coffee—by far the biggest fair trade crop—traditionally had some additional requirements to protect independent, small-scale growers. To cover the higher costs, middlemen pay a premium of, typically, 10 to 20 percent over market rates.

Does Starbucks do all that? According to its website, Starbucks and a respected environmental group called Conservation International jointly set guidelines for environmental and workplace matters at the farms that grow its coffee. By 2009, 81 percent of the beans it purchased, or 299 million pounds, met those standards, known as Coffee and Farmer Equity (CAFE) Practices, and Schultz declared a goal of reaching 100 percent by 2015. Under the CAFE Practices, outside parties must verify that there are "measures in place to manage waste, protect water quality, conserve water and energy, preserve biodiversity, and reduce agrochemical use" and must confirm that there are "measures in place that concern safe, fair, and humane working conditions." The CAFE definition for working conditions goes on to specify that "compliance with the indicators for minimum-wage requirements and [for] addressing child labor/forced labor and discrimination is mandatory." All that is fine. Nevertheless, it's not fair trade, strictly defined. The Starbucks standards don't specifically forbid child labor, forced labor, or discrimination. Moreover, relying on developing countries' minimum-wage requirements as a standard is almost meaningless since these are often far below the living wage required for fair trade certification. And what is "compliance with the indicators"?

Separately, Starbucks has set up support centers in Costa Rica and Rwanda to teach small local growers how to increase yields and improve coffee quality, and it has paid out some $2.5 million annually in small loans. But those efforts speak more to ensuring the quality of beans— a business necessity—than the quality of farmers' lives.

Starbucks does buy some genuinely fair trade coffee; in fact, it says it's the biggest purchaser in the world. (Green Mountain also claims to be number one.) As of 2009, however, that came to only about 40 million pounds, or one-ninth of the corporate total. In other words, just a small portion of the macchiatos and lattes you might drink are fair trade certified—even by the US group's more lax criteria.

Defenders say there aren't enough fair trade beans in the ground to satisfy Starbucks customers' voracious thirst. While that's true, it's circular: Starbucks has so much clout that if it demanded more fair trade beans, producers and shippers would find a way to comply. The same supposed dilemma occurred in 2002 with Ben & Jerry's and cage-free eggs (eggs laid by hens that have more freedom of movement than those in cramped traditional cages). When the Humane Society pressed B&J to use more of the humanely raised eggs in its ice cream, the company initially argued that it couldn't find enough, because 7,000 chickens are required to produce its annual supply of eggs. Somehow, however, it managed. Four years later, all the ice-cream maker's eggs were from cage-free chickens.

Some activists debate whether even fair trade does enough to protect the desperately poor people who grow the beans so beloved by customers who can afford more than three dollars for a cup of them in liquid form. When environmental consultant Fred Pearce trooped out to Tanzania for his 2008 book *Confessions of an Eco-Sinner*, coffee farmers pointed out that their fair trade "premium" price of $1.46 per pound might be 20 cents above average, but the buyers then turned around and sold that crop for the equivalent of $12 per pound retail. For a month's work—one sack of fair trade beans—a grower might get ten dollars. "No wonder that these farmers . . . struggle to send their own children to school," Pearce wrote. "No wonder their roofs leak. No wonder that no farmer I met had even a motorbike to take his beans to the shed." Similarly, in 2009 *Time* cited a survey of 179 fair trade coffee farmers in Central America and Mexico, in which "more than half said their families have still been going hungry for several months a year."

Sure, if Starbucks bought larger quantities of fair trade coffee or paid growers more, it would probably raise its retail prices. But for devotees already paying $3.20 and up, would an extra 10 cents be such a big deal?

Also on the menu are a number of noncoffee items. Starbucks' ethical policies for cocoa and tea are less developed, and it has not joined the big chocolate names Mars Inc., Cadbury Company, and Nestlé in working with the International Cocoa Initiative to set labor standards for infamous cocoa-growing countries such as Côte d'Ivoire, according to both the initiative's website and Linda Golodner, a former president of the National Consumers League. (Golodner was the consumer expert representing the United States on a special committee that wrote social-responsibility guidance for the International Organization for Standardization.)

It's important, as well, to consider what motivated Starbucks, and that probably wasn't its own conscience. The company came under tremendous criticism in the mid-1990s and again at the Seattle WTO meeting for buying beans grown by children and in other abusive circumstances. While Starbucks claimed it had no control over the growers and middlemen, it gave a token $75,000 to set up a revolving-loan fund for farmers in Guatemala, the site of the child-labor charge. Since then, it's become practically a competitive requirement for big-name brands—even McDonald's and Dunkin' Donuts—to offer some fair trade coffee.

Authors Kim Fellner and Bryant Simon separately went out to visit farmers who were selling to the coffee giant through some sort of ethical program, and each came back with a different conclusion. Fellner was more supportive, Simon more skeptical. Fellner said that Starbucks, "along with the Rainforest Alliance and a number of other NGOs, has become the toughest enforcer of environmental standards in the coffee fields," and she credited its payment premiums with saving small farmers when prices plunged in the early 2000s. Simon, meanwhile, said he could never find any "little farmers" from whom Starbucks claimed to buy its beans but instead met growers who told him that the company actually goes through large middlemen. As the book quotes one of them, "Starbucks bought almost exclusively from privately owned enterprises, from fairly wealthy investors." To add to the confusion, two of the three largest exporters of premium *Coffea arabica* beans are Brazil and Colombia, and the former is known for large, mechanized farms, while the latter relies more on small landowners. Plus, a surge in commodity prices in 2011 briefly uprooted the local-coffee cooperative system.

By 2005, Starbucks was certainly as aware as anyone of the need to maintain a socially responsible image regarding the people who were growing its basic crops (whether it deserved that image or not). That makes it hard to understand how the company could be so heavy-handed and lacking in PR savvy when it came to the farmers in the desperately poor country that discovered coffee a millennium ago, Ethiopia.

As has been widely reported by now, Ethiopia was trying to establish branding rights for certain regions famous for coffee, including Yirgacheffe, Harar (sometimes spelled Harrar), and Sidamo, so that it could trademark coffee sold with those regional names and, presumably, charge more. As Adam Kanzer, the general counsel for Domini, explained, "The names have acquired a certain value in the marketplace. It has a certain taste; it has a certain quality to it. [Ethiopian officials] felt that if they own the intellectual property, they could market the brand in a more effective way."

Many governments granted trademark protection to Ethiopia, including Canada, Japan, and the European Union, but the US Patent and Trademark Office rejected Harar and Sidamo on the grounds that Starbucks had already applied to register something called Shirkina Sun-Dried Sidamo. "Starbucks argued that you can't own the name of a region," Kanzer said. So, how could Starbucks itself register its label, if Ethiopia couldn't? The company claimed its situation was different, because it was using the word Sidamo as part of a longer, fancier brand name for a unique way of processing the coffee.

The dispute ran on for more than two years, played out in the press and public, as the Ethiopian government, Domini, Oxfam America, Trillium, and Light Years IP (an organization that helps developing countries profit from their intellectual property rights) all lobbied Starbucks. The Ethiopian ambassador wrote to Schultz; Domini brought an Ethiopian farmer to the Starbucks annual meeting; Oxfam circulated petitions and ran newspaper ads. The conflict even got a spot in a documentary about Ethiopia, *Black Gold*, that premiered at the Sundance Film Festival in 2006. Meanwhile, the National Coffee Association, a powerful trade group, filed a petition with the patent office opposing the Ethiopian government, allegedly at Starbucks's behest.

Beyond saying, "We got there first," Starbucks essentially argued that it would take better care of the farmers, and give them a bigger share of the proceeds, than their own government would. Even Kanzer conceded that "the Ethiopian government is not the most up-and-up government, and there were legitimate concerns raised about where is the revenue going to go—is it going to go to the farmers, or the government?" That may be, but how does that give Starbucks the right to the names? Kim Fellner, strongly siding with Starbucks again, asserted that the corporation meant well and that Ethiopian coffee had a poor reputation anyway.

In the end, and in the real world, there's no way a company can claim to be ethical and concerned about poor farmers, and then try to block those farmers from making money off the suddenly prestigious name of their homeland. "It's not good PR for a company to be on the wrong side of this issue," Kanzer pointed out, somewhat amazed at the coffee giant's stance. Starbucks finally saw the handwriting on the coffee-bean bag, and in June 2007 it signed a licensing deal agreeing to add the word

Ethiopia to the regional names on its brands and to promote that nation's coffees. Today, you'll find Ethiopia Sidamo coffee with the trademark symbol at Starbucks. Coffees with non-Ethiopian geographic names, like Kenya and Sumatra, don't have the TM.

However well or badly it may deal with the people who grow its coffee, Starbucks claims bragging rights regarding the people who serve it. Indeed, that's how the whole story started, going back to 1961, when Howard Schultz was seven years old and his father broke his ankle and lost his job, with no medical insurance. So, as the corporate myth goes, Schultz created a workplace where employees are treated with respect. Since 1988, the chain has offered health coverage to anyone who works at least twenty hours a week, paying 75 percent of the premiums and expanding the benefit over the years to encompass preventive, mental health, chemical dependency, crisis counseling, vision, and dental care—for unmarried partners of either sex, too. Moreover, starting in 1991—even before the company went public—employees working at least twenty hours weekly have been granted stock options.

The staff are called partners to emphasize that they can be stockholders, just like Schultz, and not mere cogs, and there are solid opportunities for promotion, plus a 401(k) plan with a matching corporate contribution. Employees supposedly have a passion for coffee and are encouraged to learn more. The perks keep improving; after Schultz's return, for instance, tuition reimbursement was added. To cater to its diverse customer base, the company hires people of all races, ages, ethnic backgrounds, sexual preference, and tattoos—although perfume is forbidden, "because coffee beans have a bad tendency to absorb odors," Schultz said.

It's easy to scoff at the claims of happy barista-customer friendships and the moniker "partners," but the perks are genuine. Business experts like Jeffrey Bernstein, a senior analyst at Barclays Capital, say Starbucks's pay is at least in line with the industry average, or even slightly above, and the health benefits are unique in the trade. Those benefits are particularly amazing considering that more than 44 percent of Americans with jobs lacked any coverage at the time Congress passed health-care reform in 2010, according to the Kaiser Family Foundation; considering the tremendous political and business opposition to that reform law; and considering the pressure on Schultz to eliminate that "frill" when Starbucks was floundering.

Starbucks has also made the *Fortune* "Best Companies" list every year

from 1998 through 2011 except for 2001, hitting as high as seventh place
in 2008. Among the typical employee comments, according to one in-
sider privy to the list making: "This place is unique because we all get
to know each other really well, but we also are able to enjoy each other's
company during work and outside of work," and "You are a partner in
every store," and even—apparently some baristas do engage in customer
chat—"Starbucks connects with customers in a way no other place does.
We see a lot of people very day, and we get to know them and we make
them feel at home." In addition, Starbucks is one of just three businesses
to qualify for the "100 Best Corporate Citizens" roster of *Corporate Responsibility* magazine every year for the first nine years, based on its performance in areas such as the environment, employee relations, human
rights, philanthropy, governance, and financial issues.

Richard Honack, the Northwestern University marketing professor
and Starbucks admirer, said its business model couldn't succeed unless
the workplace myth were true. "The employees have to buy in to the culture, and the employees do," he asserted. "When you walk in and talk to
Starbucks employees, they're doing just fine. They like their health insurance, they like their training, they like that they're brought in as partners." That's pretty much what labor activist Kim Fellner found when she
not only interviewed employees but also became one for her book, working a six-hour shift. Her conclusion: "For the most part, young workers
consider a job at Starbucks miles above a job at McDonald's, Pizza Hut,
or KFC."

"Treat people like family, and they will be loyal and give their all,"
Schultz wrote in his first book. "It's the oldest formula in business, one
that is second nature to many family-run firms."

If you want dedication, turn to author-barista Michael Gates Gill. In
his Starbucks-adoring memoir, Gill wrote that he was basically a psychological and financial mess—laid off as an executive at a prestigious
advertising firm, recently divorced after an affair, alienated from most
of his children, down nearly to his last dime, and in desperate need of
health insurance to cover an operation for a brain tumor—when he
stopped into Starbucks for a latte he probably couldn't afford and stumbled onto a recruiter. Along with a job and insurance, he gained a loving
community of coworkers and, by the way, learned to respect low-income,
poorly educated, young blacks and Latinos he would have shunned while
at the ad agency and growing up in his famous father's shadow, when he
hobnobbed with Jackie Kennedy, Ernest Hemingway, and Queen Eliza-

beth. (Really. Or so he says.) In Gill's Starbucks, the baristas are almost universally friendly and supportive, eager to help him adjust, and never jealous when one manager wins an award. As he wrote, "I could not deny the feeling of a growing happiness in my heart. This new, quiet, inner happiness kept catching me unawares in the midst of a rush of serving a big line at Starbucks." (With a job like that, who needs Jackie, Papa, or the queen?)

Nevertheless, for all the goodies—exaggerated or not—this is still a fast-food business. "The job won't give you the means to buy a house, raise a family, or even rent an apartment or make payments on a car," Kim Fellner noted. It can be physically demanding and emotionally rigorous, as customer-service work usually is; imagine chatting with strangers for six or eight straight hours. Fellner toiled hard on her shift, hauling ice, emptying trash, wiping tables, and trying to remember the damn Italianish names. Gill, behind the burbling, lays out a tough, almost nonstop regimen that sent him mopping bathrooms and carrying heavy bags of coffee grounds to the garbage whenever there was a minute's breather in the counter work. Schultz himself acknowledged, in Onward, "Being a barista is not an easy job. On their feet for hours, juggling multiple, complex drink orders." While turnover may be less than the triple-digit industry average, it's still around 60 to 90 percent.

Nor is every outside review glowing. Starbucks has never made Working Mother's "Best Companies" list—as mentioned in previous chapters, the magazine won't reveal why companies aren't listed—and it gets a mediocre 6.1 out of a possible 10 points for its overall score on GoodGuide .com, perhaps the most broad-based CSR-ranking website. Some of its lowest scores were in employee relations and working conditions.

Things got worse during the years the company overexpanded and brought in the superefficient new coffee machines, driving staff to work faster. The City University of New York's Naomi Gardberg said student baristas in her classes complained that they were no longer allowed to switch hours when they needed to study for a midterm or a final. Around 2008, Starbucks tried applying Japanese-style "lean" production methods to its counter work, such as measuring how long it takes to do routine tasks. Depending on whom you believe—news reports or Schultz's book—this was either a horribly pressured form of (ahem) beancounting micromanagement or a way of "involving employees by asking for their opinions about how to improve their own work." But even Schultz conceded that the process "was not widely embraced as a big

idea inside Starbucks." Later, in 2011—with profits booming again—
Schultz burnished his CSR reputation with new programs to provide
loans to small businesses and create jobs in poor neighborhoods, and a
vow to stop making political donations in order to protest dysfunction in
Washington, DC.

The chain's most famous labor confrontation came in 2004, when
the Industrial Workers of the World began trying to unionize four shops
in New York City. The attempt by the IWW—which used to be one of labor's radical leaders and is now nearly defunct—might seem oddly quix-
otic. As Barclays Capital's Jeffrey Bernstein pointed out, unions are rare
in the fast-food industry, because of the scattered locations, part-time
and short-term workforces, and diffuse franchise ownership. Even veteran union officials sounded tepid. Ron Blackwell, the AFL-CIO's chief
economist, praised Starbucks for its code of ethics and its benefits. Kim
Fellner—whose main career has been working in the labor movement,
not writing—cast a skeptical eye on the IWW's motivation and tactics,
implying that it was a bunch of intellectuals looking for a cause rather
than actual workers.

Aaron Kocher, a Starbucks shift supervisor in Minneapolis who was
one of the IWW's main organizers in New York City and at his own site,
seemed to fumble when asked to explain the underlying grievances. He
admitted that the company provides health benefits, the atmosphere is
"pretty friendly," and "they tend to pay slightly higher than other places."
However, he said that since the recession and the store closings, staffing
cutbacks had intensified the pressure on the remaining workers. Also,
there's no longer any time for the tastings the company used to encourage to teach baristas about their brews. And managers constantly changing shift assignments without advance warning is a perennial problem.

Facing such a half-baked effort, Starbucks could almost have ignored
the whole thing. Instead, it fought back so nastily that a National Labor
Relations Board judge in 2008 ruled that the company had broken the law.
Among other violations, the judge found that management fired three
employees for union activities; issued negative job evaluations to one of
those employees; prohibited staff from discussing the union, wages, and
other employment issues; prohibited them from posting union notices;
and barred them from wearing more than one pro-union button. Starbucks was ordered to pay back wages and reinstate the fired employees
and to end discriminatory treatment against workers sympathetic to
the union.

At the time of that ruling, moreover, there had been at least three other sets of NLRB complaints in three states, two of which were settled. Kim Fellner's book describes heavy-handed efforts by Starbucks to block the International Union of Operating Engineers from organizing one roasting plant, including screening new hires for union sympathy, plus a personal visit from Schultz. When employees signed union cards, she said, "the company capriciously changed their work shifts" and "promoted new people over them." Kocher said that at nearly every store he and his colleagues tried to organize, "we would hear people saying, 'Managers are telling workers you can't talk about the union.'" The company, according to the Wall Street Journal, has also blocked organizing efforts in Europe and New Zealand.

Starbucks doesn't just fight the creation of new unions; it has also tried to wipe out any that were already established before Schultz took control. The CEO sounded positively gleeful as he described employees petitioning him in 1987 and 1992 to decertify the union that represented a warehouse, a roasting plant (a different plant from the one Fellner described), and a few retail workers in Seattle. "When so many of our people supported decertification, it was a sign to me that they were beginning to believe I would do what I had promised," he wrote. According to Naomi Klein in No Logo, the company shut down the Vancouver distribution plant in 1997 after it unionized. Only in Chile is a sizable percentage of the Starbucks workforce unionized.

In the company's defense, Dori Jones Yang said Schultz "strongly felt that unions would get in the way. He thought there should be a high level of trust between employees and management, and management should voluntarily go out of their way to treat employees well." Fellner's book cites similar arguments, including the visit by Schultz to the roasting plant, where he brought up the well-trod story of his father's broken ankle. Such an attitude is hardly unusual among socially progressive business executives. None of the companies profiled in this book are unionized. So is it silly to focus this much on the union question? Isn't there a distinction between, say, a nonunion Walmart and a nonunion Starbucks? Is it OK for a "good" company to be nonunion?

The answer is that of course it's better to have health insurance with no union, as opposed to no insurance plus no union, but those are not the only two options, or even the key issues. "A union is also about due process. Who gets hired, who gets fired, who gets promoted, under what circumstances," says Christian E. Weller, an associate professor of public policy at the University of Massachusetts's McCormack Graduate School of Policy Studies, in Boston, and a senior fellow at the Center for American Progress, a liberal think tank based in Washington, DC. Fellner also argues that workers' well-being should not depend on the "voluntary" whims of one manager, no matter how enlightened. This topic is discussed in more detail in the introduction.

The best opportunity for Starbucks to prove its CSR cred comes in the eco-realm, because the food business probably has more impact on the environment than any other industry. On top of the standard criteria regarding carbon emissions, recycled content, packaging, pollution, energy efficiency, and on and on, there are categories like organic, pesticide free, no added antibiotics, and non–genetically modified.

Starbucks has made a lot of effort in a lot of areas—which it happily emphasizes on its website—and it has a reputation among the general public for being pretty green. Yet professional environmentalists are not impressed. "I am disappointed," said Climate Counts's Wood Turner. "It is a company that people expect to be doing things differently."

The Climate Counts ranking of companies' efforts to reduce greenhouse-gas emissions is a perfect example of this mixed reputation. Sure, Starbucks usually leads the food-services category, but so what? "It's an amazingly low bar in that sector," Turner said with a shrug. The six rated companies—the others are Burger King, Darden Restaurants (owner of Olive Garden and Red Lobster), McDonald's, the Wendy's/Arby's Group, and Yum! Brands (owner of KFC, Long John Silver's, Pizza Hut, and Taco Bell)—are largely fast-food venues, "a very disposable sector," in Turner's words, with literally tons of throwaway take-out containers. Starbucks earns only about half the points possible in most categories, including measuring its impact on climate change, setting goals to reduce energy use, and posting public information.

More positively, Turner said that Starbucks managers have "been open and very nondefensive. They are strong supporters of our process, and they often will provide new information that we may have overlooked." Moreover, in 2011 Starbucks was one of Climate Counts's twenty-five "Gold Star" companies singled out for supporting mandatory federal action on climate change.

There's a similar halfway-done sense at Ceres, the coalition that reports on companies' sustainability efforts. As of 2011, Starbucks had not taken the full step of actually joining the Ceres Company Network, which would require it to pay a membership fee ranging from $2,000 to $25,000,

officially support the group's principles, participate in some of the lobbying and publicity actions, and disclose its goals and efforts to reduce its
own emissions. The fee would obviously be peanuts for Starbucks, with
its annual revenues of over $10 billion, and even the other requirements
wouldn't seem too taxing. According to Andrea Moffat, vice president of
corporate programs at Ceres, the coffee chain has been fulfilling a lot of
the requirements anyway. Schultz headed a committee that conducted a
benchmarking study of industry rankings, and Starbucks officials have
accompanied Ceres to meet with members of Congress, helped produce op-ed pieces, and spoken at conferences, she said. As with Climate
Counts, Starbucks ranked first in its fairly crummy industry in the bench-
mark study. "I'd like them to become a member," Moffat conceded, "but
we just haven't gotten there yet."

As for other CSR organizations, Starbucks belongs to Business
for Social Responsibility, as does almost every big name you can think
of—250 of them, including ExxonMobil and Walmart—and that group's
standards are considered pretty easy to meet.

The biggest environmental problem is those ubiquitous, universally
recognizable mermaid/siren carry-out cups—which the baristas automatically give you without asking whether you're staying in or running
out. A customer who wants to be ecological has to take the effort to say,
"Please put it in a ceramic mug." The barista is then likely to grimace and
ask a coworker where the heck the mugs are. You can get a whopping
10-cent discount if you bring your own container, and the company also
now sells such containers, but you'd better shove it in the barista's face
before he or she has already poured your latte into a throwaway cup.

Baristas have told me that asking me what kind of cup I want and
searching for ceramic would reduce their efficiency. They also say that
the smaller outlets and those whose clientele are mainly take-out don't
have storage space for the rarely used mugs. Then, once the paper cups
leave the store, the staff can hardly run after them with recycling bins.
Fine, but how come the counter workers at Wendy's, Burger King, and
my local bagel store all manage to make their first sentence "Is it to stay,
or to go?"

The Starbucks website sets as a goal to "serve 25% of beverages in
reusable cups" by 2015. That's an interesting number, considering that
only 20 percent of beverages are consumed on the premises, and of those,
the website admits, paper and plastic cups "account for approximately 95
percent of our in-store beverage packaging." If it's really going to achieve
that goal, Starbucks will need to shift all of its in-store purchases into re-

usable containers plus somehow capture 5 percent of the take-out. "They will have to train the workers"—as well as Wendy's does—said Sally Greenberg, executive director of the National Consumers League. And offer better than a 10-cent inducement to bring your own.

How much damage those little mermaid/sirens cause can be estimated. It's been frequently reported that 3 billion Starbucks cups end up in landfills each year. According to the environmental group Global Green, Americans annually use 58 billion paper cups of all kinds, producing a total of 645,000 tons of waste and 2.5 million metric tons of carbon emissions, or about one-third of an ounce of waste and about 0.00004 metric tons (about 1 1/2 ounces) of emissions per cup. Starbucks's paper profligacy is thus contributing nearly one-twentieth of that mess—clogging landfills with about 32,000 tons of unnecessary waste and contributing approximately 125,000 metric tons of emissions toward destructive climate change.

The chain has taken a few steps to rein in this impact. Schultz noted that as far back as 1995, Starbucks created a "hot-cup team" to find a more environmentally sustainable container that would still allow people to hold a steaming cup of coffee. If reusing or recycling mugs wasn't feasible, was there at least a way to reduce—the first environmental R—the amount of discarded, Earth-wrecking garbage? After some experimenting, the ultimate solution, premiered in 1997, was a cardboard "sleeve" fitting over the disposable cup that required just half as much material as the double cups the chain had previously used. As a bonus, the sleeve itself was made partly out of recycled paper. A decade later, Starbucks improved on that with a cup that included 10 percent postconsumer recycled fiber, and it replaced its cold cups with ones that use 15 percent less plastic.

In 2009, seven of its New York City outlets participated in an eight-week pilot project with Global Green to test whether its cups could be recycled along with ordinary corrugated cardboard. (Answer: The cups and sleeves could, though the lids couldn't.) The catch was that this recycling only involved beverages consumed on site, in order for the cups to be collected. While the practical limitations of the test are understandable, it's almost meaningless as an environmental solution. These to-stay paper cups are exactly the ones that are unnecessary and should be replaced with reusable mugs.

And Howard, if you really want to encourage reusable cups, why are you constantly being photographed holding disposables?

———

Beyond cups, Starbucks still has a mixed record on what ought to be easier recycling and waste issues. For instance, the corporate website asserts that 70 percent of stores recycle in-house material. However, there are caveats. As the website notes, "Recycling is dependent on the availability of commercial recycling services," it's mainly for nonconsumer material like cardboard boxes, and "for stores operating out of leased spaces"—the vast majority—"it is the landlords who control waste collection and recycling." Consumer recycling is an even sadder story. Frappuccino bottles? The newspapers that get left in the armchairs? Fewer than 400 stores in all of North America had consumer-recycling bins as of 2011. "If companies aren't doing the most basic things like putting recycling bins in, it's hard for me to get impressed by other things they're doing," said Conrad McKerron, director of the corporate-accountability program at As You Sow, a San Francisco–based nonprofit organization that works with ethical-investing funds. A more successful effort is the company's "Grounds for Your Garden" policy, which allows people to take home five pounds of used coffee grounds, gratis, for composting (and which everyone seemed to mention).

The buildings themselves can be big energy guzzlers, or savers. For instance, Starbucks is slowly switching to renewable energy—that factor accounted for 25 percent of power use in company-owned stores in 2009—and it saves on air conditioning by keeping venues a tad warmer in summer. Deciding that there was "no commercially available LED [energy-efficient lighting] that met our aesthetic and functional requirements," Starbucks got General Electric Company to design a new type. Plus, it tries to install recycled floor tiles, sustainable-certified wood, and cabinets made of postindustrial recycled material in its new construction and renovation. Community-development adviser Stacy Mitchell handed out rare praise, in her 2006 book *Big-Box Swindle*, noting that Starbucks is "one of the few chains that has a record of preserving and reusing historic buildings"—a form of recycling.

The problem is that most of these efforts apply solely to locations the company owns directly, whereas most outlets are rented. What can Starbucks do in the rentals? A lot, said Wood Turner of Climate Counts. Leasing millions of square feet worldwide, "Starbucks has leverage," he said. The same way that it could, if it wanted, spur farmers to grow more fair trade coffee, "it could begin to put pressure on building owners to make their buildings more efficient."

Food sourcing is an environmental issue because of the impact of pesticides, fertilizers, genetically modified ingredients, and animal waste. "Shade-grown" and "organic" methods try to reduce the environmental impact by banning chemical pesticides. And? Starbucks buys a minuscule 14 million pounds of certified-organic coffee beans per year, according to its own accounting.

When it comes to the various sandwiches and pastries, PETA's Dan Shannon gave the chain points for seeking more humane versions of animal-based ingredients, yet he described the efforts as "baby steps." These include "starting to source some cage-free eggs," "starting to give purchasing preference" to poultry suppliers that use a new method of slaughter that's supposed to be less painful, and "moving toward suppliers" that use less-cruel crates for the pigs that become the bacon–Gouda cheese–egg frittata sandwiches. And Shannon appreciates that he can get soy milk in his coffee.

Starbucks seems to have sought creative ways to resolve a big issue for many restaurants: the water that's wasted when employees keep the faucets running to save time on washing dishes. Starbucks said it now cleans blended-drink pitchers (one of the most water-intensive pieces) with "a blast of higher-pressure water" rather than "an open tap." The company also said it's saving H_2O with a revised system for cleaning utensils and by reprogramming the way its espresso machines rinse shot glasses. What it's not doing, complained Aaron Kocher, the IWW organizer, is increasing "the amount of labor budgeted, so that perhaps workers won't feel so rushed."

Speaking of water, what on earth is Starbucks thinking with its Ethos water bottles? For every bottle sold (at, typically, $1.95 apiece), the company donates 5 cents to a special fund for "water, sanitation, and hygiene-education programs" for hundreds of thousands of people in countries without sufficient clean water. Even putting aside how small an amount that nickel takes from Starbucks's profits, any environmentalist will scream that selling bottled water in developed countries makes the world's problems *worse*, not better. More than 17 million barrels of oil are wasted to produce the water bottles Americans buy in a typical year— even while most Americans have access to perfectly safe, delicious drinking water from their own taps. The lovely lake and stream water that is poured into the Ethos bottles could have gone to those hundreds of thousands of impoverished people that Starbucks claims to be helping. No self-respecting environmental group, food co-op, or college campus will be seen with water bottles any more.

"You need to have your social issues lined up," says Conrad McKerron of As You Sow.

———

Finally, an analysis of Starbucks can't avoid the issue of price.

Of course Starbucks brews are expensive. They're meant to be. Howard Schultz made that clear from the start, happily comparing his brand to Nike, which set out "to design world-class running shoes" that could sell for $140 a pair in an era when good sneakers typically were only $20.

For the record, here are some comparisons: In my New York City neighborhood in 2010, a twelve-ounce ("tall") latte or cappuccino cost $2.49 at McDonald's, $2.69 at Dunkin' Donuts, and $3.20 at Starbucks. *Consumer Reports* found a similar range in August 2009, with $2.19 for ten ounces at Dunkin', $2.29 for twelve ounces at McDonald's, and $2.88 for twelve ounces at Starbucks. But the little, offbeat places were pricier: A twelve-ounce latte was $3.75 at Café Grumpy and a gorilla-size $4 at Café Gorilla. Meanwhile, a cup of regular coffee at a local diner went for $1.25.

During a few months in early 2011, prices throughout the world shot up as rising temperatures and volatile rainfall, probably linked to climate change, decimated the Colombian harvest—finally bringing the biggest lattes past the clichéd four-dollar mark, at least at my local Starbucks.

What do you get for that $3.20 or $4? Image.

Accountants and struggling actors, students and stay-at-home moms, Schultz's cops and construction workers could all savor the image of being richer and more worldly wise than they really were. "Starbucks gave yuppies, bobos, and their imitators a way to show off their wealth (*or their desire for wealth*), sophistication, and continental taste," Bryant Simon wrote (italics added). (Bobos are people with conflicting bohemian and bourgeois tastes.)

Not only that, but sophisticated Starbucks sippers have practically learned Italian, or at least a pseudo-Italian coffee language. "You could look at it as elitist," Northwestern University's Richard Honack acknowledged, although he prefers to consider the lingo and corporate culture "personalized." This is not an easy skill to master. Even Michael Gates Gill, the happy barista, several times admitted to getting flustered over the arcane coffee names.

No matter that very little of the image is accurate. *Grande* actually means "big" in Italian, so why does it refer to the medium size at Starbucks? *Latte* is just milk, and a glass of milk is exactly what you'd get if you ordered a *latte* in one of the real Italian cafés Schultz claims to love. A caffe latte, then? Ah, said my friend Paola, who was born in Bologna and raised in Milan, *caffelatte* is a breakfast dish, served in a bowl, consisting of espresso and lots of milk, and "the purpose of making this souplike thing is to be able to dunk bread, cookies, or pastries." And, by the way, you don't drink *caffelatte* in Italy; you eat it. Even the espresso at Starbucks is wrong, Paola said. It "lacks an essential ingredient—the *crema*, the foam that is created when the pressurized hot water goes through the coffee—not to be confused with cream."

Keep in mind, too, that coffee, Starbucks style, is not a health food. A simple "tall" latte packs 150 calories, and things pretty much go up from there: A venti, 240 calories. A grande caramel-brulée latte, 300. A venti Java-chip Frappuccino will feed you a whopping 600 calories. For one beverage. That's nearly one-third the federally recommended daily calorie intake for an average American adult.

And don't forget that basic ingredient, caffeine. The Mayo Clinic (to give one example) has warned that more than 500 milligrams of caffeine a day, which it translates to slightly over three Starbucks grande vanilla lattes, can cause insomnia, nervousness, restlessness, irritability, fast or irregular heartbeat, muscle tremors, headaches, anxiety, and nausea or other gastrointestinal problems. Nor is a "half-caff" or a decaf necessarily a free ride. When "secret shoppers" from *Consumer Reports* tested a total of thirty-six cups of decaffeinated coffee from Burger King, Dunkin' Donuts, McDonald's, Seattle's Best Coffee, 7-Eleven, and Starbucks sites near the magazine's suburban New York City headquarters in November 2007—all the cups ranging from ten to twelve ounces—the Starbucks cup had 21 milligrams of caffeine, one of the highest levels.

Sure, a hot drink—and image—isn't all that customers get. Their money pays rent on an armchair, a table, a bathroom, and free WiFi for several hours. Starbucks prides itself as well on teaching customers about the intricacies of brewing and types of coffee, if they're interested. Is $3.20 a lot to fork up for this? Maybe not if you have a steady paycheck, even as a construction worker or a cop. Certainly not if you're a lawyer or an investment banker. Among the diverse crowds that frequent Starbucks, no doubt many have the means. According to the Wall Street firm Morgan Stanley, in 2011 the average Starbucks customer earned over $75,000 a year. On the other hand, for Michael Gates Gill, ironically, right before he got hired at Starbucks, "a latte was becoming a luxury I could no longer afford." And the four-dollar latte has become the ultimate symbol of frivolous spending in virtually every retirement-advice article and book. If you skip one latte a day, that's nearly $120 per month, and starting at age twenty-two and investing that $120 in an IRA allocated 85 percent in stocks and 15 percent in bonds—why, by age sixty-five, you'd have over $300,000. *Now* is it worth the cost?

THE QUESTION: Does Starbucks deserve its reputation as an exemplar of ethical chic?

THE VERDICT: A lukewarm yes

There are two essential facts about Starbucks:

Its premise depends on making an everyday object expensive, even intimidating, and on encouraging consumers to be pretentious.

However, people don't go there only for the coffee. They go because the chain offers a community service that our government has failed to provide—a safe, inviting, all-weather public commons (with bathrooms).

I consider the second premise socially responsible and the first one the antithesis of social responsibility.

Howard Schultz probably sees both parts—and more—as socially responsible. In his view, he has given ordinary people a high-quality product plus a bit of romance, a bit of Italy, or at least an inviting place where they can take a break in their everyday lives, and for an Italian vacation it's certainly a bargain. Then don't forget the employee health insurance and the fair trade beans.

There's nothing wrong with making premium-quality coffee (or Nike sneakers) for those willing to pay. Even devotees of the not-Starbucks places told me they appreciate that Starbucks had brought the concept of gourmet coffee to the hinterland, paving the way for their little cafés. Nevertheless, I think it's stretching the definition to call that socially responsible. Culturally ennobling, maybe. Would you call Prada socially responsible for making a really good-quality, imported shoe for sophisticated consumers?

In fact, it is socially *irresponsible* for Starbucks to claim the ethical mantle while pricing out people who can't afford its wares—or even worse, as the financial advisers warn, siphoning off money that should go to more important uses. And it is patronizing to say that ordinary Joes can feel just as sophisticated as rich folks by drinking expensive joe. Even Schultz seems to be taking a step backward from the Italianate pretension. In his second book, he claimed that "for some customers, Starbucks is an aspirational brand or even a token of pride, but the latter is an unintended effect of what we originally set out to do." Yet take another look at his first justification for Il Giornale: "We would enchant customers with an atmosphere of sophistication and style and knowledge." Aspiration wasn't an "unintended side effect" back then.

Of course, price isn't the sole consideration in bestowing the ethical mantle on a business, but Starbucks's record in other aspects is similarly mixed. On the good side, its employee benefits are truly pioneering, and the consensus seems to be that, for what it is—a quick-serve eatery—the working conditions are better than most. The corporate interest in environmental issues, worker benefits, and fair trade seems to be genuine and long standing, perhaps dating back to Schultz's early inspirations from JFK, the Peace Corps, and his own father's struggles. On the so-so side, the company is obviously making some efforts to buy fair trade coffee and help struggling farmers, but there also seems to be a certain amount of hype, a willingness to let consumers believe that a lot more of the coffee is fair trade than it really is. And on the so-what side, in an era when even the hated Walmart is investigating renewable energy and pressuring its suppliers, Starbucks's measly steps to reduce energy and water use are simply par for the course.

Correction: Regarding eco-issues, Starbucks is making things worse.

With its huge market clout, it is hurting the environment by selling water bottles and automatically handing out paper cups. Would it be so hard to keep ceramic mugs under the counter and make it part of the baristas' routine to ask customers whether they're staying or going? They wouldn't even have to learn any fancy new words.

In short, Starbucks is a better-than-average company with a high-quality product that has changed the world. Not a bad epitaph. Still, I'd prefer to give my money to Café Regular or Gorilla or Grumpy or one of the other small fry that are undoubtedly having a much harder time staying in business—if they use ceramic mugs.

CHAPTER 4

Apple

The Coolest of Them All

Is ANY BRAND IN the world more cool, more hip, or more cutting edge in melding technology and design than Apple? Do any other computers look like works of art? Has any top executive, besides Apple's Steve Jobs, ever worn a black mock turtleneck and jeans?

Business managers have BlackBerrys. Artists, students, professors, techies, and other people you'd want to know have iPhones. Everyone has an iPod—or two or three or six. Apple users *adore* their Macs. PC users curse their Dell and HP clunkers.

Well, if Apple is cool, and I use Apple products, then I must be cool. And conversely, since I'm socially responsible—I recycle and I eat organic food and I care about animals—and I use Apple products, then obviously Apple must also be socially responsible.

Uh. . . .

"Apple has a very current, leading-edge brand—a drive to innovate," said Climate Counts's Wood Turner. "It's willing to change the way we engage with music and media and movies. So the consumer has always believed that the company must be environmentally and socially responsible as well. But it didn't follow. It hasn't been meeting the same bar that other companies in the [electronics] sector were." Similarly, Adam Kanzer, the general counsel at Domini, mused, "I think the perception of the brand for a long time was that this is a company that does the right thing. Apple carries that aura. But when you dig into it, we started to have some questions."

In fact, the Apple orchard isn't nearly as ethically well stocked as many people assume. Apple has historically been less environmentally responsible, less worker friendly, and much less open than other tech companies and merely average in the conditions at its overseas plants, even as it has been more beloved by the public. Nor do activists expect that corporate emphasis to change significantly now that Jobs has died. But here's the hopeful part: starting around 2005, even while Jobs was still alive and in charge, the company, concerned about its poor image, began paying more attention to environmental and sweatshop problems. And if there's one thing Apple knows, it's image.

Although the history of Apple has been widely told, a brief recap is needed to dig beneath the myths.

First, the company didn't start in Steve Jobs's garage. It started in his Silicon Valley bedroom in 1976 and then moved to the garage. And Jobs was not a tech whiz. The brains behind the earliest Apple technology was the "other" Steve, cofounder Steve Wozniak.

Jobs and Wozniak were both loners and geeks, introduced by a mutual friend when Jobs was thirteen and Wozniak was eighteen. They each stumbled around college, not graduating, eventually working at some of the Valley's earliest tech companies—video-game maker Atari (Jobs) and Hewlett-Packard Company (both).

The pair started Apple because Jobs thought they could parlay Wozniak's tinkering with phones and crude computers into something bigger. Their first order came from a local store, the Byte Shop. Jobs negotiated the deal, based on the hardware designed by Woz (as he is often known). Jobs also dreamed up the corporate name, probably in honor of some friends' apple farm in Oregon. (Whether the name was stolen from the Beatles' recording label has been one aspect of back-and-forth lawsuits since 1978.) And that was the pattern that would largely continue throughout Apple's existence: someone else designed the hardcore technology, while Jobs (sometimes disastrously, but usually brilliantly) handled the business negotiations, dreamed the long-range dreams, and crafted the image—until, eventually, he *became* the image.

Jobs "believed the computer was eventually going to become a consumer product. That was an outrageous idea back in the early 1980s," when computers were for corporations or really nerdy hobbyists, recalled John Sculley, the PepsiCo executive who in 1983 was hired as Apple's CEO and president, in an interview with *Bloomberg Businessweek* in October 2010. Nevertheless, the weird little company grew. A follow-up computer, the Apple II, was a huge success. Apple pulled itself into corporate shape, got funding from banks and venture capitalists, wrote a formal business plan, hired a professional president, and finally, in December 1980, began selling stock to the public.

Almost immediately thereafter, troubles hit. IBM Corp., which until then had focused on business clients, invaded Apple's turf in personal computers with all its 800-pound-gorilla muscle. A next-generation product, the Lisa, was a market failure. So was the Apple III. Several dozen employees were laid off, and some shaky projects were killed. With Woz on an indefinite leave of absence after a near-fatal plane crash, many questioned whether Apple could rebound.

Enter the Macintosh, lightweight and easy to use, and the answer seemed to be yes. The Mac was introduced with perhaps the most famous commercial in history even to this day, the 1984-themed Super Bowl spot, which evoked George Orwell's dystopian novel, with the Mac in the guise of an attractive blonde runner challenging IBM-as-Big Brother.

Yet a year later, in 1985, Jobs was essentially fired by his own company. Despite all the hype, Mac sales had faltered. It turned out that the first models had very little software. Jobs had miscalculated, devoting a bloated staff to his pet project, overestimating potential demand, and saddling the company with a mound of unsold inventory. In the second quarter of 1985, Apple suffered its first loss. Moreover, the management situation was tense and unsustainable. Although Jobs had wanted to be president, the board, back in 1983, had hesitated at naming a flaky twenty-eight-year-old—even a flaky twenty-eight-year-old genius who had cofounded the company—and brought in Sculley from Pepsi. Jobs was technically just running the Mac project and thus reporting to Sculley. However, Jobs was also chairman, and therefore Sculley's boss. After the Mac fiasco, the board yanked all of his operating roles, offering Jobs a face-saving title, "product visionary"—whatever that was. Jobs tried to charm and manipulate his way back to power, then finally took his multimillion-dollar marbles and left to form another computer company, called (with typically quirky Valley spelling) NeXT.

From the mid-1980s to the mid-1990s, without either of the founding Steves, Apple continued to stumble while IBM and Microsoft charged

ahead. Its market share plummeted to a measly 8 percent from 20 percent. No products seemed to catch the public imagination. One CEO after
another came and went. Red ink flowed. Bankruptcy was a real possibility. For that matter, NeXT wasn't doing too well, either, and Jobs had
gambled a good part of his Apple fortune on a struggling company that
did computer animation for movies, called Pixar.

Now, part two of the legend begins: Jobs the genius steps in to save
all three companies. Seeing the potential in Pixar, he poured in the resources to keep it alive until the first full-length movie using its technology, *Toy Story*, could bound into theaters and emerge a blockbuster. The
Apple board, in 1997, begged him to return, buying NeXT in the process.
He coyly came back as "interim" CEO, finally admitting the obvious and
becoming full CEO in 2000.

Over the next decade, everything Apple and Jobs touched turned to
gold. Even more important, they changed the world.

The new era started with the iMac, which Jobs launched almost the
minute he arrived. The iMac didn't look like a computer. It was cute,
rounded, and translucent blue. Nor did it act like most computers; amazingly, it had no floppy disks and no external hard drive, instead cram-
ming circuits, modems, plugs, monitor, and everything else into that
cute blue plastic case. It was a forerunner of what Apple would stand for:
Style. Simplicity. Radical innovation. Fun. And for only $1,300.

Moreover, according to the book *Apple Confidential 2.0*, by Owen W.
Linzmayer, a poll by the research firm Audits and Surveys showed that
29.4 percent of iMac buyers had never owned a computer before. Apple
truly had turned computers into a product for the mass market, not just
for nerds.

Still, different as it was, the iMac was a computer. The real Apple
revolution began with iTunes and the iPod, expanding the company beyond computers into technology that would take over every aspect of even
nontech consumers' lives.

Steve Jobs didn't invent the concept of downloading music from CDs
to play on computers or portable devices, of course; MP3 and Napster had
already done that, illegally. But Apple made it easy, widespread, beautiful, and legal. Most crucially, the company negotiated deals with the five
major music producers for the rights to their products at an affordable
price through its iTunes Store. And how to play that music? With typical
Jobs micromanagement and flair, Apple designed the lightweight, sleek
iPod in what would become trademark Apple white. Later, it added an on-

line music-storage-and-syncing service. Ten years after the iPod's launch in 2001, there is still no rival.

The third of the big iProducts was the iPhone. Again, the idea of a mobile phone that does more than make calls didn't originate at Apple. The stolid business executive's BlackBerry was already on the market, along with offerings from Nokia, Palm, and Sony Ericsson. And Black-Berry would continue to dominate even after the iPhone arrived in 2007. However, BlackBerry was the brand corporate managers forced their employees to use. The iPhone was what younger, more creative, more daring, cooler people chose of their own accord.

With the next innovation, the iPad, observers at first were skeptical. What did it do that an iPhone, an iPod touch, or a laptop didn't do already? And hadn't its forerunner tablet, Apple's Newton, been a much-mocked failure in the 1990s? As *Newsweek* tech columnist Daniel Lyons wrote at the official product unveiling in February 2010, "Jobs and his team kept using words like 'breakthrough' and 'magical,' but the iPad is neither, at least not right now." To make matters worse, the name sounded like a brand of sanitary napkin.

However, by the time the thing actually hit the market, two months after Lyons's column, the standard Apple adoration had kicked in. Novelist-screenwriter-actor Stephen Fry, in an April 2010 cover story for *Time*, couldn't stop drooling, comparing using the tablet to "one's relationship with a person or an animal" and "like a gun lobbyist's rifle: the only way you will take it from me is to prise it from my cold, dead hands." The night before it officially went on sale, fans lined up outside Apple Stores in New York City and San Francisco, willing to camp out all night or longer to be sure to bag their gadgets and apps. That initial day, more than 300,000 iPads were swept off the shelves. By November, *Time* had declared it one of the "50 Best Inventions of the Year." Rivals like BlackBerry, as well as Acer, Amazon, Barnes & Noble, HP, and Samsung, were months behind. Even before some of them hit the market, the next-generation iPad was released—and it sold out in major cities and online within hours.

Barely a dozen years after Jobs rode to the rescue, the once-upon-a-time laggard of the computer industry was now the undisputed champ of both the tech and hip cultures, bigger than Microsoft in terms of market capitalization, more profitable than IBM, the largest business other than an oil company in the world. It was so huge that in 2011, the Nasdaq 100 index actually had to reduce its share of the total weighting, because any blip in its sales or profits tilted the index too much. British prime minister David Cameron and his iPad were "inseparable," as *Time* put it; Russian president Dmitri A. Medvedev flaunted his iPhone and iPad. Everyone except the family of Microsoft cofounder Bill Gates, apparently, has an iPod. (At least Melinda Gates, Bill's wife, claimed in an interview with the *New York Times Magazine* in October 2010 that her household was iPod-free.)

True, it's tough to stay number one in all areas forever. Google's Android operating system overtook the iPhone in 2010, and its $12.5 billion purchase of Motorola's cell phone business the following year put its smartphone power on steroids. Microsoft—finally—learned about marketing, launching its Windows 7 in 2009 with ads that challenged Apple for hipness. On the other hand, Apple is constantly branching into new fields and adding updates; at the same time that Google and Microsoft were beefing up, Apple put out an improved version of its middling TV device and won an important victory that will inhibit Android. Even with growing competition, it has, by a long shot, more smartphone applications than anyone. Each iteration of the iPhone immediately sells out. And no gadget maker—never, nowhere, nohow—makes products as beautiful, as easy to use, or as beloved.

In short, the story of Apple has everything you'd want in a heroic myth: David versus Goliath. Near-death and resurrection. Beautiful heroine (or products). Brilliant young hero-genius, misunderstood by the common world, who dares to challenge the status quo. And, apparently, a happy ending.

Until the hero is struck down at the height of his powers.

If there's a myth, then there must be true believers. This is not the same thing as having a huge customer base. Apple has that base, as the range of buyers from the Kremlin to 10 Downing Street proves; but so do Walmart and Toyota and, yes, Microsoft. What Apple also has are fans whose homes, cars, and offices are stocked with every version of the brand's merchandise, who read magazines and follow blogs solely about the company, who wait in long lines to grab each new product as it comes out.

Fast Company magazine, in July 2010, dubbed Apple "the Coolest Company Anywhere," citing, in part, the "religious fervor among its adherents." The iPod is virtually a character in Arthur Phillips's 2009 novel *This Song Is You.* Apple was one of just nine companies, people, or other entities that met the strict criteria for being "premier" cults as defined by consultants Matthew W. Ragas and Bolivar J. Bueno in their book about cult branding. (The rest were Harley-Davidson, musician Jimmy Buffett, the Linux operating system, Oprah Winfrey, Star Trek, Vans shoes, Volkswagen, and World Wrestling Entertainment.) This devotion can go beyond a desire for mere physical products. "The real Apple believers see some sort of 'I'm in touch with the universe' thing, that 'my computer is spiritual,'" claimed David Eiswert, a stock analyst who manages T. Rowe Price's global technology fund. (When I interviewed him in October 2009, Apple comprised 5.5 percent of the $350 million fund, the largest single holding.) Some branding consultants studied the brain activity of Apple users through functional magnetic resonance imaging and found amazing similarities to the way the subjects' brains responded to images of rosary beads and the pope or to the proximity of a girlfriend.

To meet such true believers, go to Macworld, the annual convention of Apple customers and vendors. Even in a year like 2010—when Steve Jobs, although still alive, didn't attend—more than 30,000 devotees poured into San Francisco's Moscone Center. Many of them had taken time off from work and were paying with their own hard-earned cash, $195 to $1,595 apiece in registration fees alone (depending on how many events they wanted to access), plus hotel, food, transportation, and other travel costs. I talked with people from Chicago and Las Vegas, from Arizona and Minnesota, and from throughout the length of California. They were mostly white but of all ages, sporting styles from polyester to pierced noses. There were couples with babies and local high school students; would-be iPhone app sellers and IT geeks; teachers and graphic designers; and at least one yoga instructor, one archaeology professor, one US Navy welder, and one Greek Orthodox priest. Only one of more than a dozen I interviewed thought she might go to a similar conference for another company's products. Consider some of them:

Mary Lee and her husband have a PowerBook G4, an iPhone, a Mac Pro, two Apple TVs, and an assortment of Mac computers in their Chicago home. "It's more than just a company that makes products that I buy," said the forty-one-year-old Lee, an IT assistant. "I feel some kind of connection to the company. I feel happy when they do well."

George Van Houton, age sixty-two, an electronics technician from Las Vegas, was at his tenth Macworld. "You see products you wouldn't be aware of" otherwise, he said. With three iPods, a Mac Pro, two Mac minis, and countless other Macs at home, he was eyeballing an iPod touch and more memory for his Mac Pro. "Why do rock fans go to a rock concert? Macworld is my version of Woodstock."

John Swayze, a forty-five-year-old welding-program manager for the Navy, likes Apple products because they're easy to use: he should know, since he and his family own seven iPods, an iMac, a laptop, and a Power-Book. He had driven the five hundred miles from San Diego to every Mac-world since 2001, making a whole extended-family vacation of it with his kids, brother, nephews, nieces, and other relatives.

Leo Gesday, forty-six, manages a consumer-electronics store and had been at all the Macworlds save one since they began in 1985. "There's nothing so pervasive in my life as the products from Apple"—a laptop, a Mac mini, an iMac, an iPhone, and four iPods.

I found the same kind of devotion among people waiting overnight for the inaugural iPads in New York City. At 9 P.M., twelve hours before the gadget officially went on sale, there were already about twenty people in line, with sleeping bags and folding chairs, including a half dozen who had preordered and were thus guaranteed one no matter how late they came by, but who wanted accessories or the shared experience of an Apple all-nighter. Dean Vassallo, a twenty-seven-year-old systems engineer from Long Island, was among the latter. He had taken the day off work, arriving at around noon—but that was nothing. For the first iPhone, he had camped out for two days. "I've owned almost every single product Apple has come out with since before Steve Jobs came back," he said. "Apple is in a class of their own. They're magical devices."

Woodstock. Magical. Can you imagine standing in line nearly twenty-four hours to pick up something you've already reserved? Can you imagine being happy when your washing machine company does well?

Experts use a lot of jewelry analogies when talking about Apple. The iPod "likens itself to a watch and pendant," said Michael Myers, the advertising veteran from upstate New York. For Michael Tchong, a technology-trends consultant who founded the trade journal *MacWeek* and ran it from 1987 to 1991, "Tiffany comes to mind. There are so many tiny details [in the iPhone], like the elegant little drop shadows around the lettering."

Even when Apple messes up, fans blame themselves, or the store where they bought the item, or United Parcel Service, or Microsoft, or the weather—anyone except Apple. For instance, the iPhone got so popular by late 2009 that all those millions of Americans texting, downloading, video streaming, Web surfing, and talking overwhelmed the network of its sole carrier at the time, AT&T. Particularly in New York City and San Francisco, calls and other services were dropped and delayed.

And? AT&T took the blame. "People are still buying iPhones," T. Rowe Price's David Eiswert said at the height of the turmoil. "But people don't like AT&T's network." Many customers were waiting for AT&T's exclusive contract to end in early 2011; however, after Apple added Verizon, that carrier, too, warned of undercapacity.

It was harder, in June 2010, for Apple to dodge a different case of dropped calls and other reception trouble with the iPhone 4. For a while, the company tried to dismiss the situation as an old software bug that simply displayed the wrong number of reception bars or even say it was the customer's fault for holding the phone wrong. Finally, in July, when venerable *Consumer Reports* said that it couldn't recommend the phone because of a hardware flaw with the antenna, Apple conceded that it had a problem. Sort of. Jobs held a rare news conference at corporate headquarters to admit that there was an antenna issue and to temporarily offer free bumpers that would wrap around the rim of the phone, which seemed to improve the reception. "We are human, and we make mistakes sometimes," he said. Then he promptly went on to claim that other smartphones had the same flaw, iPhone complaints were rare, the media were exaggerating, and the iPhone is the greatest phone in the world anyway.

And? Customers rushed out to buy more iPhones. Less than a week after the mea culpa press conference, there was a three-week wait for the gadgets. Apple has "created that community, so no one cares," said branding expert Robert Passikoff. "That's the beauty of getting the benefit of the doubt." Steve Wozniak himself can't figure it out. "Apple has a community, millions of people who love its products. I don't know why it's loved," he admitted when I met him at a conference in 2010.

It's not just the products that are the object of Apple fans' devotion. So is Steve Jobs.

No wonder, really. A guy rated one of "The World's Most Influential People" by *Time* in 2010, called one of "27 Brave Thinkers" by the *Atlantic* in 2009 and one of just 21 in 2011, listed under "Revolutionaries"—not merely zillionaires—in the 2009 *Forbes* "400 Richest People in America" roster, even hailed as "CEO of the Decade" by *Fortune* in 2009. The book *Apple Confidential 2.0* describes the reaction at the 2000 Macworld, when Jobs announced that he would be the permanent CEO: "The Mac faithful that filled San Francisco's Moscone Center rose to their feet, chanting, 'Steve! Steve! Steve!'" There were similar frenzies when he introduced the Mac in 1984 and when he came back to Apple from exile in 1997. Stephen

Fry—the writer-actor who drooled over the iPad in *Time*—offered that "I have met five British Prime Ministers, two American Presidents, Nelson Mandela, Michael Jackson, and the Queen. My hour with Steve Jobs certainly made me more nervous than any of those encounters."

So when Jobs got a rare form of pancreatic cancer in 2004, then inexplicably lost weight and took a mysterious health leave in 2009, followed by a liver transplant, and again in early 2011 announced that he was taking another indefinite leave of absence to deal with medical issues, terror coursed through the Apple world. What if he didn't . . . ? The thought was too horrible to contemplate. The stock price gyrated with each medical report, shooting up after the liver transplant, plunging briefly at the news of the 2011 medical leave, rising smartly again when Jobs interrupted his 2011 leave to introduce, in person, a new version of the iPad. At his first news conference upon returning to work after the transplant, employees and even journalists (journalists?) gave Jobs a standing ovation.

Then, in late August 2011, the first unthinkable happened: Apple announced that Jobs was stepping down as CEO, to be replaced by Chief Operating Officer Timothy D. Cook—although Jobs would presumably keep a lot of fingers on the keyboard as chairman of the board.

The universe shook: The announcement led the news at the *Wall Street Journal* and other newspapers; hundreds of thousands of messages were posted on Twitter and elsewhere, fans flocked to Apple stores in a kind of makeshift wake, and the stock slid more than 5 percent in after-hours trading. The *New York Times* called him "the da Vinci of our time."

Things calmed down within a couple of days. The stock picked up nicely; after all, the company's product line was strong, and it had some $76 billion in cash to cushion any problems. The experts' consensus was that there were enough Jobs-created gizmos in the pipeline to carry the karma another two or three years, and Jobs would still be sort-of around as chairman, but a key issue was how many other people would leave. The headlines faded, replaced by a hurricane on the East Coast and the ongoing fall of Libyan dictator Muammar Qaddafi.

Still, the Apple world was holding its breath. "If Wall Street says, 'Jobs is gone, so Apple is dying,' then it loses the hipness," Northwestern University's Richard Honack suggested. From Wall Street, T. Rowe Price's David Eiswert was a bit reassuring, on the Street's unique terms. "Apple has built a culture and philosophy that's bigger than Jobs," he said. "The stock will go down, but it's a buying opportunity."

Less than two months later came the even-more-dreaded follow-up blow: Jobs died of complications from his cancer. There could be no more fantasies that he might still hover over the shoulders of Apple designers.

Now the tributes were even more intense. His photo was splashed on the covers of magazines ranging from the *New Yorker* to *People* to the *Economist* to *Rolling Stone*, while *Bloomberg Businessweek*, *Fortune*, and *Newsweek* each devoted an entire issue to tributes to him. President Barack Obama hailed him as one of "the greatest of American innovators." The State of California declared an official Steve Jobs Day.

Although Jobs was still CEO when I went to Macworld, I had asked the attendees about the dire possibility. They weren't about to dump their iPhones and PowerBooks if Jobs were to leave—"The Apple products would have to get really bad, or Microsoft would have to get really good," Ann Pfaff-Doss, a retired graphic designer, told me—but they would definitely be nervous. "When he's there, I'm more reassured that things are going to go in the right direction," said Jeffrey Boerner, a graduate student in math at the University of Iowa who had written some iPhone apps and who had come to the conference with his wife and mother.

Of course, there's nothing ethically wrong with selling products that people love. And consumer and political movements often rely on building a sense of community, seen in groups like food co-ops and MoveOn.org. So, why does the Apple fan club make a lot of activists nervous?

Perhaps it's because they worry that love and community can too easily edge into blind devotion—when community risks becoming a cult. And there are hints of cultism in the way no one seemed to blame the company for the iPhone problems in 2009 and 2010, in the Jobsmania, in the loving comparisons to Tiffany and jewels, and, most troubling, in the company's extreme secrecy.

Jobs and his spokespeople were coy—verging on outright lying—about his second medical scare. When they couldn't hide his severe weight loss any longer, they initially claimed that he was suffering from a "hormone imbalance," then conceded only that he was taking time off because, as Jobs put it, his "health-related issues are more complex than I originally thought." The third medical leave, too, followed months of mysterious weight loss and was announced in a terse, six-sentence e-mail sent to Apple staff on a federal holiday, Martin Luther King Jr. Day, when many employees and reporters were presumably not working. Jobs didn't return journalists' phone calls. While he certainly had a right to medical privacy, that didn't include a right to lie, especially when so many people thought the company's fortunes—and maybe the value of their stock holdings, their paychecks, or the warranties on their products—were directly tied to his heartbeat.

When I wrote an article in 2009 about the company's lagging environmental policies for the website Portfolio.com—details on that topic follow a little further in this chapter—and again for this book, the company never responded to my repeated requests for an interview. OK, that happens with reporters all the time. Then, the minute my environmental article posted online, a press person called to complain that I hadn't said enough about the good things Apple is doing. That, too, happens regularly. Now, here's the weird Apple twist: the press person said I was not allowed to quote her, nor would she let me talk to anyone else at the company. What's the point of complaining to the press if you don't want the public to hear your side?

The obsessive secrecy has grown worse over time. Michael Tchong told me that when he was in charge of *MacWeek* during the non-Jobs years, from 1987 to 1991, "people would come to our booth at trade shows and tell us if it weren't for us, they wouldn't know what was going on. People would get fired if they talked to us. [Members of Apple management] were checking phone records, checking for our number in San Francisco." Still, Tchong and his writers were able to glean some information "because it wasn't as insane as it is today. I could not publish *MacWeek* today." The book *iCon*, by Jeffrey S. Young and William L. Simon, picks up the story from there, saying that after Jobs returned he instituted "an absolute ban on talking to anyone outside the company who uses words as a tool of his trade," with limited exceptions. That remark proved more prescient and ironic than the authors could have foreseen: presumably annoyed that it couldn't control what was being written in that book, Apple removed *all* titles published by *iCon*'s publisher, John Wiley & Sons, from Apple Stores—even though this particular book ends up quite positive about Jobs. (Conflict-of-interest alert: I guess the Apple Store ban would include four of my books, which were published by Wiley or a firm subsequently acquired by Wiley.)

In spring 2010, an unfortunate employee accidentally left a prototype of the not-yet-released iPhone 4 in a Silicon Valley bar. As news reports later revealed, another customer found it and sold it to the tech blog Gizmodo, which then posted photos and a story. Although Gizmodo returned the phone, as the company requested, Apple immediately filed a criminal complaint, and the next thing anyone knew, the county sheriff's office had raided the home of the Gizmodo blogger who'd written the post. It took more than a year before the local district attorney finally announced that he wouldn't be filing charges against the blogger.

Apple's secrecy is internal as well. Multiple articles have been written about the oversight systems, ID badges, numeric-code door locks, and security cameras. New-product R&D is as shrouded as nuclear weapons development in Iran. The *New York Times* reported in June 2009, "Some Apple workers in the most critical product-testing rooms must cover up devices with black cloaks when they are working on them, and turn on a red warning light when devices are unmasked." According to *iCon*, when the iPod was under development, "Steve was manic about leaks, so each unit was sealed in a separate reinforced plastic box, much larger than the actual unit—closer to the size of a shoe box. Wires for the controls were strung to random spots on the exterior of the box. On some, the scroll wheel was on the side, for example, and the screen on the top; anyone looking at the box would have no idea how the controls were placed on the actual unit."

Sure, no company likes bad publicity, no company agrees to every media request, and many companies insist that a PR person be present at all interviews. To a certain degree, secrecy is even a standard business tactic. The hush-hush build-up to a product launch can—so executives hope—create a sense of drama and then stoke demand. Apple, however, takes these common uses of secrecy too far.

And when it comes to social responsibility, extreme secrecy may be the single most anti-responsible quality a business could have, because without information, how can activists know whether a company really is providing decent working conditions, cutting back on energy use, or undertaking any of the other efforts considered responsible? That's why "report" is one of the four areas Climate Counts measures when it analyzes companies' efforts to reduce emissions, asking questions like, "Is the company publicly reporting on emissions, risks, and actions?" And why union officials like Mark Levinson insist that outside organizations need to monitor overseas sweatshops and then issue detailed descriptions. The consumer movement began, in part, with a demand for information, such as data about the pollutants that local businesses were discharging into the air and water. Nor is it socially responsible to treat your employees like potential spies.

Openness is especially important to investors, and not just ESG types. The foundation of the modern financial industry is full and fair

disclosure, the concept that everyone has access to the same information at the same time. Particularly with such a leader-driven company,
investors during Jobs's long illness needed to know more than "Steve is
still the CEO." For instance, how much was he actually working? Who
was being groomed as a successor? "Apple would benefit from Jobs giving
more of the limelight to the best talents," suggested Jeffrey Sonnenfeld,
a senior associate dean at the Yale School of Management, in an article
in *Newsweek* soon after the 2011 medical leave was announced and before Jobs stepped down. Even one member of the Apple board—Jerome
B. York, a former top finance officer at IBM and Chrysler, who died in
2010—criticized the company in 2009 for being so tight-lipped regarding
Jobs's health, according to the *Wall Street Journal*. An official at the giant
California Public Employees' Retirement System pension fund (Cal-
PERS) was quoted in another *Wall Street Journal* piece saying that the federal Securities and Exchange Commission should require all companies
to disclose more information about a chief executive's serious illness.
The commission briefly investigated whether Apple's corporate disclo-
sure had been sufficient but took no action.

Brushing aside such advice, Apple management beat back a shareholder resolution in early 2011 that would have required it to disclose its
succession planning, claiming that would give rivals an unfair advantage; nevertheless, the resolution garnered 30 percent of the stockholders' votes, which is an amazing figure considering that resolutions not
proposed by management usually disappear unseen.

"A company that considers itself progressive shouldn't resist transparency of reporting," said the ICCR's Laura Berry. "Apple tends to be
resistant to the whole idea of anyone outside of Apple telling them what
to do." Her group of religious investor-activists filed a shareholder resolution in 2009, also opposed by management, pushing Apple to be more
open about its sustainability efforts and attracted an impressive 8 percent yes vote. As You Sow's Conrad MacKerron gave the example of companies that install a code of conduct for overseas sweatshops: "You can
have a code of conduct in place, but unless you can show us how it's being carried out, we can't know the companies are rigorously enforcing it.
Like everything else, the devil is in the details."

Lack of information was consistently a key factor dragging down
Apple's scores in Greenpeace's Guide to Greener Electronics, an industry ranking, as well as, until recently, Climate Counts's lists. "Disclosure
has probably not been their strength, compared to their competitors,"

said Casey Harrell, a coordinator for Greenpeace's global electronics campaign. MacKerron said that Dell and HP publicized lots of details about worker-injury rates, energy efficiency, greenhouse-gas-emissions goals, and corporate philanthropy; Apple was silent. Students and Scholars Against Corporate Misbehavior, an organization in Hong Kong that investigates working conditions, found HP more open to monitoring groups, according to Jeff Ballinger, the antisweatshop activist.

The only privacy Apple seems to ignore is that of its customers. A transatlantic furor erupted in spring 2011 over the discovery that iPhones, iPads, and Google products were secretly collecting information on users' locations. Although the data were supposedly anonymous, to be used for targeted ads and geography-based services, Steve Jobs was forced to leave his sickbed and admit that the project was mishandled.

The obsession with control—and its ethical implications—also plays out in Apple's basic business philosophy. Under the dominance of Microsoft, and spurred by the Internet, technology has long thrived via widespread sharing. Any computer maker can install Windows. Anyone with a browser can surf the Web. But Apple historically hasn't shared.

It provides almost everything itself: the hardware, the software, and the doorway to content. Because it controls the spigot, the company can control what flows through the spigot. Notoriously, it has refused to allow certain political or pornographic material, often without explanation, including an app with cartoons about golf superstar Tiger Woods, another mocking President Obama, and one by a Republican challenger to California Congress member Henry A. Waxman—although, in fairness, it later relented on the last two. When Apple released its first guidelines for its App Store in September 2010, supposedly to clarify the rules, some of the standards remained vague and micromanaging: "Apps that are not very useful or do not provide any lasting entertainment value may be rejected" and no apps will be allowed if they look like they were "cobbled together in a few days." To avoid potential hitches, *Playboy* removed most of the photos from its iPad version. (*Playboy* without the centerfold?)

Business strategists could reasonably debate the effectiveness of this approach. Apple claims that if it doesn't control every step, it can't be sure that outside contributors meet the superhigh quality standards for which it is famous. But from an ethical standpoint, this strategy is wrong. In fact, there's a well-known word for it: censorship.

Trillium Asset Management—which runs about $900 million in ESG investments for churches, endowments, foundations, nonprofit organizations, and individuals, including shares in Apple—wrote to Apple in late 2009 asking "why and what you're doing to avoid making political determinations" in vetting apps, according to Jonas Kron, deputy director for shareholder advocacy at the firm. "It's an opaque process," he added in an interview. "They're the gatekeeper, and it puts them at the forefront of issues relating to freedom of speech and expression and association and privacy."

"Buy into the World According to Steve, and you're making a Faustian bargain," warned Daniel Lyons, the *Newsweek* tech columnist and a longtime critic of the Apple model. "You sacrifice freedom for the sake of a lovely device that (mostly) works just the way it's supposed to."

Even fans are starting to grumble. While they may adore Apple's quality, innovation, stylishness, ease of use, and former CEO, they're the ones who aren't getting the *Playboy* centerfolds or Tiger Woods cartoons. "Rejections from the Apple Store should only be for very obvious, glaring reasons," John Gruber, who writes the blog *Daring Fireball*, devoted to Apple issues—and who usually loves the company—said at Macworld. "It should only be about quality control, not content control. That's one of the lines they've crossed that rubs people the wrong way."

In any case, the wall may be cracking. Between summer 2009 and summer 2010, according to news reports, the US Department of Justice and the Federal Trade Commission launched investigations into whether Apple was blocking various sorts of outside content, while the Library of Congress ruled against the company in another blocking case and European and US regulators, in 2011, began looking into possible antitrust issues with Apple's subscription requirements for the iPad dating to September 2010. Apple caved a bit by issuing the App Store guidelines and relaxing its requirements for outside applications for the iPhone and the iPad, even allowing long-banned Adobe some limited access. Moreover, as powerful players like Google, Microsoft, and Motorola bring out smartphones and tablets with features and prices as good as or better than the iPhone's and the iPad's, Apple will be ruling a smaller and smaller piece of turf.

Other than the ultrasecurity and black cloaks, working at Apple is, more or less, like the cliché of working anywhere in Silicon Valley. Devotion, excitement, and adrenaline. Ping-Pong and stock options, but long hours. Creativity and independence—as long as Steve Jobs didn't interfere. For that matter, it's the same kind of passionate commitment I found when I interviewed veteran employees of the pharmaceutical maker Merck & Company for my book *The Merck Druggernaut*, as they described the glory days of the mid-1980s to mid-1990s, when Merck was discovering one groundbreaking medicine after another.

At Apple, "it wasn't just a job," recalled Kristina Woolsey, who was a senior engineer, director of a multimedia lab, and an HR official from 1985 to 1998. "It was a calling or a fascination or a passion. It became a way of life. People had a common vision in terms of wanting to change the computing environment." Her sentiment was shared by Kris Lawley, a senior service manager in the Austin, Texas, office who has spent more than two decades at Apple. "You work hard on a project, and then it ends and you take a vacation," Lawley said. "And then you plunge in again." In a rare inside look at the place, *Fortune*, in 2011, quoted a former designer this way: "If you're a diehard Apple geek, it's magical. But it's also a really tough place to work."

Employees have some flexibility in choosing which hours they work. "You could take the afternoon off and go see a movie, as long as you're there the core hours" of 11 A.M. to 4 P.M., said Lawley's mother, Gail, who recently retired as a quality-control manager in Tucson. The famous Silicon Valley perks were available: Kris Lawley mentioned Ping-Pong, Nerf guns, and nap rooms; at the Cupertino headquarters, said Woolsey, "they set up an incredible cafeteria," with everything from health food to pizza. Woolsey even nursed her infant daughter at the office.

However, *Fortune* claimed that "the vibe is the opposite of the jocularity that Google—with its wear-your-pajamas-to-work day and all-you-can-eat cafeterias—has fostered." If so, that may stem at least in part from the secrecy and micromanaging. At the Apple Store, according to the *Wall Street Journal*, employees are given a detailed script for almost every interaction with customers. Certainly, it was no picnic to answer to Steve Jobs, who could stalk into a lab and tear up a design or demand an impossible change at the drop of a chip. Some of Gail Lawley's colleagues left as soon as he returned in 1997, she said, "because they didn't want to work with him." Authors Jeffrey Young and William Simons, in *iCon*, described how employees tried to avoid the boss: "You didn't want to encounter him in a hallway, because he might not like an answer you gave. . . . And you sure as hell didn't want to get trapped on an elevator with him, because by the time the doors opened, you might not have a job."

Janet Gray Hayes didn't work *for* Jobs, but she sometimes had to work *with* him when she was the mayor of San Jose—the biggest city near Apple headquarters—from 1975 to 1983. One time when he came to her office, "he lay on my table, like he was the center of the universe," she sniffed in an interview with me, years later. More diplomatically, Kristina Woolsey offered, "He manages to the product. He doesn't manage [in order] to be a nice guy." But she never felt he was looking over her shoulder, she added.

Moreover, not everyone gets the same perks. The initial Mac developers directly under Jobs famously were a privileged group, with cars, video games, their own basketball court, subsidized babysitters, and free massages. Other employees resented those deals, but then again, the Mac team resented the non-Mac staff's higher pay. When Apple first went public by selling stock in 1980, and again with Pixar's initial public offering, some longtime colleagues were inexplicably left out or got a measly allocation of shares, according to the books *iCon* and *Apple Confidential 2.0.*

Labor expert Christian Weller is a bit skeptical about the perks but sympathetic on the whole to the workplace style. Things like Ping-Pong are "flim-flam," he scoffed. "When people move into their thirties, a Ping-Pong table becomes a lot less important, and health care and work-flex rules become more important." In that sense, he added, "one place where Silicon Valley companies tend to be very good is giving workers plenty of flexibility in the hours they work."

To its credit, Apple has not been a major actor in the tech industry's biggest workplace controversy, the use of "permatemps"—long-term contract employees who work almost identical jobs and hours as full-timers yet are denied benefits. Microsoft, by contrast, had to pay a $97 million settlement in a class-action lawsuit in 2005.

In another crucial way, however, Apple is worse than the rest of Silicon Valley. Microsoft, Google, IBM, HP, and other rivals regularly appear on *Fortune* magazine's "Best Companies to Work For" list. Apple has never been seen there (although it was included in a 1984 book by the same journalists who compile the *Fortune* project). What's wrong with Apple? Since companies must proactively apply, it's possible Apple wouldn't even deign to ask a magazine to judge it. Or, it's possible that the staff actually doesn't like working there. Because the editors of the list won't discuss why companies don't qualify, we'll never know.

Domini's Steven Lydenberg offered a historical explanation for Apple's omission from the "best" lists. In the early days, he said, "it had a reputation for being a great place to work, better than any other Silicon Valley place. It had AIDS education in the workplace and a big community volunteerism program; it was good on diversity issues." Then the revenues and stock collapsed, and "all the socially responsible programs were understandably set to one side, and they just concentrated on getting their business model and getting back on line," he suggested. (Apple constitutes about 3 percent of Domini's $1 billion holdings.)

It's still too soon to tell how much the atmosphere may change under the new CEO, Tim Cook. Descriptions of him emphasize his skill at operations and efficiency, which may sound a lot more boring than inventing the iPod but could also mean a more grueling working environment without much time for Ping-Pong. Cook is also described as intense and a workaholic—no change from Jobs there. On the optimistic side, he is considered calmer and more polite than his predecessor. In any case, it's probably safe to assume that Jobs's handpicked successor is no flower child.

Stressful as the milieu at headquarters might be, matters are far worse, of course, in the developing-world factories where Apple products are manufactured. In fairness, Apple is hardly the only company outsourcing. Everything we use nowadays seems to be made in sweatshops in China or in other desperately poor locales like Bangladesh, El Salvador, Honduras, and Vietnam. Tech factories like Apple's can be especially dangerous because of the lead, beryllium, and other toxic materials that go into a computer or iPhone. And don't expect the facilities always to provide safety gloves or masks. But again, to be fair to Apple, the whole electronics industry "was kind of late to the game in terms of dealing with overseas-labor issues," trailing the apparel industry, according to Adam Kanzer, the general counsel at Domini.

Even with those caveats, Apple was a step behind the rest of the Valley. Dell, HP, and IBM cofounded the Electronic Industry Citizenship Coalition (EICC) in 2004 and crafted a code of conduct for monitoring working conditions in the supply chain, but Apple didn't join until 2006.

According to Kanzer, in 2004, Domini began writing to Jobs about the factory conditions, emphasizing an angle that the investment firm figured would appeal to the image-conscious CEO. "They have such a strong base of young consumers who probably care about these issues more than most," as Kanzer put it. "This could have a significant impact on the company. What if people found out something like, children were making iPods?" Domini followed up with a shareholder resolution seeking a corporate code of conduct for the supply chain and a system of monitoring and reporting. Perhaps the threat of looking like an ugly capitalist got Apple's attention, or perhaps it was the $21.5 million worth of its stock Domini holds; in any case, Apple said it would consider the ideas. Then negotiations dragged on for a year and a half. Domini agreed to withdraw its resolution if Apple adopted a code, Apple missed the deadline for doing so, and Domini refiled the resolution. Drafts went back and forth. Finally, in November 2005, Apple adopted a code.

True to Apple's modus operandi, when it finally came out with a product—in this case, a code of conduct—it was arguably the best on the market. One key area involves freedom of association and union activity, which too many codes omit. The EICC version requires participating members "to respect the rights of workers as established by local law to associate freely on a voluntary basis, seek representation, join or be represented by Works Councils, and join or not join labor unions and bargain collectively." Apple's is more pointed in placing similar freedom-of-association requirements on *suppliers*—not just on itself—and in specifying that suppliers may not fire or refuse to hire people because of union membership. Moreover, within four years, Apple had audited 288 supplier factories, cutting ties with 3 that hired underage workers—and, perhaps most amazing, issuing public annual reports on its suppliers. "I was impressed how quickly the company got up to speed," Kanzer said.

Apple soon had a test of its intentions. Barely six months after its code was adopted, a British newspaper published an investigation of iPod factories in China run by the subcontractor Foxconn Technology, charging, among other things, that people worked fifteen hours a day for less than $50 a month and were housed in crowded dormitories, forced to work overtime, guarded by armed police, and punished harshly.

It took Apple a mere two months to investigate and post a detailed report on its website. According to that report, its audit team "interviewed over 100 randomly selected employees" and "visited and inspected factory floors, dormitories, dining halls, and recreation areas," as well as reviewing "thousands of documents." The upshot was fairly tame. Apple claimed that "we found the supplier to be in compliance in the majority of the areas audited," including "no evidence whatsoever of the use of child labor or any form of forced labor." However, the company-that-never-apologizes did concede a few "violations to our Code of Conduct," most notably that "employees worked longer hours than permitted" by the code. The report additionally cited "impersonal" and crowded conditions at three dorms—ah, trust Apple to notice the decor!—and a pay structure that "was unnecessarily complex." To remedy these problems, Apple hired the respected outside monitoring firm Verité.

Scandal struck Foxconn and Apple again four years later. A dozen young Chinese workers at two Foxconn plants committed suicide in winter and spring 2010, most of them dramatically by leaping from corporate dorms. Tens of thousands of other unhappy workers had quit, charging long hours, low pay, military-style drills, forced overtime, verbal abuse, and harsh punishments. This time, Apple wasn't alone; Foxconn made products for Dell, HP, and others as well. By summer, as the headlines raced around the world, several of the tech giants promised to investigate. Apple sent an inspection team led by Tim Cook (not yet the CEO) that interviewed, by its own count, more than one thousand workers. Foxconn denied that its working conditions had any connection to the suicides but nevertheless responded by doubling salaries, setting up a twenty-four-hour counseling center, and installing yards of netting.

In China, sadly, tales of horrible workplaces don't end. Six months after the Foxconn controversy seemed to die down, Apple acknowledged that some 137 laborers at another subcontractor, Wintek, had suffered nerve damage, weakness, headaches, dizziness, and other serious injuries from a toxic chemical used in manufacturing iPhone screens in 2009. Apple claimed it had ordered Wintek to stop using the chemical and to improve safety and said it would monitor conditions. Wintek said almost everyone had recovered, but employees told the *New York Times* that they had never heard from Apple, even as the subcontractor was pressuring them to quit, take cash settlements, and shut up. Students and Scholars Against Corporate Misbehavior, the Hong Kong advocacy group, also accused Apple of dragging its feet.

The area where Apple should do best—and disappoints most—is the environment. For a lot of reasons, the tech industry is usually a star of the green world. "The electronics sector, since Day One, has had the highest average scores of any sectors" in the Climate Counts ranking of large companies' carbon-emissions policies, said Wood Turner, the organization's former executive director. As he explained it, "People that are early adopters of technology are typically the leading edge of thinking on issues, whether it be the gadget they're using or how business should be focusing on sustainability." Similarly, Greenpeace's Casey Harrell opined that "you've got a much younger industry that's built around a lot of means of innovation. Comparatively, they're relatively green." Three of the top four companies cited by Ceres (the group that reports on business sustainability efforts) are tech companies. So were the first three—and six of the first nine—of Newsweek's "100 Greenest Companies in America" in 2010, and three of the top five in 2011.

But not Apple.

The company didn't make Newsweek's 2009 and 2011 lists at all and came in at a paltry Number 65 in 2010. It consistently ranks at the bottom of Climate Counts's twelve names in its industry. When IBM, Nokia, and Sony, among others, formed the Eco-Patent Commons in 2008 to share new environmental ideas, Apple was AWOL. It has refused to join Ceres, despite years of discussions. "Apple was one of the personal-computer companies that was later to the table in terms of allowing recycling of older computers," said the ICCR's Laura Berry. As noted by As You Sow's Conrad MacKerron, Dell and HP are more open about disclosing goals for all sorts of environmental issues, such as emissions cuts, energy efficiency, reduced packaging, and greener packaging, and Greenpeace specifically targeted Apple in a special consumer campaign called Green My Apple in 2006.

This is not the image people expect of Apple. Not the Apple where former US vice president Al Gore—winner of the Nobel Peace Prize and an Academy Award for his global-warming film An Inconvenient Truth—sits on the board. Consider the name, with its evocation of nature, trees, organic fruit, and the precursor farm owned by Jobs's friends. "A lot of people think Apple is an environmental leader just because it's Apple and it's a cool company," said Conrad MacKerron with a sigh. "When you scratch below the surface, I would not say they are an environmental leader."

Along with many activists, MacKerron suspects that Apple's culture has gotten in the way. The secrecy and insistence on handling everything itself make it harder for environmental advocates to figure out exactly what Apple is doing. "A lot of companies would have given a nod to shareholders on those issues, saying, 'We've been glad to work with our partners' [to fix environmental problems]," suggested Trillium's Jonas Kron. "Apple didn't see the shareholders as useful partners." Even worse, Wood Turner, of Climate Counts, worries that Apple's obsession with being the hippest, most innovative guy on the block could keep it from being the most ethical guy on the block. "They have to be first, and once they're not the first, I think they fight tooth and nail against being pressured into doing anything," he said. So, if all of its tech rivals are already recycling old computers or pressuring their suppliers to reduce packaging, Apple certainly isn't going to copy them, no matter how much better that would be for the environment.

Of course, the reverse could be true. It might be that Apple is doing a lot more than the critics realize, but because Apple keeps it hidden, nobody knows.

And in other ways, Apple's culture works both for and against greenness. The tendency toward minimalist design and packaging means that fewer ingredients need to be mined to create the gadgets, less is dumped in a landfill at the end, and less energy is consumed in manufacturing and shipping. That's the good part. However, all those efforts are undermined by the imperative to constantly produce newer, more innovative versions of whatever is already on the market. Each time the next iPhone or iPod comes out, fans must have it. How much energy and how many resources are used up in that serially speedy obsolescence? And what happens to the outdated models?

The situation began improving around 2006. Perhaps Apple wasn't immune to the shareholder resolutions, poor rankings, and comparisons with hated rivals. Conrad MacKerron's group, for instance, finally managed to meet with Al Gore and (it took a year longer to arrange) with Jobs. In October 2009, Apple, along with a handful of lesser-known companies like California utility PG&E, dramatically quit the US Chamber of Commerce to protest the chamber's foot dragging on climate change. And in 2011, it was one of only twenty-five companies, out of the nearly one hundred ranked by Climate Counts, to get an extra gold star for supporting mandatory federal action on carbon emissions.

Environmentalists said they have even noticed a greater willingness by Apple to share information. In some cases, it's now an industry leader, rather than a follower. The corporate website has product-by-product environmental statistics, including greenhouse gas emissions in kilograms and power consumption for various operating modes. Greenpeace's Casey Harrell particularly praised the company for educating suppliers about less toxic alternatives. "They did a lot of the early-adapter costs," he said. "They pulled the rest of the industry along." It was the first company to stop using lead-containing monitors, a pioneer in banning glass containing arsenic, and at least a year ahead of HP and Dell in getting rid of toxic PVCs. Neither Harrell nor other activists expect Tim Cook to alter this trend, in part because Cook and Jobs both said as much.

The Apple PR person who wouldn't let me quote her (so I'll paraphrase) emphasized three areas where, she asserted, my Portfolio.com article hadn't given the company enough green credit: detailed environmental reports about each product; elimination of brominated flame retardants, PVCs, mercury, and other toxic ingredients; and measurement of the emissions when people use the products, in addition to the emissions from manufacturing and corporate headquarters. Moreover, she claimed that the company had been doing some of this for years. As a result of these efforts, and more, Apple jumped a whopping forty-one points on Climate Counts's ranking from 2008 to 2009. It briefly flew up six notches on the Greenpeace guide in January 2010, from eleventh to a five-way tie for fifth out of seventeen, then dropped four places the following October, and then shot back up to fourth in November 2011.

Yet Apple's efforts start from such a low point that it still has a long way to go. It remains the worst-ranking electronics company on Climate Counts's list.

Secrecy continues to drag down its Greenpeace rankings. "Apple would score more points on the other criteria with greater transparency of its data" regarding suppliers' emissions and use of dangerous chemicals, the November 2011 report said. On the Climate Counts chart, the worst ratings come in the most important category, that of setting goals and actually doing something to reduce emissions—as opposed to simply mouthing off about federal mandates and such. Moreover, as the ICCR's Laura Berry and Climate Counts's Wood Turner mentioned, Apple lags rival big tech firms in enabling customers to return old computers for recycling.

(The issue of recycling is separate from the problem of obtaining the tantalum, coltan, tin, tungsten, and other minerals that are vital components of tech products like cell phones. Many of these are dug up in habitats of endangered animals or war zones controlled by vicious militia leaders, or else mined in ways that pollute the environment. In this controversy, Apple shines no brighter—but no worse—than any other manufacturer. It says it is seeking to ensure that its raw materials don't come from regions with human rights abuses or in the midst of fighting.)

A major dispute centers on how to measure emissions. The company argues that customer usage must be included because the gases emitted after an iPhone, MacBook, or anything else leaves the Apple Store—

taking it home, manufacturing the battery or providing the electricity that powers it, disposing of it—account for 46 percent of the total carbon footprint. Jobs, in a rare interview that may indicate how important this topic suddenly became to the company, told *BusinessWeek* in October 2009 that measuring emissions without including the end user is "like asking a cigarette company how green their office is." He added, "A lot of companies publish how green their building is, but it doesn't matter if you're shipping millions of power-hungry products with toxic chemicals in them." Apple may want to include this part of the emissions trail because it claims its gizmos are the most energy-efficient in the world, as detailed on the website. And the company knows this, the unquotable spokesperson said, because it microanalyzes even down to the level of how much power goes into each keystroke.

Activists like MacKerron and Turner are skeptical about this whole argument. First, they question whether product usage really has such a significant greenhouse impact. By Apple's own figures, after all, the nonconsumer aspects like manufacturing and transportation from the factory to the store are responsible for 54 percent of the emissions. "Extraction of raw materials, design, production, a vast distribution network, retail stores—there's a huge amount of energy that goes into getting that product into the consumer's hands," Turner said. "How much are you pressuring your supply chain [to reduce this energy consumption]?" There have been contradictory studies of whether reading something electronically is greener than using old-fashioned paper, but even if it is, skeptics don't necessarily buy Apple's assertion that its electronic products are the greenest. And finally, even if all of Apple's claims are true, customer usage is one area the company really doesn't control. Maybe fans love its products so much that they use them more than they would use clunky PCs and BlackBerrys, in which case Apple is actually increasing total emissions.

Ideally, Apple could leverage its customers' devotion to really move the industry. Greenpeace aimed to do exactly that with its international Green My Apple campaign, beginning in 2006. The environmental group found Apple users by going to Mac trade shows and reaching out online "through the echo chamber that is the Mac fan world," as Casey Harrell put it. It directed them to a special website, where users were asked to design an Apple ad campaign that would emphasize environmental topics. Greenpeace stepped carefully, knowing the fans' feelings. "Our campaign wasn't, 'Apple, you're horrible.' Our campaign was, 'Apple, you're great, but we want you green,'" Harrell recalled. For instance, the home page said, "We love Apple. Apple knows more about 'clean' design than anybody, right? So why do Macs, iPods, iBooks, and the rest of their product range contain hazardous substances that other companies have abandoned?" Customers were thrilled at the chance to design an ad for their idol, Harrell said, and the campaign ended up with thousands of submissions. (He conceded that there was also "a subsegment of the population that said, 'Piss off, Greenpeace, Apple can do no wrong.'")

Did the campaign work? Naturally, Harrell said yes. But so did Jobs, in the *BusinessWeek* interview. At any rate, it was around that time that Apple began to change.

And why did Greenpeace choose to target Apple instead of Dell or Motorola or Sony? Partly because of the fan base. Partly because it was a laggard. And, Harrell said, because "we hoped it will have a domino effect on the rest of the industry."

Maybe critics are defining "social responsibility" too narrowly.

When describing Apple's efforts in classically CSR areas like overseas sweatshops or green initiatives, Domini's Steve Lydenberg used cautious terms like "incrementally" and "satisfactory" and "phasing in, in an orderly manner," and he admitted that the company had taken "what I would not necessarily call a leadership role." Nevertheless, his ethical-investing firm has taken a $21.5 million bite of that Apple. So what makes it a socially responsible investment? "We value innovation and customer quality and service, and Apple has always been a true leader in that area," Lydenberg explained. "We look for innovations that are related to access." In particular, he cited mobile phones, the Internet, and computers in general as technologies that have "had a tremendously empowering and economically positive effect in the developing world."

Journalist Chrystia Freeland made a similar point in a 2011 cover story in the *Atlantic* about what she called the global superelite. She distinguished techno-zillionaires like Jobs (and Bill Gates), who built their fortunes on "advances that have broadly benefited the nation and the world," from "TARP-recipient bankers," who took federal bailout money in the Troubled Asset Relief Program during the 2008 financial crisis.

Certainly, there are many uplifting stories of schools in Africa, Asia, and Latin America that are able to run solar-powered laptops or of impoverished farmers who have established cell phone networks to market their produce and crafts. Even some American schools have found that students focus better if they get their assignments via iPad. One iPad app helps children who have cerebral palsy. The Iranians who took to the streets in June 2009 to protest their country's stolen presidential election used cell phones to organize and send information to the outside world, and undoubtedly many of those were iPhones. The same goes for the Facebook- and Twitter-wielding protestors in Tunisia and Egypt who brought down their authoritarian governments in 2011. If all that is CSR, Apple clearly fits.

It's not only political protesters and impoverished farmers who benefit sociopolitically from Apple technology. In an era of information aggregation and Web surfing, experts ranging from *New York Times* media columnist David Carr to Unilever's chief marketing officer to Walter Isaacson, author of the only authorized biography of Steve Jobs, have predicted that the iPad may be the innovation that will keep books, magazines, and newspapers alive (no small matter for this author and freelance writer). Perhaps the $4.99 copy of the *New Yorker* on the iPad is the middle ground between the $5.99 print edition and free downloads to a computer or a smartphone, allowing readers the convenience of e-versions while still funneling some income to the publishers and authors. (And if the first-round prices for tablet editions were too close to the print ones and if publishers didn't like Apple's subscription terms, those are basically problems of monopoly and technology that competition and more tech can solve; indeed, pressure from publishers forced Apple to alter its subscription policies within less than a year.) The iPad is easier to read than a smartphone, the picture quality is better than on a computer, and the pages look identical to the hard copy. Probably most important to publishers in the long run, the tablet offers the kind of flexibility that the digital world demands, including interactive ads, multimedia links, and ways to measure consumer viewing of ads.

Condé Nast, for one, decided the iPad made it worthwhile to revive its defunct magazine *Gourmet*, albeit as a mobile app, not the original publication. Rupert Murdoch even created a brand-new newspaper, the *Daily*, specifically for that platform. As for e-books, publishers hoped that Apple, by breaking Amazon's Kindle monopoly, would give them pricing leverage down the road, even if the publishers' and authors' royalties were actually lower at the beginning. In fact, one day after the iPad was introduced, Macmillan Publishing forced Amazon to raise its e-book prices by threatening to pull its titles (and, presumably, transfer to Apple). True, competition from Google and Barnes & Noble could accomplish those same goals—but Apple was first.

But speaking of old-fashioned virtues like reading: whatever happened to the concept of walking down the street or in a park, noticing the people around you, smelling the flowers, listening to the birds, letting your mind daydream, or thinking deep thoughts? No time for that anymore, because we're plugged into our iPods 24/7. Steve Jobs and Apple have a lot to answer for in that destruction of social responsibility.

When it comes to more mundane aspects of community service, ironically, Apple seems far less polished. Outside of a few standard-issue gestures, like donating a portion of the proceeds from specific iPod and iTunes purchases to fighting AIDS in Africa, it's not particularly known for its philanthropy. According to a long analysis by noted *New York Times* business writer Andrew Ross Sorkin—in the same 2011 article in which he called Jobs "the da Vinci of our time"—Apple doesn't even do standard big-company actions like matching employees' charitable donations, and Jobs shut down the existing philanthropic programs when he returned in 1997. Furthermore, Sorkin pointed out, Jobs didn't join fellow famous moguls Bill Gates and Warren Buffett in the Giving Pledge, in which superwealthy families promise to give away at least half of their fortunes. Nor did his cancer turn Jobs into a public advocate for health issues. In fairness, of course, he and Apple could have been handing out a ton of money anonymously.

Apple has been busier on the political side. Since 1998, it's been steadily increasing its profile and now is "a significant lobbying force," according to Dave Levinthal, who until 2011 was the spokesperson for the Center for Responsive Politics, the nonpartisan research group that's considered the best source for this sort of data. By 2008, the company was spending $1.71 million on nineteen lobbyists, including, said Levinthal, "some very high-powered" outside firms. It's been a bit stingier with campaign donations, but by 2008 it reached number 16 in the tech industry. (That was obviously a busy year for Apple.) Nearly 90 percent of the money goes to Democrats. Jobs and his wife, Laurene, were major Democratic Party donors for years, and Laurene was even a delegate to the Democratic National Convention in 2000. Among specific beneficiaries, the Human Rights Campaign's Eric Bloem praised the company for being one of the few to give money in 2008—that same busy year—to defeat Proposition 8, a constitutional amendment in California banning same-sex marriage. (The measure passed anyway.)

The scorecard on shareholder governance issues—the G in ESG—is fairly weak, perhaps because governance by its very nature means being open to pressure from outsiders, in this case shareholders. Rubber-stamp though the process usually is, management does have to bring resolutions and board elections to a public vote, while shareholders get the opportunity to bring up their own issues. Remember all those resolutions and threatened resolutions about Apple's environmental initiatives and the global supply chain? Another popular activist target is the board membership and the process of electing it, since directors throughout the corporate world are notoriously cozy with their CEOs. CalPERS, the giant California pension fund, managed—against Apple management's opposition—to push through a resolution in February 2011 changing the rules so that directors running unopposed couldn't simply assume re-election; they would actually have to win a majority of the votes. On any board, gender and racial diversity makes a symbolic statement to activists, and Apple's lack of both long bothered ESG investors like the ICCR and Domini. Apple didn't get its first nonwhite or nonmale board member until 2008, when it managed a twofer by appointing Andrea Jung, the chair and chief executive of Avon Products.

Cost has always been the big rap against Apple, because its high price tags discriminate against lower-income people. "They are the product of choice of elite, preppy Ivy Leaguers who have the money to afford the price," Sally Greenberg of the National Consumers League asserted.

But look again at those issues of quality and service Steven Lydenberg mentioned. Apple desktops, in a *Consumer Reports* survey of 62,500 users between 2005 and 2009, required the fewest repairs among seven leading brands. Putting aside the antenna problem with the iPhone 4, "Apple has been at or near the top consistently" in *Consumer Reports* computer rankings, according to a spokesperson. David Eiswert, the T. Rowe Price portfolio manager, compared the 12-inch MacBook Pro ($1,200, when we spoke) with an equivalent PC (maybe $750). "With MacPro, you get ease of software, iMovie and iPhoto, and a seven-hour battery. That's what people want," he said. "It would take you an hour just to install the software in the PC." The computers famously get hit by far fewer viruses than Windows-using rivals (although that may be due less to Apple antivirus wizardry than to virus mongers' calculation that its single-digit market share isn't worth attacking).

Plus, Apple customers and noncustomers alike have access to more than three hundred beautiful, airy, glass-and-steel Apple Stores, where

they can use the restrooms, the display Macs, and the WiFi, no purchase
necessary. Best of all are the stores' Genius Bars, whose technicians will
answer almost any question and fix almost any problem at no cost. Compare that with what most tech companies offer: a call center somewhere
in Mumbai or Bangalore, or no live voices at all, just computerized answering services or websites that never return messages.

The price issue may finally have gotten to Apple. By 2011, it was mull-
ing a cheaper version of the iPhone, and the iPad sold at a lower cost
than rivals for its first year. (More likely, however, the iPhone move was
spurred by the competition from Google, not CSR guilt, and the iPad
was no doubt partly subsidized by fat profits from all the other pricey
gizmos.)

For true believers, all this microanalysis is beside the point. They know
that Apple is socially responsible, because—well, because Al Gore is on
the board, and Gandhi was in the 1997 "Think Different" ad campaign,
and all the cool people they know use Apple products. "It's equated with
California, and California is organic food and driving a Prius," Michael
Tchong, the former *MacWeek* publisher (and former California resident),
said with a laugh.

The people I met at Macworld didn't spend much time fretting about
the company's social responsibility. Jeffrey Boerner, the grad student
from Iowa, was vaguely aware that Apple was taking some steps on recycling. His wife, Nora, accepted the company's claims about its environmental efforts at face value, because, as she put it, "I do believe they are
the leader in so many ways."

"It's not the compelling thing for me," said Lynn Goldstein, a fifty-
nine-year-old archaeology professor at Michigan State University. "The
compelling issue is how easy it is for me to do the things I do" on Apple
products.

THE QUESTION: Does Apple deserve its reputation
as an exemplar of ethical chic?

THE VERDICT: Inching closer to yes

Because its image of social responsibility is so much more glowing than
Apple deserves, the first temptation is to issue a flat-out negative verdict.
And that would have been accurate in the early 2000s. Today, however,
any analysis has to be a combination of maybes, yes-buts, and back-and-
forths.

For instance, the company deserves recognition for the improvements it has made on the environmental and sweatshop fronts, even if the green ones don't go far enough. In some ways, it's ahead of its peers, and in some ways behind. That's OK, but can a company be hailed as socially responsible if it's average? And how much credit should it get if the action was forced on it by public pressure? For a company to be truly ethical, CSR concerns should be built into the corporate culture. The purchasing manager shouldn't even have to ask whether to buy recycled or virgin-tree paper.

Another yes-but involves working conditions. While Apple isn't the most nurturing place to work, prospective employees either buy into the pressured creativity, or they don't have to apply. It can be invigorating to work ninety hours a week when you feel as though you are changing the world. Still, can a company be considered socially responsible if employees live in mortal terror of a mercurial and micromanaging CEO? In this case, the answer will now depend on our evolving insight into the new CEO.

Steven Lydenberg, Chrystia Freeland, and David Eiswert have a point in saying that it's socially responsible to help the public—to expand access and communication, to go overboard in making products easy to use, and to offer prompt help. That may be the most unsung value of all. Yet is that CSR, or just good business?

Maybe most important, there is the question of corporate soul. The secrecy. The self-satisfaction. The obsessive need for control. Can any company really be socially responsible if it's so secretive that no one can be sure whether it's even doing the socially responsible things it claims? This trait is particularly troubling if Apple is arbitrarily rejecting apps for the iPad and iPhone because of their content, whether political, pornographic, or otherwise. While government investigations, competition, and public protest seem to be eroding some of the micromanagement at the edges, the changes are not hitting the core. Even worse, they are not self-motivated. Apple doesn't really want to change.

Will things be different now that Steve Jobs is no longer around to smother the corporate culture with his personality, paranoia, and whims? Here's one reason for hope: because Tim Cook does not start out with Jobs's cultlike following, he will need to nurture goodwill, love, respect, and adoration. It may be easier to accomplish that by actually talking to reporters, investors, activists, and customers. Moreover, Andrea Matwyshyn, a professor of legal studies and business ethics at the

University of Pennsylvania's Wharton School, predicted that, as is often the case when a strong founding leader leaves, the company is more likely to be run by a team leadership, and a team pretty much requires some communication. Indeed, a whole bevy of executives, not a solo Jobs, was hauled before reporters to announce the iPhone 4S, just one day before Jobs died.

Now, here are all the reasons not to hope: the *New York Times*, *Newsweek*, and other publications regularly describe Cook with words such as "intensely private," and Cook and Apple both clammed up, Jobs-like, about the former CEO's health every time he took a medical leave. Apple also refused to make Cook available to the press when Jobs made his farewell announcement. Besides, why should Apple change its culture? It's worked at least since Jobs returned in 1997.

As long as the pixie dust holds out.

CHAPTER 5

Trader Joe's

Are We Having Fun Yet?

IF YOU BRING YOUR own shopping bags, a cashier in a navy-and-white flowered shirt told the customer ahead of me in line, you can enter your name in a lottery.

"What's the lottery prize?" I butted in.

"A cryogenic chamber," deadpanned the cashier.

When I gave him a skeptical glance, the cashier laughed. He was an athletic-looking blond, maybe in his twenties. "A twenty-five-dollar gift certificate and a Trader Joe's bag," he amended.

"But I wouldn't need a bag, because I brought my own," I pointed out. "That's how I'd get in the lottery."

"Yeah, Joe didn't think about that. But he's still a nice guy."

Shopping at Trader Joe's is like that. The employees will slip into easygoing conversations at the drop of an organic banana. And if there are no organic bananas, there may be Formosa papaya, heirloom leaf lettuce, six types of pita bread, nine varieties of mushrooms, seven kinds of feta cheese, free-range organic chicken, no-antibiotic/vegetarian-fed chicken, and minimally raised chicken. Plastered on the walls are nautical and South Sea knickknacks such as surfboards, fake-bamboo picture frames, and Polynesian masks, plus perky sayings written on wooden signs. By the lettuce bin: "The fact 'Romaines,' TJ's has unbeatable prices on salad! 'Lettuce' be your go-tos for greens." At the meat section: "You can 'butcher' bottom dollar that TJ's meat values are a 'cut' above the rest."

No one *loves* grocery shopping, not the way Paris Hilton might love cruising through the Sydney Michelle boutique. But people love Trader Joe's.

Before an outlet opened in New York City in 2006, Willa Edwards, a credit-collection clerk then in her mid-sixties, would take a one-hour bus ride from her Manhattan home once a month to get to the Trader Joe's in the Westchester suburbs. The *New York Times* found an even more devoted Brooklynite who regularly trekked five hours round-trip via train and bus in pursuit of the chain's egg rolls and minestrone.

Those bereft of a local Trader Joe's beg for one. The *Times Union*, in Albany, New York, in 2008 wrote about a group called We Want Trader Joe's in the Capital District—the Capital District is the region that encompasses Albany, the state capital—and reported that some locals "believe the Capital Region cannot become a center for technology or high-wage employment until it has stores like Whole Foods, Trader Joe's, and Nordstrom."

There are as many varieties of shoppers and reasons for shopping at Trader Joe's as there are types of feta cheese and mushrooms. My mother goes there, and so does my vegetarian cousin. According to a 2010 cover story in *Fortune* magazine, "[Y]oung Hollywood types like Jessica Alba are regularly photographed brandishing Trader Joe's shopping bags—but Supreme Court Justice Sonia Sotomayor reportedly is a fan too." Willa Edwards cited "the gourmet food," including honey-plantain strips, and the fact that the offerings are "natural, no MSG or any of that crap." Tatiana Boureau, a twentysomething dance student, likes the chain "because it's cheap," while Ronnie Worthen, a forty-nine-year-old corrections officer from Brooklyn, mentioned the assortment of nuts, berries, organic breads, and vegetables. I know one couple who go out of their way for the low-sodium lox. Anton Chatterji, an associate professor at Duke University's Fuqua School of Business, is happy to find prepared, ethnic-Indian food like chicken tandoori. It seems impossible to find anyone who doesn't love Trader Joe's.

But which Trader Joe's do these fans love?

"They didn't bill themselves as a socially responsible company, just a well-run company in the gourmet and natural business. Well run, and ethical."
>   —Tom Chappell, the Tom of Tom's of Maine,
>   whose toothpaste is sold there

"A commercial version of the neighborhood store."
>   —Arthur Caplan, chair of the University of
>   Pennsylvania's medical-ethics department

"A Tiki Room with Aisles of Discounts"
>   —the headline on the *New York Times* article
>   when the first outlet opened in that city

"The corporate culture can be described as dorky."
>   —a different *New York Times* article by
>   a different writer, ten days earlier

"They combine almost a warehouse-grocery experience, which on some level feels hip and green, with some unique foods."
>   —Michael Myers, president of the ad agency
>   Palio Communications

"An offbeat, fun discovery zone."
>   —*Fortune* cover story, 2010

"They're not a supermarket; they're a specialty market."
>   —consumer-branding expert Robert Passikoff

"Your Neighborhood Grocery Store."
>   —the Trader Joe's website

The Rough Guide to Shopping with a Conscience essentially throws up its hands, saying that "[w]hether Trader Joe's, incidentally, is classified as a 'health food' store or 'specialist foods' retailer seems to vary according to what source you read."

Some basic facts appear to be undisputed: The chain specializes in unusual foods not available in standard supermarkets, often imported or at least with international-style names, and in particular, precooked frozen entrees that can be easily warmed up for a quick, gourmet-seeming dinner. A "tasting panel" scours the globe to bring back exciting new treats. The company stocks mainly its own private-label products, which, by and large, cost less than national brands. A few famous names are available, but Trader Joe's deliberately does not try to sell all things to all people—no diapers, no baby food, no Diet Coke. Where a typical grocery store might carry 30,000 to 50,000 SKUs (stock-keeping units—essentially, items), Trader Joe's could have a mere 4,000. The stores themselves are small by industry standards, with a decor variously described as Hawaiian, Polynesian, Tahitian, South Seas, nautical, and tropical kitsch, and a superfriendly staff. Beyond that, let's take a closer look at some of the popular images.

Image: "A well-run company in the gourmet and natural business" that
      "on some level feels hip and green"
For its 3,000 private-label goods, which constitute about 80 percent of the items on its shelves, Trader Joe's indeed sets stringent "natural" and "green" standards, including no trans fats, genetically modified ingredients, or artificial preservatives, colors, or flavors. A lot of the house products are fully organic, as are about half of the fruits and vegetables. Since 2005, all TJ's-brand eggs must be laid by cage-free hens—that is, hens not crammed into the horrendous cages of mainstream egg factories. According to PETA, Trader Joe's does not test its products on animals.

These promises apply solely to the specific Trader Joe's labels, however. The outside brands could well be full of chemicals or produced in inhumane ways. The Hebrew National hot dogs on Trader Joe's shelves contain sodium nitrite, which has been linked to cancer, as well as heapings of fat, saturated fat, and salt. Some non-TJ's eggs are laid by mistreated hens. "They could certainly do a lot more, as companies like Whole Foods have done," said the Humane Society's Michael Markarian. For instance, he'd like the chain to use roomier crates for pigs. It's also important to remember that when tasting-panel members scout out a perfect tiramisu on the coast of Italy, they're not focusing on whether it's organic or free of GMOs (genetically modified organisms). They simply want a mouth-watering dish that isn't available commercially in the United States.

(By the way, the shelves have more national brands than shoppers realize. Many products are actually made by big manufacturers like Kiss My Face and Tasty Bite, with a TJ's label slapped on.)

And some of the most well-known ethical requirements, including the GMO ban and the cage-free eggs, were instituted only after pressure from groups like Greenpeace and the Humane Society. Perhaps the nastiest food fight involved fish. According to Casson Trenor, a senior markets campaigner at Greenpeace who specializes in seafood, the Trader Joe's seafood section at one time was "appalling." It was selling species like orange roughy, Greenland halibut, Alaska pollock, Atlantic cod, South Atlantic albacore, and yellowfin tuna, all of which are endangered, at risk, or caught in environmentally damaging ways, Trenor said. (The respected Monterey Bay Aquarium Seafood Watch and Blue Ocean Institute seafood guide are a lot more forgiving, urging consumers to avoid orange roughy and some types of Atlantic cod and yellowfin tuna but permitting or not commenting on the rest of Trenor's list.)

While admirers said TJ's tuna was caught without nets, to protect dolphins, Trenor argued that the fishing process used a long-line network of thousands of hooks that could unintentionally snag endangered species, rather than the less-destructive, though less common, pole-and-line system, which has fewer hooks. Furthermore, Trenor accused the company of putting an "egregious" sign right above a pile of orange roughy proclaiming that "all of our seafood was caught in a sustainable and environmentally friendly manner." (Trader Joe's rarely talks to the press and declined to comment for this book.)

For eighteen months in 2008 and 2009, while Greenpeace pelted Trader Joe's officials with e-mails, phone messages, and surveys, the company "stonewalled us," Trenor claimed. So the environmental organization went public, urging shoppers to contact corporate headquarters in Monrovia (a town on the outskirts of Los Angeles), and briefly set up a website called Traitor Joe's. "Groups of people went up and down the West and East Coasts engaging with their customers and staff in front of different stores," according to Trenor.

Apparently, the pressure worked. In March 2010, Trader Joe's posted "A Note to our Customers" on its website declaring that "all of our seafood purchases will shift to sustainable sources by December 21, 2012." The company said, in fact, that it had already ceased selling orange roughy, Chilean sea bass, and red snapper. The announcement added that the company promised to work with "third-party, science-based organizations to establish definitions and parameters" for its sustainability goals and to include information on the seafood's procurement or production method in its policies.

OK, maybe the food isn't all pure. But doesn't Trader Joe's deserve green credit for rewarding customers who supply their own bags? That's one of the biggest issues among environmentalists, who point to the trees that are chopped down to become paper bags and the oil that's drilled to make plastic bags, which most shops—including Trader Joe's—blithely hand out. Yet, once again, Trader Joe's seemed to give a few eco-inches only after public pressure. The Rainforest Alliance, back in 2004, was planning demonstrations against some Trader Joe's branches because the grocer obtained its paper bags from Weyerhaeuser Company, which the Alliance and the Forest Stewardship Council had singled out for using particularly destructive lumbering methods. Then, Trader Joe's dropped Weyerhaeuser. The chain claimed that was purely for business reasons, to consolidate its paper bag purchasing nationwide.

In any case, Trader Joe's is not as ecologically progressive as Costco, which provides no packaging material at all except the empty cartons in which the food was delivered. San Francisco, Seattle, and other cities ban standard plastic bags completely at most grocery stores, while many supermarkets refund shoppers two cents for each bag they bring from home. As a final indication of how pale green Trader Joe's really is, the ethical-ranking website GoodGuide.com gave it a lousy score of 5.8, out of a possible 10, for environmental issues.

Image: *"Your neighborhood grocery store"*
Perhaps this was true back in 1958, when it all began. An entrepreneur named Joe Coulombe, four years out of business school, bought a small chain of three convenience stores near Los Angeles known as Pronto Markets. It was great timing: Southern California was at the beginning of its postwar boom, fed by Hollywood, sunshine, the federal highway system, and the aerospace industry. Pronto prospered.

Unfortunately for Coulombe, by the 1960s, the much bigger chain of 7-Eleven convenience stores had discovered California. To fight off the incursion, Pronto needed a gimmick. So in 1967, Coulombe reinvented his little company. It would be offbeat, off-price, and sophisticated. He scouted out overstocked and discontinued gourmet food items from manufacturers, distributors, and importers, then sold them at steep discounts. In addition, Coulombe redecorated, establishing a Polynesian decor and renaming the business Trader Joe's. The "Joe" part would seem to be in honor of himself. But why Polynesian? Len Lewis, a veteran trade journalist and author of a fawning book about the company, *The Trader*

Joe's Adventure, cited a couple of common theories. "Legend has it that Coulombe was vacationing on a beach somewhere in the Caribbean, trying to figure out what to do about this new competition" from 7-Eleven. Or, "He also took inspiration from the novel *Trader Horn*"—written in 1927 by Alfred Aloysius Horn—"which chronicled the travels of a trader and adventurer in Equatorial Africa during the 19th century."

Over the years, Coulombe tweaked the product line, bringing in more organic food and starting the private labels in 1972. Yet the basic image remained. The chain added the brands Trader Ming's (for its Chinese food), Trader José's (Spanish), and Trader Giotto's (Italian). Things seemed to be going great. But in 1979, Coulombe sold the whole shebang to a reclusive German billionaire, Theo Albrecht, who along with his older brother, Karl, owned the Aldi discount-grocery chain in Europe.

Why he sold remains a big retail mystery, and the answer may never be known, since Coulombe shuns interviews. Money was presumably a motive, although the purchase price has not been publicly revealed. Coulombe could have been bored with the business, yet he stayed on for another decade. Maybe Albrecht wore him down. Various accounts have said that the German magnate pursued the purchase for two years.

With about two dozen stores at the time of the deal, all in Southern California, Trader Joe's was already too big to be "your neighborhood grocer." It might have been accurately described as a small regional chain, until that, too, changed. Gradually, it moved into Northern California, Arizona, Oregon, Washington, Nevada, and then cross-country in 1996 to Boston. By 2011, there were more than three hundred and fifty locations in thirty states plus the District of Columbia, from Maine to New Mexico, from Minnesota to South Carolina, with new branches constantly opening. If it's not as huge as Kroger Company, Safeway Inc., or, of course, Walmart, it's about the same size as, or maybe larger than, Whole Foods.

More broadly, Trader Joe's is part of a supersecretive, $68 billion global conglomerate, the eighth-largest retailer on Earth. Its owners, the Albrecht brothers, who divided Aldi in 1960, each qualified for *Forbes* magazine's ranking of the world's billionaires, until Theo died in 2010 at age eighty-eight. At that time, *Bloomberg Businessweek* reported that Theo had made just three confirmed public statements in his lifetime and that the last known photograph of either brother dated from the 1980s. (Understandably, Theo grew especially publicity shy after he was kidnapped and held for seventeen days in 1971.) Officials of the parent company, like those of the TJ's subsidiary, almost never grant interviews.

In keeping with the brothers' personal secrecy, the company is privately owned. There are plenty of pros and cons about private versus public ownership of a business, which will be discussed in more detail in chapter 7, but a key issue is that secrecy is the antithesis of social responsibility. Secrecy makes it impossible for shoppers to learn about the sourcing of the paper bags, tuna, eggs, chicken, or any other products unless management decides that it's in its own interest to reveal the information. Yes, Trader Joe's succumbed to the Greenpeace campaign about sustainable fish, but it would have been forced to reply—and perhaps change—a lot sooner if it had to face questions from shareholders at an annual meeting. If you go on the Trader Joe's website and read its timeline, you will learn when it put handles on its paper bags (1992). However, you would have no idea that it was ever sold to Theo Albrecht.

Then why does the little-old-general-store image stick? For a combination of genuine reasons (the limited selection and square footage) and phony ones (the corny signs). "It's a marvelous coup on their part to have created branding like that," Greenpeace's Casson Trenor said, "this company that feels like it's owned by a couple of surfers from San Diego, when in reality it's owned by a couple of octogenarian billionaires from Germany." (In fairness, he said this while he was still fighting over fish and at the height of his annoyance with the firm.)

After the *Times Union* ran its article about the Albany-area group begging for a Trader Joe's, an advocate for local shopping replied on the newspaper's blog that, while she loved the nuts, coffee, and olive oil, "I am under no illusions that this international corporation is my hometown neighborhood grocery store. . . . It is an international chain, trying to make lots of money for the home office in Germany."

Image: *"A Tiki Room with Aisles of Discounts"*
Producing and selling ethical products is almost always more expensive than doing things the standard way, as discussed in the introduction. Items are often handmade, rather than in bulk. Animals raised grass-fed, cage-free, or free-range need more space and more expensive feed than those in factory farms. Fair trade workers overseas are paid better than sweatshop wages.

Except, magically, for Trader Joe's.

One of the most common reasons customers give for shopping there is its low prices. Particularly famous is Two-Buck Chuck, the award-winning wine that sells in many TJ's outlets for a mere $1.99 per bottle. After all, discounting was an essential part of Joe Coulombe's gimmick for fighting off 7-Eleven, way back when.

This is one image that is, in fact, largely true. In *Consumer Reports* surveys in 2008 and 2009, Trader Joe's ranked as one of only eight and six (respectively) national chains that "gave our readers the biggest bang for the buck," as the magazine wrote in April 2008.

I tried to do some market-basket comparisons over a three-day period in October 2009 and a six-day period in December 2010, taking an actual basket around six stores within a three-and-a-half-mile radius: Whole Foods, Trader Joe's, my local food co-op, Costco, and two regular, regional chains: Key Food (in the New York City area) and Pathmark (Delaware, New Jersey, New York, and Pennsylvania). By definition, it was tough to find identical items to compare, since Trader Joe's prides itself on its unique lineup. Forget the canned vegetable soup, which I thought would be a staple; did I want Trader Joe's low-sodium minestrone? Organic vegetable and lentil? And don't even get me started on the eggs: Cage-free omega-1? Cage-free organic omega-3? Large organic free roaming? Cage-free large? Cage-free extra-large? Brown large cage-free? Brown large organic? Making matters even more difficult, most Trader Joe's fruit is sold either by the piece or in unit-priced bags, whereas other stores typically sell it per pound.

Still, I was able to pull together fifteen similar-enough items in a variety of food groups, and the result was that Trader Joe's was the cheapest in six categories and tied with Whole Foods in a seventh—the best showing of any contender. (The items were a pound of nonorganic baby carrots, a loaf of raisin bread, a six-ounce container of yogurt, an eleven-ounce package of Hebrew National hot dogs, barbecue-flavor potato chips, and organic Fuji apples and nonorganic Granny Smith apples, but only if you buy those last two in bags of two pounds and five pounds, respectively.) From all these comparisons, however, shoppers would have to subtract any double coupons and special discounts that rivals might offer, because Trader Joe's doesn't stoop to such measures.

To the degree that Trader Joe's genuinely keeps prices down, how does it manage? Part of the explanation is precisely that it doesn't sell only goods that are organic, pesticide-free, cage-free, and all those other socially responsible qualities that cost more to produce. Moreover, in many locations, especially the original ones, it saves on rent by seeking out-of-the-way sites, like mini-malls without big-name anchor tenants. The dearth of expensive national brands helps, too.

Moreover, the basic business model includes some inherent savings. If a store carries merely two brands of toothpaste or three brands of bar soap—and one of them is the house brand—rather than a dozen or more, as at a traditional big supermarket, then it's probably buying from just two or three suppliers. (Many manufacturers make more than one brand of the same type of product, so the number of brand names is a little misleading as a strict guide to the number of sources, but the essential principle holds.) Add to that the fact that by offering only a few choices, Trader Joe's is probably selling more of each choice than a traditional supermarket, even if that bigger market sells far more toothpaste tubes or soap bars per week in total. Thus, the odd little store probably has more clout per item and can exert more price pressure on each supplier. Then add one more factor: As much as possible, Trader Joe's sources directly from the manufacturer rather than via distributors, thereby avoiding extra distribution fees.

A double socially responsible area of savings is that Trader Joe's runs almost zero advertising. It's not spending its money trying to persuade customers to spend their money on things they don't need. Furthermore, according to the records of the Center for Responsive Politics, the chain apparently wastes very little on political contributions and lobbying. (It also, obviously, spends nothing on a PR department.)

Maybe it's skimping too much on its social responsibility. "Trader Joe's makes it crystal clear that it does not buy advertising, program space, or tickets to [charitable] events under any circumstances," Len Lewis wrote in his book. "It also does not underwrite any organization . . . or donate gift certificates . . . it is simply being practical and holding down unnecessary costs."

And take a second look at that beloved Two-Buck Chuck: the name comes from Charles F. Shaw, an investment banker who owned a vineyard that he sold to another vintner, who now produces the wine for Trader Joe's. According to *The Trader Joe's Adventure*, Shaw has publicly protested the use of his name on a cheap wine that, he said, unfairly competes with classier labels bottled by his friends. Other critics complain that the whole concept of discount wine has turned an art form into a commodity.

Image: *"An offbeat, fun discovery zone" (for workers)*
For a lot of objective reasons, Trader Joe's wouldn't seem to be a fun place to work. Len Lewis wrote that "to control labor costs, overall store payrolls are kept down by having a lower head count in each location per

dollar of sales." That sounds like the notorious practice of speed-up, or pushing fewer workers to do extra tasks that should be shared by more people, without added pay—in other words, lousy working conditions.

Nor has the company apparently made it onto the major "Best Companies" rosters. Although Lewis claimed in his book that "*Fortune* magazine has consistently ranked the company among its 100 best places to work," I couldn't find a single mention of it in a search of the entire *Fortune* "Best Companies" database when I was given special access. Like most retailers, Trader Joe's might be at a disadvantage in these contests by following a business model that typically relies on part-timers who don't qualify for benefits. However, after *Working Mother* launched a special list for hourly workers in 2010, Trader Joe's still didn't make the cut—even as companies like Marriott International, with lots of hourly workers, actually get on the regular list. Meanwhile, GoodGuide gave the chain a middling 5.2 (out of a possible 10) in its overall rating, and a dreadful 4.4 in the "workers" category, dragged down by "labor and human rights" and "workplace diversity." The "working conditions and benefits" subcategory was a better 6.7. Maybe the Trader Joe's scores are hurt by its union situation. Supermarkets are one of the last bastions of union strength in the US business world. The United Food and Commercial Workers International Union represents 70 percent of the labor force at large national supermarket chains. But Trader Joe's isn't among them.

Why not? For one thing, the union hasn't tried very hard. Although a few small, unsuccessful efforts have been reported in California, in 1998 and 2003, Jim Papian, a UFCW spokesman, said, "I don't think we made a major attempt on a national basis. We had our hands full with Walmart and other major operators." Certainly, Walmart is a much bigger, juicier, and still-unreached target, with a long roster of accusations, including sex discrimination, cheating workers out of pay, illegally denying them breaks, skimping on health benefits, and much more. Papian further said he's not surprised at the lack of unions at Trader Joe's, given the tough organizing climate nationally. The chain was also a target of several farmworkers' groups in 2011 for refusing to sign agreements to improve working conditions and pay for the laborers who pick the tomatoes it sells.

Of course, another reason unions haven't taken hold could be that workers like Trader Joe's just fine the way it is. Pay and benefits, for instance, appear to be at least as good as those at unionized shops. As of 2005, Len Lewis said that the average Trader Joe's salary was about 15 percent above the union average. Five years later, *Fortune* reported that "full-time crew members"—which the company defines as supervisors working 40 to 47.5 hours per week—"can start in the $40,000 to $60,000 range." That could be noticeably more than the median pay for "first-line supervisors/managers" at grocery stores, which, according to the US Bureau of Labor Statistics, would come to about $35,150 for a 40-hour week and $41,750 for the longer hours.

(The BLS publishes hourly pay, so to get an annual comparison, I multiplied the BLS rate by Trader Joe's lowest and highest weekly hours and then multiplied those two figures by fifty-two weeks. Two caveats: The BLS median is for all grocery stores, nonunion as well as union, but with the high unionization rate in the industry, it's probably fair enough to consider the BLS numbers equivalent to union rates. Also, the most recent BLS data at the time of the 2010 *Fortune* article were two years older, dating to May 2008; however, inflation was virtually nonexistent then, so raises between 2008 and 2010 would have been low, and the year-to-year comparisons are reasonable.)

Less clear was an article in the *Atlantic* in 2011, which reported that "Trader Joe's sets wages so that full-time employees earn at least a median income within their community." But that community median could be a very low, nonunion rate.

To those wages, add in the benefits. Trader Joe's has been putting an amount equal to 15.4 percent of pay into a 401(k)-style retirement plan for years. That's a heck of a lot more generous than the typical 401(k) formula, whereby companies contribute just 3 percent of pay, and only if the employee contributes first. In addition, the Trader Joe's website says that "eligible" full- and part-time employees get medical, dental, and vision coverage. It doesn't define "eligible," except to say that "most" people qualify after a couple of months.

Many on-the-spot reports are positive. Sally Greenberg, of the National Consumers League, said that a niece and a friend's wife who have worked at Trader Joe's "seem really happy" with their jobs and pay. "If you ask them," said Patricia Werhane, a senior fellow at the University of Virginia's Olsson Center for Applied Ethics, "employees say they really do love to work there. They can chat; they can do what they want. They seem to not have so many rules." When I got to know a checkout worker well enough to feel comfortable asking a few questions, the one thing she complained about was pressure to wear turkey hats at Thanksgiving.

Personally, I don't put much stake in the celebrated hats, flowered shirts, and nautical names as proof of good working conditions. Trader Joe's staffers are called captains, first mates, crew members, and so on. Other than having a theme, how is that any different from Starbucks's "partners" or Target's "team members"? All the cute titles are simply ways to pretend that these aren't low-status, low-paid employees working at tedious jobs. And the so-called Hawaiian shirts? Well, McDonald's, Starbucks, Target, and many other retailers have uniforms, aprons, or dress codes for their workforces (by whatever name). Supposedly, the Trader Joe's flowered version is more playful. However, the designs have been getting steadily less flowery, and in any case it's not fair to call them Hawaiian, because they are nowhere near as garish as a genuine Hawaiian shirt with a splash of loud colors.

It's also debatable whether people are really enjoying their work if "Have fun!" is a mandatory part of the job description. I've certainly run into Trader Joe's staff who don't seem to be having the best time of their life, like the bored-looking woman sitting at the free-samples counter who never offered any samples. But those are rare. Then again, perhaps the most sullen staffers get hidden in the stockroom.

Image: "An offbeat, fun discovery zone" (for shoppers)
Yes, it's a show. And maybe you hate the too-adorable signs as much as I do, or you don't even notice the plastic lobsters and fake bamboo any more. Still, those props are not what create the Trader Joe's milieu. The real differences between Trader Joe's and just any old store are genuine customer service and personal warmth.

There's usually free coffee and some exotic free sample. I saw one worker at a New York outlet take several minutes to explain the different varieties of vitamins to a shopper, and a staffer at another store, rather than waiting for harried customers to grab her in desperation, walked around asking, "Does anyone need help finding anything?" One cashier in California got to know my mother so well that she called her "Nana" and gave her a plant at Christmastime. Restrooms are available, with prominent signs. Even the customers seem to pick up the mood. At the Chelsea site in New York City, a total stranger who saw me at the soap shelf suddenly started telling me which scents of soap she preferred and how much she liked the layout of the aisles.

If all the types of eggs are confusing, a sign at the egg display at the flagship Union Square outlet in Manhattan outlined the differences among organic, cage-free, white, and brown. At the Brooklyn store, a sign asked and answered the question "What is free-range chicken?" While the *Fearless Flyer* newsletter may lack coupons, it explains why Northern California's climate is good for growing orchids and where Fuji apples come from. Respondents in the 2009 *Consumer Reports* survey, in addition to citing low prices, gave Trader Joe's top marks for service. And the magazine singled it out, along with Wegmans, as "among the most satisfying chains to shop at."

The main consumer complaint involves the notoriously long lines. You could look at that as proof of the store's popularity or of its penny-pinching in not hiring enough cashiers.

The real problem with Trader Joe's isn't that it doesn't live up to its image. The problem is the image itself—the subtle implications of the chain's basic operating principles: a limited selection of exotic food, carefully plucked from around the world, precooked and ready to eat. We need to take a second look behind the scenes:

Limited selection. Yummy as the food may be to most shoppers, we all need more than low-sodium lox and honey-plantain strips. Like toothpaste (which not all outlets carry). Scouring pads (ditto). Maybe some of us (me) drink Diet Coke. Maybe we would like more than two choices of cake mix (lemon or chocolate). Therefore, customers will have to make an extra trip to a "real" supermarket now and then, and in almost every city or state where Trader Joe's is located—especially in California—that means driving. Thus, Trader Joe's customers must waste gas and spew unnecessary carbon emissions by shopping double. This could negate any environmental benefit from bringing reusable shopping bags.

Exotic food. Average Trader Joe's shoppers, according to a finding by researcher and ratings guru ACNielsen cited in Len Lewis's book, are childless younger couples, young singles, middle-aged singles, or middle-aged childless couples. Elsewhere, the book discusses an analysis from another lifestyle-and-shopping research firm, Scarborough Research, showing that "the typical Trader Joe's customer in the Pacific Northwest is a college-educated, white homeowner with a median age of 44 and a median household income [in the early 2000s] of $64,000. . . . About two-thirds have no kids at home."

These are not descriptions of the average American supermarket customer. Most notable is the lack of children. Remember, Trader Joe's doesn't carry diapers or baby food, and it's not clear how many three-year-olds really want double cream champagne brie. On the other hand, if your kid *has* to have the little packages of chocolate chip cookies that everyone else brings for lunch at school, but Trader Joe's doesn't sell that brand, you're in big trouble.

Jill Kickul, the director of the entrepreneurial program at New York University, pointed out another demographic issue: "[I]t's not located in some of the lower-income communities." Although the company may have sought cheaper sites off the fashion track in its early days, by the time it got to New York City in 2006, it was pitching its fake-bamboo tent poles in such reliably yuppie areas as Manhattan's Upper West Side and the edge of Brooklyn Heights.

In short, if you're an average American who needs staples to feed your family, Trader Joe's isn't interested in you. Or, to put it another way, Trader Joe's is elitist. Can being elitist also be socially responsible?

The focus on exotic food troubled me for one more reason. Until I walked into an outlet and leafed through the *Fearless Flyer*, I had no idea that things like chicken *chilaquiles* or inside-out carrot-cake cookies existed, let alone that I might want to try them. So, Trader Joe's has created a false demand for unnecessary consumption. Isn't that socially *irresponsible?*

That theory doesn't seem to bother consumer activists. On the contrary, many consider that one of Trader Joe's best qualities, since it can teach insular Americans about other cultures—and far more authentically than Starbucks. "Consumers want choices, and it opens consumers to a whole range of ethnic choices they may never have known about," said the National Consumers League's Sally Greenberg.

Carefully plucked from around the world. In 2006, the *New York Times* described the work of the fifteen members of Trader Joe's tasting panel who "perpetually travel the world visiting all kinds of food businesses— restaurants, farmers' markets, artisanal pasta makers, street stalls, and supermarkets—and then translate their finds to the stores." They bring back grass-fed cheddar cheese from New Zealand, goat's-milk cream cheese from France, and lime-and-chili peanuts from Thailand. That means it isn't only customers who are racking up the carbon emissions and burning gallons of fossil fuels. Trader Joe's completely violates every tenet of the locavore movement, which advocates buying locally grown food—usually defined as being within one hundred to two hundred miles—in order to support neighborhood businesses and to limit the environmental impact of shipping the food. Again, this makes it hard to describe Trader Joe's as green.

Precooked and ready to eat. The more processing involved in a food product, the more energy and packaging it usually demands. Fresh fruits and vegetables can pretty much go straight from field to carton to truck to produce bins at the store. By contrast, Climate Counts's Wood Turner pointed out that Trader Joe's uses a lot of excess packaging to ship its cleaned, shelled, diced, sliced, sautéed, mixed, and otherwise cooked foods from their exotic locales to the cute store aisles—while admitting that he likes being able to "buy products that don't have tons of preservatives and maybe are organic, in some cases at a lower cost than I might otherwise get."

"I wouldn't call them environmentally friendly," said Russell Winer, chair of the marketing department at New York University's Stern School of Business, "because they sell a lot of fast stuff in plastic packages— convenience foods."

Even the noncooked items are overpackaged. In its quest to make meal preparation a breeze for customers, Trader Joe's is increasingly switching to precut, prewashed salads and other veggies, all in plastic bags rather than loose in bins. As one of the world-traveling tasters told a *New York Times* reporter, in a rare occasion when the company granted any access, "Who buys head lettuce anymore?"

I know that these precooked meals can be a great option for busy shoppers, healthier than TV dinners, and less expensive than restaurant take-out. Yet I worry: What will happen to the old-fashioned art of home cooking?

THE QUESTION: Does Trader Joe's deserve its reputation as an exemplar of ethical chic?

THE VERDICT: No, but who cares?

Hey, I like going to Trader Joe's. You can drool through the unusual entrees and cheeses, and the staff really makes you feel happy to be there. There is a clear public value to a business model that emphasizes friendly, helpful service. As Sally Greenberg asserts, Trader Joe's may be increasing Americans' awareness of other cultures, which also is an important social value. If people never cook any more, Trader Joe's isn't the cause; blame dual-working families and the fast-food culture—in which case, it's a lot better to serve a Trader Joe's salmon mojito-marinated filet than a Big Mac with fries. And really, even if the whole atmosphere is too cute by half, what's wrong with making grocery shopping fun?

So, fine; it's a nice set of stores. Nevertheless, very few of the good points have much to do with social responsibility.

On the contrary, the carbon footprint is horrendous, while the few gestures toward greenness are trivial. Other stores do a lot more to encourage customers to bring their own bags, for instance. Although Trader Joe's may carry more organic, cage-free, and natural-type food than the average supermarket, the whole industry is moving in that direction. Virtually every major chain now sells big-name, factory-organic brands like Horizon milk and Earthbound Farm baby carrots, along with cage-free eggs. Moreover, for all the image of open friendliness, Trader Joe's is way too secretive about issues that really matter to the public.

Perhaps most important, this is an industry where ethical shoppers have lots of good choices, including food co-ops, farmers' markets, health food stores, community-supported-agriculture programs, local specialty shops, and—the easiest of all—unionized supermarket chains. Surely we can find enough to eat in those places.

CHAPTER 6

American Apparel

Sex and the T-Shirt

THE CORAL-COLORED, SEVEN-STORY FACTORY towers over its neighbors in the industrial downtown of Los Angeles—the LA Wholesale Produce Market, Bravo Brand Food, Canton Food Company, Angel Toy Corporation, a *Los Angeles Times* printing plant. A set of long-abandoned trolley tracks runs alongside, down Alameda Street. It's a far cry from the Santa Monica oceanfront or the fashionable streets just east of Beverly Hills where shops sell the clothing made at the coral-colored factory, although geographically they're only about fifteen miles away.

On the outside of the factory, huge signs proclaim "Legalize LA" and "Immigration Reform Now" and (in English and Spanish) "American Apparel Is an Industrial Revolution." Inside, in large, open, light-filled rooms, hundreds of middle-aged Latina women stitch skimpy shorts and tight-fitting T-shirts under blown-up photos of women crouched on all fours, pulling out their T-shirt necklines to reveal their cleavage, and suggestively shoving their hands down the waistbands of their jeans.

All of this—the industrial grime and retail chic, the outreach to immigrants and the outright sexualization, the hip, the socially responsible, the socially irresponsible—are equally part of the image of American Apparel. Indeed, they are the most famous aspects of its brand.

Theoretically, CSR activists should admire American Apparel for stubbornly resisting the garment industry's trend to shift production to the lowest-paying sweatshops in the poorest countries in the world, workers' rights be damned. Every piece of American Apparel is created in the United States, from fabric to ad photos, nonunion but with what is widely considered union-quality pay and benefits. If its ads are really, really sexy, well, that's what sells fashion.

Yet for all its advocacy of immigrants' rights, its subsidized lunches and bus passes, its free bikes and English classes, American Apparel makes liberal activists squirm.

"*American Apparel?*" I heard repeatedly, in horrified tones, when I rattled off the list of companies for this book. And: "It's soft porn." On top of that, by 2011, the company's finances were such a mess that it was in serious danger of shutting its doors, and it wasn't clear how much was due to standard business problems like overexpansion and the recession, and how much came from the same self-indulgent lawlessness and carelessness that the founder, Dov Charney, has allegedly exhibited in sexual harassment of his employees.

This was undoubtedly the most controversial of my picks.

"Made in Downtown LA—Sweatshop Free" proclaim the ads. It's true, and it's important. Five thousand workers at the coral-colored factory, an adjoining warehouse, and two smaller knitting-and-dyeing facilities nearby churn out the company's entire line: some 1.2 million brightly colored, snug-fitting, highly fashionable T-shirts, leggings, tank tops, miniskirts, button-down shirts, short shorts, swimsuits, jeans, sweaters, underwear, and more each week. These wares are then sold by another five thousand or so sales clerks at over 285 company-owned stores throughout the world—including China, thus putting American Apparel in the rare, and possibly unique, position of shipping clothing *from* the United States *to* China. The company claims to operate—and no one disputes this—"the largest garment factory in the United States."

By contrast, its competitors mainly send the drudge sewing work to Bangladesh, China, Honduras, Vietnam, and other countries that pay workers a fraction of US wages. The typical rate in these countries might range from 15 cents an hour to $1, judging by news reports; meanwhile, the US minimum wage was $7.25 an hour in 2010, and American Apparel at that point was paying $9 to $10 an hour as a base, plus productivity bonuses that, the company asserted, brought its average hourly wage to $13 to $18. Here's another comparison: the standard US workweek is 40 hours; in overseas sweatshops, it's easily 100 or more hours, with a typical schedule running sixteen-hour days, seven days a week.

After laborers at electronics and auto factories like Apple's in China staged protests and even jumped to their deaths in a rash of suicides in 2010, they got their pay hiked from around $130 per month to $176. However, as Chinese wages rose "too high," manufacturers moved operations to cheaper Bangladesh and Vietnam. Even for an (unlikely) forty-hour week, that "raise" would bring the pay rate to little more than $1 an hour. Workplace conditions in these countries are also much, much worse than at American Apparel, with the toxic materials, sexual abuse, and lack of breaks described in earlier chapters.

Some social-justice advocates, such as *New York Times* columnist Nicholas Kristof and author Fred Pearce, argue that these jobs are actually good deals in countries where any paycheck is a luxury. The alternatives—trying to scrabble a living from a tiny family farm, prostitution, scrounging in dumps, starvation—are worse.

While Kristof and Pearce raise important issues, and companies like Apple and Nike are trying to improve conditions, American Apparel undeniably spends more and offers better conditions—which we'll get to shortly—by basing its manufacturing in California. And if it's depriving women in Bangladesh, China, Honduras, Vietnam, and other struggling countries of job opportunities, it is providing those opportunities for low-skilled Americans and preserving the last remnants of what was once a thriving sector of the US industrial base. "American Apparel is showing that you can produce domestically," said Mark Levinson, the economist from the SEIU, whose affiliate Workers United represents textile-industry workers. However, his praise is qualified, and organized labor's relationship with American Apparel is complicated, as will be discussed a little later.

Having spent twenty years fighting sweatshops, Jeff Ballinger is more accustomed to castigating clothing makers than complimenting them. Yet he echoed Levinson's qualified appraisal of American Apparel: "For me, it boils down to 'Are people making a living wage?' I think it's a terrific operation, because it's built a factory in Los Angeles. You can't pay [Los Angeles workers] less than $300 a week. They showed that you can compete [by operating in the United States] and win."

Let's not go overboard with the praise. American Apparel chose to centralize its operations in the United States not for charitable reasons but because it believes this arrangement offers solid business advantages. As the company itself emphasizes, it is "vertically integrated"—that is, it can oversee every step of the production process in one spot and thus, presumably, ensure quality. By sewing in California, it also saves on shipping costs and can get supplies to North American stores fast to keep up with ever-moving fashion trends.

Moreover, these vaunted American jobs are boring, repetitive, and sometimes physically demanding. It's an assembly line, not Wall Street or Silicon Valley. "Teams" of five to twenty-five men and women sit at long tables of sewing machines doing the same limited task over and over: Sew a pocket on a pair of jeans. Sew a sleeve to a T-shirt. The noise level varies, depending on the number of machines clacking away, but it can be roughly the decibel level of a New York City subway train arriving in a station, brakes screeching. Many workers wear face masks or ear plugs. There's little chitchat.

Still, as factories go, the American Apparel version—a converted railroad warehouse—is particularly pleasant. Sunlight streams through floor-to-ceiling windows filling three or even all four outer sides of the block-long work rooms—windows that workers are actually allowed to open. One full side of windows looks out on a panoramic view of downtown Los Angeles. The inner walls are painted white, which adds to the sense of airiness, and a few green plants are scattered about.

Most incredible are the benefits: A subsidized health clinic next to the main lunchroom, open two days a week for ten hours each day and available to workers' families, too. Free on-site English and yoga classes. Discount bus passes and catered meals (in several ethnic choices, including Spanish and Korean). Free ten-minute massages during breaks, plus a voluntary twenty-minute exercise routine—on company time—before the shift begins. A bank of three or four phones on every floor for free international calls. (Ryan Holiday, a company spokesperson, said that perk alone probably costs American Apparel "hundreds of thousands" of dollars.) A few hundred free bicycles that can be used for pleasure as well as for commuting. This is not merely the official list outlined by Holiday; on a tour, I saw much of it in action, such as an exercise session, the phone banks, a food truck, two massage therapists, the health clinic (closed that day), signs about the buses and bikes, and the cavernous lunchroom with plenty of microwave ovens, hot-storage facilities, and vending machines.

(This description applies only to the factory. The milieu at the retail outlets is a totally different and more controversial matter, which will be discussed later.)

The company brags about its egalitarian philosophy, as well. Chief executive Dov Charney's office is on the same floor as one of the main sewing areas, past the "development room" with its bolts of fabric for making samples, then through a set of industrial double doors. Workers call him Dov, and he holds a weekly phone conference with the retail managers, in which any store staffer supposedly can join. "There's no middleman between the employee and the CEO," boasted Holiday (who doubles as head of Web design and also works on advertising). A 2005 article in *BusinessWeek* described how "anyone can walk into the boss's office at any time."

"A lot of them love him. He will walk the floor, and they will hug him," said Angelica M. Salas, executive director of the Coalition for Humane Immigration Rights of Los Angeles (known as CHIRLA), an immigrant-advocacy organization, who has known Charney since he came to Los Angeles in 1997. One time when she was visiting, she recalled, a worker came up to Charney with an offer to go from town to town in Mexico selling T-shirts. As Salas recounted it, Charney told the worker, "'If you can have a plan for me, go for it.' The worker was so happy," Salas added. "He was basically going to be a distributor."

For all the "Dov-ing" and hugs and phone chats, however, there is clearly a caste system. The lower-skilled staff—sewers, maintenance workers, guards—are mainly Hispanic men and women (especially women, at the sewing machines) who look to be in their thirties and older. The office jobs—marketing, advertising, technology, Web design—go to Anglo twentysomethings. These latter employees work in offices that were cooler than the sewing floors on a hot summer day, with doors that can shut out the subway-brake noise.

Another negative: American Apparel has never appeared on *Fortune* or *Working Mother*'s "Best Companies" lists, and it's impossible to know why. The benefits would certainly seem to rank up there with the "best." Nor can size explain the omission, since *Fortune* requires merely that a company have more than one thousand employees, which American Apparel does, and the list has at times included companies with similar or lower sales volume, such as the Container Store, the Atlanta-based law firm Alston & Bird, and Shared Technologies, a Texas telecom. In 2010, *Working Mother* even added a list for hourly workers, giving American Apparel a second shot. No go.

With the subsidized meals, bus fare, and other fringe benefits, does it matter that American Apparel isn't unionized? Neither are its overseas sweatshop competitors, after all. Nor, for that matter, are 93.1 percent of private businesses in the United States. Yet in an industry that was one of the keystones of the nation's labor movement—a movement forged by the infamous Triangle Shirtwaist Factory fire of 1911—are American Apparel's wages, benefits, and overall atmosphere so good that, as it claims, a union is unnecessary?

Jason Coulter is now pastor of Chicago's Ravenswood United Church of Christ. However, for thirteen years in the 1990s and early 2000s, he was an organizer for the old Amalgamated Clothing and Textile Workers Union and the textile union UNITE. In 2003, he came to American Apparel.

It was an unusual target from the start. "Some of our members had family members that were working there, and they described kind of a crazy scene," Coulter recalled. "The owner would ride around the factory on a skateboard. He was a gringo from Canada who spoke Spanish and didn't wear a suit and tie, the classic patrón model: you drive people hard and then show great fits of generosity. He led a group of hard-driving Mexican supervisors and then would say, 'We're having a fiesta!'" Contrary to American Apparel's image now, Coulter said that "the wages and benefits at that time were maybe at standard or below standard, comparable to nonunion local wages." And the vaunted health-care coverage, he claimed, consisted merely of arranging for "one of those county health care trucks to come by the plant" once a week. Still, he said the union didn't see the company as evil. It just wanted to find out what was really happening.

(The sole person American Apparel would make available for an interview was Holiday, the spokesman, who basically cited all the workplace benefits when I asked about working conditions.)

Once UNITE got serious and started holding meetings and handing out leaflets, the charmingly erratic T-shirt maker "behaved exactly like every other nonunion company," Coulter charged. "They sought to have us thrown off the property. They restricted the workers' access to information. They tried to find out who had signed union cards and monitored closely those people who were union supporters, to see who they were talking to." For instance, he said, company officials ordered organizers off the public sidewalk outside the factory and refused requests to hold informational meetings on the premises or post union information on factory bulletin boards.

As Coulter told it, when Charney, the CEO, finally met with union officials at UNITE's Los Angeles office, it was a disaster: "He was an incredibly difficult guy to talk with. He never lets you speak, he's so blustery and controlling and domineering. He accused us of manipulating the workers and misrepresenting how well he treats them. He held on dearly to this belief that he is this lovable and benevolent employer that everyone would want to work for. He started attacking the union, [saying] all we were out for was dues money."

By late 2003, UNITE filed a complaint with the National Labor Relations Board, alleging that American Apparel illegally attempted to block the organizing drive. The two sides settled, with the company paying no financial damages and acknowledging no wrongdoing but agreeing to post a notice on site stating that it promised not to interfere with the workers' right to organize.

What that meant was that Charney won. UNITE gave up. Coulter conceded that "at some level the *patrón* model of management, throwing people a few crumbs here and there, can be effective in forestalling unionization, especially if people feel they have to risk their jobs in order to have a union." He nevertheless claimed some credit, saying that the union efforts forced the company to improve its pay and health coverage. American Apparel, of course, would argue that those "crumbs" are exactly the point: the wages and benefits it voluntarily gives are far better than anyone could get in a typical labor contract.

Portfolio magazine, in a long article in November 2008, wrote that in light of the decent pay, benefits, and working conditions, "union leaders in LA have arrived at a kind of cease-fire with Charney." Some top labor officials seemed to confirm that assessment, although it may simply be that they're not very familiar with the situation. For instance, Carl Proper, communications director for the UNITE HERE offshoot that remains independent of the SEIU, said he didn't know why the organizing drive failed at American Apparel and conceded that "it's plausible" the pay and benefits were generous enough to dissipate any interest. "They paid fairly well, for a nonunion place" was his recollection. Another major labor leader, who didn't want to be named because praising a nonunion shop could be politically delicate, described the company as "formed with a worker-friendly attitude, trying to mine that niche in a very dirty industry." The SEIU's Mark Levinson, however, bristled at the *Portfolio* description, asserting that the American Apparel fight "was as vicious an antiunion campaign as you can find." Despite his praise for the company's effort to "produce domestically," he added, "I wouldn't rule out [another organizing drive] by any means."

But as labor leaders like Levinson, Coulter, the AFL-CIO's Ron Blackwell, and the Center for American Progress's Christian Weller point out, wages and benefits are not the only criteria for judging a company. There are also important considerations like respect and the ability to speak out. "An essential aspect of a good place to work is the people have a right to join a union," Blackwell said. "Whether they do [join] or not depends on their choices." In the International Organization for Standardization's detailed definition of human rights, under "Fundamental principles and rights at work," the first item listed is "freedom of association and collective bargaining," even before important principles like nondiscrimination and the elimination of forced labor and child labor. In Levinson's and Coulter's view, American Apparel, for all its freebies, didn't provide that basic freedom.

American Apparel's other unique claim to socially responsible fame, in addition to keeping presumably well-paying garment jobs in the United States, is its strong advocacy of immigrant rights.

Until around 2006, it wasn't unusual for US businesses to welcome high levels of immigration, including unskilled factory, farm, and construction workers. However, that was simply as a source of cheap labor. If the immigrants didn't have legal papers, well, companies winked and gave a quick glance at forged Social Security cards, and the workers didn't dare complain about low pay and poor conditions.

After 2006, even that sort of immigration-exploitation tolerance became rare, as the federal government cracked down on the hiring of workers without proper documentation. The mood grew nastier over the next few years when recession rolled in, unemployment spiked past 10 percent, and politicians revved up fears about Latinos swarming across the border to "steal" jobs. Polls showed wide national support for an unprecedentedly harsh law passed by Arizona in April 2010 that made it a crime to be an illegal immigrant and actually required local police officers to check the immigration status of anyone they stopped for any cause, if they had "reasonable suspicion" of the person's status.

That pervasive mood of suspicion and antagonism is what made—and still makes—American Apparel so different. It actively tries to help its Spanish-speaking workers. The free English classes, subsidized *arroz con pollo* lunches, and bilingual signs throughout the building are part of it. In addition, the plant gives staff time off on May Day to march in Los Angeles's traditional immigrant rights parade. Sometimes Charney joins. He likes to point out that after all, he's an immigrant, too—albeit from Canada—and one year he let the immigrant rights group CHIRLA use his own green card in a fund-raising ad. The corporate website has myriad links to pro-immigration news articles, fact sheets, interviews, photos from the May march, a TV series, and more. Among the rare logos allowed on its T-shirts are political ones, like "Legalize LA"—meaning the city's immigrant workforce. CHIRLA's Angelica Salas said Charney has donated thousands of T-shirts to her organization and others and to the marches, as well as at least $50,000 in cash to her group, and has opened the factory to CHIRLA speakers to talk about workers' legal rights. Other immigrant advocacy groups also say the efforts seem to be genuine and serious.

Toward the end of 2007, in the heat of the federal crackdown, American Apparel began a major advertising push, featuring its own Latino workers and supporting immigrant rights in strong language. "The government and politicians exploit and misrepresent this matter to advance their own careers," newspaper ads declared. And, "At what point are we going to recognize that the status quo amounts to an apartheid system?" Union organizers, too, praise American Apparel for that part of its philosophy. The AFL-CIO in the mid-1990s officially dropped its historic opposition to immigration, and Mark Levinson of the SEIU (which represents a large number of foreign-born members) said that American Apparel's "view on immigration is the same as ours: all workers, regardless of status, should have the same rights in the workplace." Still, Jason Coulter, the organizer turned pastor, maintained some skepticism about the company's motives. "LA is a teeming mass of people who, because they don't have papers, can't negotiate the same type of employment situation" as legally documented workers, he said. "American Apparel benefits from that."

In the furious politics of the early 2000s, it was inevitable that a company as in-your-face as American Apparel would be busted.

Sure enough, in January 2008, the federal Immigration and Customs Enforcement (ICE) agency demanded to see the company's personnel files. Over the next year and a half, American Apparel cooperated with the feds as they pored through the records in search of phony Social Security cards and other suspect IDs. By September 2009, the company had axed some 1,500 employees who couldn't prove their legal status, more than one-fourth of its manufacturing workforce—or, as Ryan Holiday, the spokesperson put it, "Because of a broken immigration process, American Apparel was forced to lay off 1,500 hard-working employees and lose

1,500 good jobs. Some of the workers had worked for the company for ten years." Holiday said the people weren't immediately replaced, in part because it was the middle of a severe recession, and in part because of the helter-skelter nature of the firings, with some teams decimated and others almost intact. "That really threw off the production process," he said. Nine months later, about 1,000 spots had been filled.

The whole episode was awkward for a company that had so proudly advocated against the very laws it was now forced to obey. Still, matters could have been far worse. In other well-publicized cases—most notably at the Iowa-based slaughterhouse Agriprocessors in 2008—government agents have swooped down in surprise raids and arrested company officials on criminal charges. American Apparel's relatively clean record— the fact that it didn't seem to have knowingly hired undocumented workers and had no history of abusing its workforce—undoubtedly protected it from worse legal treatment, its own lawyer said.

Politicians' reactions immediately afterward summed up the extremes of the public mood:

The mayor of Los Angeles, Antonio Villaraigosa, a Democrat of Hispanic background, was quoted calling the firings "devastating" and telling ICE to focus instead on employers that mistreat their workers. Meanwhile, a Republican congressman from nearby San Diego, Brian P. Bilbray, said that American Apparel managers "seem to think that somehow the law doesn't matter, that crossing the line from legal to illegal is not a big deal."

Even before the federal probe, hints had popped up in the press from time to time implying that Charney's passion for immigrant rights was cooling. *New York Times Magazine* columnist Rob Walker asserted in his 2008 book *Buying In* that the company had deliberately switched its marketing strategy away from emphasizing social values like being sweatshop-free to trumpeting its sexiness. *Bloomberg Businessweek*, in August 2010, indirectly quoted the CEO saying that, among the things he could have done differently to avoid the serious financial weaknesses facing the company at that point, he could have moved "manufacturing offshore while he resolved his worker problems."

Yet it's hard to see any CSR de-emphasis at the company itself. A year after the firings, signs throughout the factory were still in English and Spanish. Employees chatted in Spanish; guards' uniforms were emblazoned with the word "security" in both languages. The staff had marched on May Day, as always. There was a new line of "Legalize Arizona" T-shirts, protesting that state's anti-immigration law. Ryan Holiday said the company continued to hire Latino workers, although he conceded that HR might now check identification "more strenuously." Pointing to the huge banners on the building, he claimed, "I don't think American Apparel has toned down its ads in any way."

Ultimately, when discussing American Apparel, the elephant in the room—the naked elephant—is sex.

Of course the fashion industry reeks of sex. And it's not the fashion world alone. Sex sells, and always has sold, everything from Coke to cars, from cigarettes to Cialis. Former *Esquire* editor-in-chief Lee Eisenberg described in his 2009 book *Shoptimism* the advice that Ernest Dichter, a pioneering social scientist who specialized in consumer marketing, gave to *Esquire* editors years ago: They should tell potential advertisers that when men look at photos of nearly nude women, such as those in *Esquire*, "their pupils open wide, which in turn makes men 'more attentive to visual stimuli' of any sort," such as ads on the next page.

Whether or not Dov Charney has gotten bored with CSR, he certainly knows that sex, not immigrant rights campaigns, is what draws his customers. So American Apparel's ads, website, in-store posters, and mannequins show people (or figures) in provocative poses revealing lots of flesh. That goes without saying. The real question should be, "Are American Apparel's displays significantly worse than those of other companies?" A fair and comprehensive answer has to consider three elements: the clothing itself, the marketing, and the working conditions.

Are the clothes sexy? That depends on which clothes.

American Apparel sells crotch-high shorts and skimpy bikinis, bodysuit thongs and see-through blouses, skintight pencil skirts and strapless "dresses" no bigger than an oversize shirt. It also markets plenty of modestly cut crew-neck T-shirts, button-down Oxford-style shirts, and zippered hoodies. Like it or not, body-clinging or androgynous, this is what fashionable young women in their teens and twenties wear. People could debate whether a thirteen-year-old should dress like a twenty-eight-year-old, but plenty of them aim to, and that's a problem that would exist even if American Apparel didn't. (Judging by the customers—and their mothers—that I interviewed, along with marketing experts and college professors with a sense of their students' wardrobes, the typical American Apparel customer ranges from about thirteen to thirty-two.)

Overall, these are the same sorts of clothes available at American

Apparel's rivals, places like Abercrombie & Fitch, Aéropostale, Forever 21, the Gap, Hollister, H&M, and Urban Outfitters. The last-named offers backless shirts and bustiers. Hollister displays short shorts and spaghetti-strap tops. H&M has short shorts and tight, short skirts. As their customers might say, "Duh."

Perhaps American Apparel's wares are a tad sexier. After all, it's known for its form-fitting T-shirts that are cut for women, rather than boxy and unisex like most. Loretta Lurie, a veteran advertising executive in New York City and Chicago—and the mother of a teenage girl, Sydney Bornstein, who considers the brand "cool"—grimaced a bit. "You go into Hollister and Abercrombie, and then American Apparel: Their shirts are cut a little lower. The dresses are too short or too tight. It encourages teenage girls to dress like sluts." Not surprisingly, one of her daughter's friends, fifteen-year-old Faye Honig, agreed with the daughter, not the mother, about the chain's coolness; nevertheless, certain American Apparel items were too much for her. "Some of the stuff you laugh at. Who would wear that netted, see-through stuff—which if you'd buy, you'd layer?" (And what mother and teenage daughter will ever have the same opinion about which clothes are appropriate?) Meanwhile, from the opposite point of view, Rachel Gilman, a thirty-three-year-old New York City advertising stylist, said she likes American Apparel's turtlenecks and tank tops because "they make them long, not cropped"—that is, *less* revealing of the midriff.

In any case, American Apparel clothing has more attributes, unrelated to sexiness, that make it popular among the target audience. The T-shirts are softer than most others and of higher-quality fabric, often all-cotton. They don't have silly logos. "They're a step up from casual T-shirts," Jessie, a thirty-two-year-old New York City nursing student, commented. "I can wear the shirts out and not feel like a slob."

The biggest problems are the occasional children's items that seem to copy the adult versions. In fairness, most of the gear is age appropriate ('tween girls like to wear leggings and tank tops) or even too sedate (try getting a squirming two-year-old into an Oxford button-down). But the slinky rib racerback dress? The baby rib spaghetti tank dress? It's one thing for a thirteen-year-old to dress like twenty-eight; it's another matter for an eight-year-old to do so.

Is the marketing sexy? Consider the following examples.

The window displays of an American Apparel store on the Upper East Side of Manhattan in April 2010: One female mannequin stands with her hand on her buttocks, her blouse unbuttoned so far down that half of one breast is revealed. A real woman, in a blown-up poster, is perched on hands and knees, her rear end high in the air. However, a half dozen other mannequins are posed much more innocently, arms and legs akimbo, striding, or even slouching almost pigeon-toed like shy little kids.

The window and outside-wall displays of an H&M store a few blocks away, the same day: Headless mannequins are set in positions similar to those at American Apparel—for instance, one has a hip thrust out, with her feet pigeon-toed. Huge posters show head-and-shoulder shots of attractive youths who look to be in their teens and twenties. They're usually fresh faced and fully clothed, but in one strategically placed poster, the much-larger-than-life-size crotch of a blonde in a tight, short skirt is right about at a passerby's eye level.

The window displays of an Urban Outfitters store in the same neighborhood, same day: The mannequins lack heads and sometimes arms and legs, which inherently renders them fairly sexless. However, the posters make up for any sexual slack. There's a blow-up of a young blonde woman in a vest with deep cleavage, and in another, a woman is seen from behind walking on a beach, wearing high boots and bikini panties that reveal generous portions of her buttocks.

The window display for Abercrombie & Fitch, Northridge Mall, in Northridge, California, March 2011: A huge black-and-white photo shows a blonde teenage girl lying on top of a bare-chested teen boy, almost kissing, with his hands stroking her hips.

The window display for Forever 21, same mall, same day: The mannequins are wearing miniskirts and short shorts, but their mops of curly hair, lack of faces, and playful stances evoke a completely asexual, childlike mood.

The back-page ad for American Apparel in the *Onion*, June 3–9, 2010: A brunette arches her back in an impossible yoga-style pose on the sand, wearing a black swimsuit that reveals plenty of buttocks and torso, her legs stretched apart suggestively, her head leaning back so that it almost touches her upraised bare foot, eyes closed in ecstasy, as her curly hair cascades down.

The back-page ad for American Apparel in the *Onion*, April 22–28, 2010: In a series of three photos, a young, long-haired Asian woman in beige slacks and a plain white, short-sleeved, somewhat loose-fitting blouse kneels demurely, with her head tilted in a different direction in each shot, her arms usually down at her sides.

A full-age ad for H&M in *Seventeen*, December 2009-January 2010: Three women strut or lean against each other, clad in various configurations of body-hugging black leather, silk, spandex, and other clingy fabrics—a very short skirt, bicycle-style shorts, a front-zippered minidress, a half-unbuttoned blouse.

A double-truck ad for H&M in *Teen Vogue*, March 2010: Two young women with frizzy red hair, laughing, arm in arm, are sporting bright yellow-and-pink striped sweaters with black skirts.

Seductive? Yes, some of the American Apparel images certainly are. And some of them are playful or straightforward. Furthermore, they're not noticeably different from the ads, posters, and mannequins of rival brands—and far, far less raunchy than ads in the same magazines for Valentino and Jimmy Choo.

So, is American Apparel's marketing sexy compared with the competition's?

To answer that, I pored through a stack of copies of *Allure*, *Girls' Life*, *Harper's Bazaar*, *InStyle*, *Marie Claire*, the *New York Times Magazine*, the *Onion*, *Seventeen*, *Teen Vogue*, and the *Village Voice*, from October 2009 through July 2010, and studied window and store displays at American Apparel, Banana Republic, the Gap, H&M, Hollister, Uniqlo, Urban Outfitters, and Victoria's Secret throughout the course of several months. (It's a tough job, but somebody's got to do it.)

In analyzing the various examples, it's important to remember that American Apparel has a wide target market, encompassing readers of *Girls' Life* and of *Allure*. The ads in *Girls' Life*, *Seventeen*, and *Teen Vogue* ought to be more demure than those in magazines aimed at adults. American Apparel solves the problem to some degree by not advertising in the PG-13 publications. Going for edgier outlets, like the satirical weekly the *Onion* and the *Village Voice* (famous for its sex-of-all-sorts classified ads), it gets more leeway. Yes, thirteen-year-olds may read Mom's *Allure* rather than *Seventeen*, but that's another one of the broader social problems that can't be blamed on American Apparel.

For that matter, American Apparel doesn't push the limits as far as it could. Take another look at those back-page ads in the *Onion*. Of a half dozen from February through June 2010, four were not sexual at all, or were only minimally so. The models were sitting or standing in casual positions, with serious or cheerful faces, not come-hither looks. Two of them were fully clothed in slacks and shirts, and the others—one in a bikini top and jacket, and one in a black lace blouse—still didn't look any sexier than someone wearing a "Legalize LA" T-shirt. They seemed almost bored with their poses. (By contrast, the two more provocative back pages featured a young woman in a short skirt and form-fitting long-sleeve shirt, and the yoga-stretching model described above.)

Too sexy for teens? Hardly. These six ads could have fit comfortably into the November 2009 issue of *Teen Vogue*, which boasted a demure profile of a young woman in a lacy-sleeved white blouse and jeans, for PRVCY Premium; the back view of a young woman modeling Emu boots and wearing a white bikini bottom that revealed as much of her buttocks as American Apparel's yoga performer displayed; and eight pages of ads for Jimmy Choo shoes "for H&M" that included (among other images) a couple of women sprawled seductively in black leather, a woman with half of one breast falling out of her dress while she caressed a partner, and a seated woman with a black skirt slit up to her crotch.

Moving up (or down) the ladder of raunchiness, American Apparel's website is certainly more erotic than those of rivals like Hollister and Urban Outfitters. However, it's a crapshoot. Clicking onto the American Apparel page for women's dresses, you might see a woman in a slinky tank dress sprawled on an unmade bed. Or you might see a woman sitting on a chair in a pink dress with a wide, twirly skirt.

Most troubling are the store displays, because they are harder to avoid. While no one has to buy a magazine or surf online, anybody walking down the street or the mall, from age three to eighty-three, can see the mannequins splayed in sexy poses, maybe lying on one side or sitting with legs stretched wide. The display photos are usually worse, showing lots of black lace and up-on-all-fours poses. Yet the mannequins are just as likely to be unobjectionable, merely standing, striding, even (apparently) doing jumping jacks or gymnastic stretches and wearing long sleeves, jackets, and slacks in a splatter of bright colors.

The colors actually gave American Apparel a more innocent look than H&M and Hollister on that April day. Those other two stores exuded an air of sophistication and sexiness—H&M with its sultry black-white-beige-brown color scheme, and Hollister with its black-painted walls and wafts of incense. At the Hollister door, moreover, shoppers were met by bikini-clad greeters.

Certainly, American Apparel has a reputation for being worse than its rivals, and that reputation can even alienate the target audience. Faye Honig, the teenager, complained that in its marketing, "it's like, whoa! It's crazy, they're showing off underwear, and they're basically naked.

They show everything." A fifteen-year-old boy in Manhattan told me that when American Apparel ads are on the Onion's back page—which can be every other week—it's so embarrassing that he won't read the newspaper on the subway. His friends called the ads "weird" (from a boy) and "pornographic" (a girl). When I visited the Hastings Center, a think tank in suburban New York that specializes in ethical issues relating to health and the environment, one researcher said she felt uncomfortable bringing her teenage niece to the stores, while another said the shops "are known as a place to go look at soft porn."

Viewing the marketing strategy from a hard-nosed business angle, Robert Passikoff, the branding expert, said, "It does provide some level of image differentiation for the brand, but it's a dangerous game."

Yet the bottom-of-the-line reputation is not universal. Several mothers of teenage girls I talked with didn't think American Apparel's ads are particularly different from those of other stores or manufacturers. Although Loretta Lurie (who is married to Peter Bornstein, the artist who wears Timberland shoes) considers the clothing sexier, she said the commercials blend in with the TV programs where they're featured— something she should know about, as an advertising expert herself. "Didn't Abercrombie & Fitch set the bar on sexy marketing?" asked Carol Holding, the brand-strategies consultant. "They had ads where the men's pants were cut so low that you can see the pubic hair." The New York Times media writer David Carr, too, pointed to other examples, noting in a January 2011 column that "Abercrombie & Fitch built a brand out of writhing, half-naked teenagers, as Calvin Klein once did."

Defending their company, Dov Charney and Ryan Holiday argue that the extra-sexy reputation actually stems from American Apparel's policy of using its own employees in its ads, rather than professional models. "I don't think the sexuality of American Apparel is necessarily any more explicit or extreme than any other fashion company," Holiday told me, "but because we are not using professional stylists and they're not Photoshopped, people are sometimes caught off guard by the realness of our ads. They conflate that with being more explicit." Indeed, the manufacturer is proud of the policy, claiming it proves that the clothes are for real people. "We try to use our employees and friends, because that's who we design our clothes around—not what people should look like, but what they are," Holiday said.

Then, essentially conceding that the marketing might in fact be extra edgy, he added, "These are the images we choose to use because we think they are evocative and interesting and exciting. We consider our ad space as a conversation. Sometimes we use our ad space to speak out about politics like immigration." And sometimes, apparently, sex.

In truth, sexuality in marketing and fashion alike has grown increasingly explicit over time. A century ago in Europe and the United States, a glimpse of a woman's ankle was risqué; now, bikinis barely cover what's still considered the tiniest scrap of private parts, and if you want more, just see what people voluntarily post on YouTube without even getting paid. What in the American Apparel repertoire can hold a candle to the Neiman Marcus ad in *Marie Claire* where the model—close-up, full-frontal view almost to the navel—is wearing nothing except a couple of strategically placed necklaces?

Okay, so sex sells. Fashion designs, store displays, clothing ads, and even nonclothing ads use sex. That still leaves the most serious charge against American Apparel, and the one that most sets it apart from its competitors—that the work place itself oozes sex.

The tales have been repeated in news articles and lawsuits for years and to some degree even confirmed by Dov Charney. Allegedly, he walks around nearly nude in the office and has held business meetings in a similar state of undress, calls employees "sluts" and "whores," favors staffers who sleep with him, hires young women on the basis of their looks, screams at employees, grabs their hair, describes graphic sex to them, and more. The *Portfolio* article talked about a half dozen male employees in their twenties who lived with Charney in his mansion, including one "loud, pear-shaped" PR apprentice who called the boss "Daddy." *New York Times Magazine* consumer columnist Rob Walker wrote in his book that he was in the CEO's office with one male and two female staffers while "Dov Charney was naked from the waist down"—but the punch line is that Charney was trying on prototypes of a new line of men's underwear. He has certainly dated female staffers, at least three of them seriously. Most notoriously, writer Claudine Ko, in the June–July 2004 issue of *Jane* magazine, described a female employee presumably performing oral sex on Charney in a hotel room in front of Ko. A week afterward, the article continued, Ko was in a corporate apartment with Charney while the CEO masturbated and "we casually carry on our interview, discussing things like business models, hiring practices and the stupidity of focus groups."

Nine female employees or ex-employees have filed lawsuits or legal complaints officially asserting sexual harassment. One was dropped, one was settled, and the rest were pending at the time of this book's publication, one of them for years.

Nikky Yang—a former girlfriend of Charney's who, according to her lawyer, Keith A. Fink of Los Angeles, helped found the clothing chain—charged that the company had created "a hostile work environment based on sex." For instance, "while working naked Mr. Charney grabbed his penis and stated to Ms. Yang, 'pet my dick.'" In another situation, Yang's lawsuit accused Charney of "forcing Ms. Yang to sit and watch him shower to discuss business." (The lawsuit includes nonsexual issues, as well, alleging that the CEO screamed at her, physically abused her, and cheated her out of pay.) Although Fink would not discuss a second client, Mary Nelson, whose case was still pending, published reports have mentioned claims that Charney made sexual advances and inappropriate comments to her and "wore a skimpy thong that barely covered his genitals."

Yet more Fink clients have filed cases that include sexual angles almost as a side charge. In December 2008, Bernhard-Axel Ingo Brake, who was hired to set up American Apparel's retail operations in Europe, sued the company and Charney mainly for issues relating to wrongful termination, breach of contract, failure to pay bonuses and commissions, and emotional distress. However, he also claimed that "American Apparel employs many women who have had sex with Mr. Charney. These women are commonly referred to as 'Dov's girls,' his 'girls,' 'lovers of Dov,' or 'F.O.D.' (meaning 'Friends of Dov'). 'Dov's girls' receive preferential treatment from American Apparel due to their 'special relationship' with American Apparel's largest shareholder."

Brake said that Charney would send these women to "take over management tasks [in Europe] despite their lack of qualifications," leading to "mismanagement of the retail store operations to the financial detriment of American Apparel and its shareholders in the hundreds of thousands of dollars"—and, not coincidentally, making it difficult for Brake to do his job. The lawsuit further alleged that Charney "purchased hundreds of sex videos using company funds," saying they were for research, and "attempted to charge his payment for the services of a prostitute at his hotel to American Apparel."

Things seemed to quiet down for a couple of years, until, within less than three weeks in March 2011, five more women filed charges. Most dramatically, a New York City woman claimed that when she was only eighteen, she'd been "held prisoner" in Charney's apartment for several hours and threatened with being fired if she refused to perform sex acts over the next eight months.

The fact that some of the women say they felt forced to have sex with Charney in order to keep their jobs ties in with the controversy over using employees in ads. Even without any sex, there's always an implicit coercion when your boss asks you to do a task.

If the charges focus on Charney, it's impossible to separate him from the company. He founded it, nearly destroyed it, revived it, saw the potential of form-fitting and no-logo shirts, set the sexually charged mood, and still is the public face and ultimate arbiter of everything from designs to hiring to advertising to immigration advocacy.

As Charney himself lays out the history on the corporate website, he essentially launched the business through the back window while he was a high school student at the elite Connecticut prep school Choate Rosemary Hall. He would buy up huge numbers of "iconic" Hanes T-shirts when stores like Kmart had supersales, then load them onto trains bound for his hometown of Montreal for resale, undercutting the official Canadian distributors. He carried the business concept over to his dorm room at Tufts University, where a partner—a local Hanes wholesaler—conceived the name American Apparel. (That partnership didn't last long. By Charney's own admission on the website, the wholesaler "thought I was a little difficult to deal with," and Charney had to return the man's $16,000 investment.)

During Charney's sophomore year, American Apparel began manufacturing its own unique garments in the barn of a South Carolina farm. Charney eventually dropped out of Tufts and moved to South Carolina to devote himself to the burgeoning business full-time. Already, the firm was becoming known for its fitted designs, in contrast to the standard unisex cut. At that point it was a wholesaler, not a retail brand, often selling to companies that would imprint their own logos.

However, in 1996, Charney filed for bankruptcy. This is one portion of his history that the CEO does not discuss on the website—although he manages to find space to muse about his mother's Syrian roots and his favorite bagels. Outsiders have variously attributed the problems to low-cost imports and Charney's disorganization, both of which would become recurring themes in his career.

In any case, by 1997 he was in Los Angeles, starting over, thanks to the financial backing of either one or two Korean partners, depending on who's telling the story. The brush with bankruptcy apparently didn't sober him. Airily, Charney wrote on the website, "The Korean garment community was vigorously supportive of my work . . . . Many suppliers extended me credit even after I bounced so many checks on them and continuously failed to pay them on time." Still, the company seemed to do well enough—at least for a while—that in 2003 Charney decided to open his own stores, rather than sell through middlemen.

That decision changed everything: it made the chain famous, but it also opened the door to the notorious advertising and probably overexpansion that are among the company's worst problems today.

Sexual or not, Charney is clearly a charismatic and hands-on (no double entendre intended) manager. According to published reports, he selects some of the employees to pose in those sexy ads and may even photograph them himself. (For that matter, spokesman Ryan Holiday said that Charney's two dogs have been featured in spots.) During my visit, employees were constantly checking his opinion on things like a marketing plan, and the *Portfolio* article describes him striding through downtown Los Angeles handing out job fliers. Jason Coulter, the erstwhile union organizer, said that when he and his labor colleagues met with Charney, "he tried to seduce us"—not literally, of course.

Thus, nine lawsuits. That may not seem like a lot, within the context of 10,000 employees and 285 stores. Yet there are larger companies with fewer, or none.

Charney's main defense has been essentially that the whole industry is motivated by sex, that fashion workplaces are inevitably sexually charged, so why pick on him? For instance, responding to Mary Nelson's lawsuit, he asserted, as *Portfolio* put it, that "in addition to being the company's creative director, he is also one of its fit models—a simple explanation for why he would stride around his offices half-dressed. . . . He has also said he 'test-drives' the underwear to see how it fits 'in action.' . . . In a deposition, he said he 'frequently' had been in his 'underpants' because he was 'designing an underwear line' while Nelson was working at the company."

That jibes with Rob Walker's account, as well.

In other specific cases, Charney has claimed that the women suing him did substandard work or that they were trying to extort money from him. "Dov Charney's celebrity status in the fashion industry is being publicly exploited," the company said in a statement to the press, in response to the New York teenager's lawsuit in 2011. Regarding the four women who jointly filed soon afterward, Charney showed reporters sexually explicit e-mails, text messages, and photos that he said the women had sent to him—in other words, *they* were hounding *him*, not vice versa.

Others in the industry scoff at his "everybody does it" defense. Sure, famous models regularly hang out in design studios in various states of semidress. That doesn't mean the company owner fondles them or strolls around in thongs himself. "I have been in Liz Claiborne shops, in a bunch of other places," Jason Coulter said. "They are run professionally." Karen Erickson has been part of the industry since she started New York City–based Showroom Seven, a designer-fashion sales firm, in 1983. "Everyone I know who is in fashion works too hard to have affairs in the office," she snapped. "My husband has been working with me for thirty years. He would be backstage helping with models; he sees top models naked. Whether I have problems with him? Absolutely not, any more than a gynecologist's wife has problems with him seeing patients naked."

Still, there is other evidence to indicate that all is not sex and foreplay at American Apparel. When I visited the Los Angeles factory, I saw no one running around half-naked or flirting, nor anyone who looked drop-dead gorgeous. In fact, some of the white-collar, younger, presumably hip employees were unfashionably chubby, and the two massage therapists who were starting their work shift—one middle-aged man, one twentyish woman—were modestly dressed in pale-blue T-shirts and shorts. Angelica Salas, the immigrant rights advocate, said that she's never heard any complaints from factory workers she talks with. "In my own interactions, personally, as a woman, he has always been super respectful of me," she added. (She was twenty-six when she first met Charney in 1997, presumably within his target age for hitting on.)

The website Gawker.com, in June 2010, posted a couple of supposedly leaked American Apparel memos spelling out the guidelines for employee grooming, and the requirements were, if anything, amazingly modest. For females, "Makeup is to be kept to a minimal [sic]. . . . Liquid eyeliner, pencil eyeliner and eyeshadow are advised against; mascara must look very natural. . . . Blush must not be overdone—should not have glitter or sparkles. . . . Please do not use a shiny gloss on your lips; any lipcolor must be subtle. . . . Hair must be kept your natural color." And among the "guidelines for dudes" are the warnings that "[h]air should look natural. Excessive product to the extent of creating stiffness and an unnatural or greasy appearance to your hair is advised against."

In describing the look that the company seeks in its staff, Ryan Holiday said, "The idea that we're hiring on attraction is false. We hire based on a sense of personal style: How do you hold yourself? What do you wear that with? It's that they're stylish and creative and expressive with their clothes."

The teenage employees I interviewed who had worked at the retail stores, males and females alike, didn't report any uncomfortable situations. For instance, Matt Jacobs (not his real name) spent about six months as a part-time stock clerk and sales clerk at an outlet in Manhattan's Greenwich Village during his senior year in high school in 2006. In addition, friends of both genders worked at other American Apparel stores. True to the stereotype, he said that the sales staff upstairs were thin, pretty, young white women, while the stockroom employees in the basement were older, often Hispanic and black, and often married with kids themselves. "There definitely was a [sales-clerk] look," Jacobs said. However, it wasn't always a sexy look: "There were different body types. A lot had tattoos. They were interesting looking. Hipster." And, yes, he heard plenty of rumors about Charney sleeping with employees or taking photos of them. When Charney paid a call, people were on their toes, the same as anyone would be at any company when the boss comes by. Still, the mood never took on a sexual edge, with or without the presence of the CEO. "It wasn't uncomfortable at all. I liked how everyone worked together. There wasn't that kind of [sexually charged] feeling," Jacobs said with a shrug. "I don't know where that whole reputation comes from."

The charges in the lawsuits are serious, yet anyone can claim anything in legal papers. The proof is in the end result—and even that can be ambiguous. Of these American Apparel suits, one was dismissed at the request of the woman who filed it, which might or might not mean that it was baseless; sometimes lawsuits are dropped because a big, rich, corporate defendant applies so much pressure that the plaintiff can't hold out any longer. Another American Apparel case was settled, which usually implies either that there was some merit or that the company just paid off the plaintiff to get rid of the nuisance. A third lawsuit had been pending for years at the time this book was published, which could simply indicate obstinacy on both sides. One had gone against the company in the first round with the federal Equal Employment Opportunity Commission, but lawyers on both sides were negotiating. Five others were too new to have been resolved in any fashion.

Keith Fink, the attorney for the two longer-pending suits, has a controversial history of his own. According to various news reports, he has been fined for fabricating evidence, has repeatedly sued famous people to obtain quick nuisance settlements, has stalled and changed his mind on an arbitration offer, and has demanded money from American Apparel. The clothing company has reportedly countersued, charging him with extortion. Fink proudly told me, "I represent all sorts of celebrities," although the ones he cited are hardly household names, other than bad girl/rock musician Courtney Love. He claimed that American Apparel has paid people to write negative articles about him and manipulated Google's search optimization. "They will stop at nothing" to badmouth him, he said. So, which side of the legal debate is sleazier?

In a way, my visit to the corporate headquarters epitomized the contradictions. There were the airy and well-lighted production floors, the free bikes, the subsidized food, the professional-looking massage therapists. And then there were all those middle-aged seamstresses, probably from traditional Latino backgrounds, soberly dressed themselves, sewing skimpy shorts and bikinis under huge photos of woman crouched seductively on hands and knees. The store clerks may be cool with this. But are the factory workers comfortable?

As for other topics often of concern to socially responsible shoppers, American Apparel doesn't have much of a reputation either way. On balance, it ends up slightly on the positive side of the ethical spectrum.

The only social issue on which the company has publicly taken a major stand, besides immigration reform, is gay rights. After its home-state voters approved Proposition 8, a constitutional amendment to ban same-sex marriage, in 2008, American Apparel jumped into the ensuing protests. It produced and donated tens of thousands of "Legalize Gay" T-shirts, put those shirts in its store windows, cosponsored a march in Washington with the Human Rights Campaign, donated some proceeds from sales of the shirts to the HRC, and advocated on its website.

That kind of sensitivity to sex-based discrimination might seem out of alignment with the charges of sexual harassment and the ads that exploit women. However, it fits an industry where homosexual designers are a cliché and customers are often young and unafraid of breaking taboos. As the American Apparel website declared, "With many of our employees and customers identifying as gay, lesbian, bisexual or trans-gendered, we are a company that is vocal about our support for the protection of gay rights." Both the immigration and gay rights advocacy have helped make the chain popular with San Francisco–area teenagers I interviewed. And if American Apparel is about anything, it's about in-your-face sexuality, whether it's half-nude women in sexy poses, or two women kissing.

To the HRC's Eric Bloem, the anti–Proposition 8 activism (and no doubt the cash from the T-shirt sales) earns the company a lot of breathing room to make up for the allegations of sexism. While HRC's annual survey asks large companies about all sorts of policies regarding gay, lesbian, transgendered, and bisexual employees and consumers—topics like their domestic-partner benefits, marketing, and donations—Bloem said that sexual harassment is "not so much in our portfolio." He went on, "Obviously, we do not condone any sort of sexual harassment, but with the firm stance [American Apparel] has taken on LGBT inclusion, we'd like to try to see if their policies match up with the programs they have in place. I'd like to see what the allegations are." He didn't know exactly what policies American Apparel has or how it might rate on the various human resources issues, since the company isn't big enough to be actually included in the annual survey.

Meanwhile, its environmental record is mixed. It's also too small to qualify for Climate Counts's rankings, although Wood Turner, the organization's founder and former executive director, said he wears some of the T-shirts because "they're sweatshop-free, and that matters to me." By not shipping garments all the way from China or other far-off points, the company certainly uses less fuel and produces fewer emissions than other brands.

The Rough Guide to Shopping with a Conscience gave American Apparel credit for "offering its most popular styles in certified organic cotton and recycling, according to its own count, over a million pounds of fabric scraps every year." The recycling part may be true. Company officials say that T-shirt fabric left over from adult shirts goes into making smaller items such as bathing suits (which, at American Apparel, can get really small), children's clothes, and hair bows. The littlest scraps are used to tie up bundles of garments. "Everything is designed to reduce waste," Ryan Holiday said.

The cotton claim is more dubious. Consumers often rave about how much of the clothing is all-cotton and thus not made from petroleum-based synthetics, with the mess of attendant environmental and political problems that come from using oil. That's only partly true; obviously, the leggings and other stretch garments are synthetic. Moreover, cotton creates plenty of its own environmental damage as well as human rights violations. For starters, instead of propping up Russia or Saudi Arabia, cotton buying probably supports the police state of Uzbekistan, one of the world's three main sources of raw cotton, which uses forced labor. Standard cotton growing demands huge amounts of chemical fertilizers, insecticides, and water, and Uzbekistan has drained the Aral Sea to feed this industry. What about American Apparel's supposed use of organic cotton? In a search for "organic cotton" on the company's website, a mere fourteen items emerged. Only three of those were specifically labeled for babies, a category where many customers think being organic is most important.

PETA and the Humane Society give the brand credit for not using fur or leather, although that's rather meaningless, considering that the vast majority of its products—T-shirts, button-down shirts, underwear, jeans, bathing suits—aren't normally made of animal skins. Then PETA subtracts points for wool, which it doesn't like due to the painful mulesing and shipping processes. On balance, however, PETA calculates that the lack of fur and leather tips the scales in favor of American Apparel; indeed, the chain makes some of the T-shirts PETA sells.

On another important ethical topic—free speech and politics—the record is similarly mixed. American Apparel has never been a big force in political lobbying or donations, according to the Center for Responsive Politics. Of course, the company asserts that its whole attitude toward sexuality is really about being open and frank. But Keith Fink, the lawyer handling some of the sexual-harassment suits, accused American Apparel during our interview of forcing newly hired staff to sign arbitration provisions far more restrictive than the norm. Although arbitration agreements are common enough among "sophisticated employers," he said, the usual formula is that employees must accept the ruling of a private arbitrator and keep the charges and settlement from the public. "Nobody else has in their agreement the provision that American Apparel does," Fink added. "[New hires] are forced to agree not to discuss with the media anything that goes on with American Apparel."

Price is also a CSR issue, albeit one too often ignored. It's hard to figure out where to place American Apparel in that category. Among customers I talked with, there seemed to be a general feeling that its most stylish clothes were probably worth the somewhat high cost but that twenty dollars—a typical American Apparel price tag—was a little dear

for a plain T-shirt. Several New York City teenage girls singled out Urban
Outfitters as usually cheaper, while another rival, H&M, is known for
bargains. Then again, some American Apparel T-shirts were just fifteen
or eighteen dollars at the time I wrote this book, and I talked to shoppers
who actually go to the chain for what they consider its low prices. Carol
Holding, the brand-strategies consultant, said her twenty-two-year-
old daughter likes American Apparel clothes in part because "they're
disposable—they cost nothing."

A fashion designer wondered how it could be competitive if it's paying such high, nonsweatshop salaries. Company officials say they save
money by controlling the whole design-to-retail process through their
vertical integration. As the American Apparel website proclaims, "A
smaller portion of the margins goes towards fuel, transocean container
ships, middlemen, boxes, pallets and entropy." The best answer is probably that, while it's no discount house, it's not the most expensive shop
in town.

A discussion of American Apparel's ethics also needs to consider its finances. There are serious questions of fiscal irresponsibility, or at least
really lousy judgment. It might seem that a key requirement for a socially
responsible company would be honesty about basic business issues. A
second requirement might simply be to stay in business.

From the prep school beginnings, American Apparel's corporate history is sprinkled with ethical envelope pushing (the resales to Canada)
and shaky finances (the 1996 bankruptcy). The newest problems probably
go back to what seemed like its era of greatest success, the happy days
in the early 2000s when the reincarnated company was expanding into
retail. The initial three stores burgeoned to over 280 in seven years. The
stock started trading on the then American Stock Exchange (now part of
the New York Stock Exchange), by virtue of the fact that, in 2007, American Apparel was bought by a publicly traded special-purpose acquisition
company—essentially, a shell that exists to buy other companies—called
Endeavor Acquisition Corporation. The chain hired an industry veteran
as vice president of operations, praised by author Rob Walker as "quiet,
serious, soft spoken."

Then, as 2010 wended its way into summer, the house of T-shirts
began unraveling. As numerous press reports have recounted, its accounting firm, Deloitte & Touche, quit, with a warning of "material
weaknesses" in the internal controls, and the company revealed that the

Securities and Exchange Commission and the US Justice Department were investigating. It teetered on the brink of violating the covenants of a private equity loan, the second time it had had trouble with a key lender. On top of all that, it risked being kicked off the NYSE for repeatedly filing its quarterly papers late. The stock price plummeted.

By year-end, the manufacturer had cobbled together fresh financing, brought in a new acting president and chief financial officer, and rehired its old, pre-Deloitte auditor, but Charney had to buy up nearly $4 million worth of shares to keep things going. And that didn't seem to be enough. The debt kept rising, sales and revenue fell, thirteen underperforming stores were closed, two board members left, angry shareholders filed class-action lawsuits, and loan terms were repeatedly renegotiated. Losses for 2010 reached $86 million. In its annual SEC report in March 2011, the company warned that it might have to file for bankruptcy. Again, financial salvation arrived at the last minute—at least, temporarily—in the form of a package of stock purchases and warrants to purchase more, worth up to $43 million, from a group of Canadian investors.

Maybe it was all just a mix of overexpansion, recession, and sloppiness, aggravated by the need to quickly hire and train 1,500 new employees to replace the ones forced out by the immigration raid. The company claimed—plausibly enough—that such a mass talent search hurt its productivity. Charney told *Bloomberg News* that with replacement workers now in place, seventy new stores set to open, and a program to sell its wares at other retailers, the company was poised to return to profitability. The bankruptcy warning, he claimed, was just a technicality.

Maybe. However, some of the lawsuits filed by Keith Fink go beyond bad luck and run-of-the-mill poor business decisions to allege actual malfeasance. For example, Bernhard-Axel Ingo Brake, the head of American Apparel's European operations, brought incendiary charges against Charney. Brake alleged that, in addition to hiring incompetent "Dov's girls" and using company money for sex videos, Charney ordered him to avoid paying French taxes by illegally attributing part of employees' salaries as reimbursement for expenses; tried to inflate the value of the stock by lying about the prices of goods that were sold; and demanded that he fiddle with the way rent and other expenses for unopened stores would be booked. Another plaintiff, Roberto Hernandez, said he was fired for refusing to manipulate the inventory figures.

———

THE QUESTION: Does American Apparel deserve its reputation
as an exemplar of ethical chic?

THE VERDICT: No (but it's not hopeless)

To oversimplify, the debate comes down to this: is extreme sexism so
egregious that it outweighs American Apparel's efforts to improve its
employees' work lives in other ways, including giving them jobs in the
United States to begin with?

If many of my friends think the answer to the sexism question is obvious, activists had a much harder time. They seemed to find the question
excruciating. They really wanted to endorse the company for its support
for immigrants and gay rights, keeping jobs in America, not using leather,
or whatever other ethical reason. They wanted someone to prove that the
sexual-harassment charges weren't true; failing that, they avoided answering by pleading lack of information (especially since the company
is too small to hit the radar of a lot of "Best Companies" surveys). Or
perhaps nine lawsuits really aren't so many? Eric Bloem of the Human
Rights Campaign mused that if female employees are treated crudely, "it
may be indicative of a lack of appropriate human resources policies and
procedures." Nevertheless, he added that he couldn't be sure.

Nor has the ICCR (the shareholder activist group for religious institutions) paid much attention to the clothing manufacturer. "We have been
aware of more general concerns regarding images in advertising," said
Laura Berry, the executive director. "There are definitely members who
are concerned about pornography and violent media portrayals." But, after all, American Apparel's photos and harassment are nowhere near as
horrible as child sex slavery. "We choose our battles," she added.

Aaron Chatterji, the Duke University professor, even used the
company—along with ExxonMobil!—in a guest lecture at California's
Monterey Institute of International Studies in November 2009 as an example of how difficult it can be to juggle competing aspects of CSR. Pre-
tending that he was discussing four anonymous companies rather than
just two, he told the students, "Here's a company with the best safety
record in the industry, here's a company that's a bad polluter, here's a
company that has good working conditions, here's a company that's
been sued for sexual harassment. Which do you value more?" The students quickly nixed the supposed companies with pollution records and
sexual-harassment lawsuits, favoring the "other two." Then Chatterji revealed that the safe company and the polluter were actually both Exxon-

Mobil, and the good working conditions and the lawsuits both applied to American Apparel.

To some activists, however, the very fact that American Apparel aspires to be seen as socially responsible in areas like workers' rights and immigration gives it an extra obligation to be a good citizen all around. The charges of sexual harassment are even more troubling than they would be at a less socially active employer. So American Apparel considers itself a protector of immigrants? Well, pointed out the National Consumers League's Sally Greenberg, "immigrant women are very vulnerable. [Charney] has to clean up his act." In other words, Latina employees at American Apparel might be doubly at risk.

In a typical company, the sexually charged image "would not raise an eyebrow. It would be 'Yeah, look at the clothes, these are sexy clothes,'" suggested Carol Holding, the brand strategist from Seattle. "But because this brand is so rooted in this social ethos, all of a sudden, it becomes a very big deal. It negates the whole social-responsibility thing."

Certainly, American Apparel deserves acknowledgment for what it does right. It seems to be genuine about providing decent benefits (albeit without allowing unions) and fighting for better treatment of immigrants without exploiting those who are illegal. These qualities are in its DNA. And to his credit—or perhaps as a result, finally, of the bad PR backlash—Charney has apparently toned down the underwear parades and other particularly outrageous flaunting.

Nevertheless, CSR is a little like the Hippocratic oath: first, do no harm, before you try to whitewash your harm with good works. Were the robber barons of the late nineteenth century good guys if they built libraries and universities? Is Goldman Sachs a paragon if its CEO, Lloyd Blankfein, donates $1.3 million a year to philanthropic causes, even as the firm sold risky subprime-mortgage-backed loans to customers without revealing that a key client was hedging against those same loans, ultimately paying a fine worth five hundred times Blankfein's yearly donation?

Winning the sexual-harassment trials (if they ever happen) wouldn't solve American Apparel's problem, because those cover only a few examples. The sexuality is the company's whole identity.

To earn a social-responsibility badge, American Apparel would have to take a major step: dump Charney.

OK, OK, he's the founder and head designer and inspiration and guiding light and micromanager and chief underwear model, so ease him upstairs as founding CEO or chief consultant or CEO emeritus. In fact, let him keep suggesting designs and colors. And then hire a real CEO with management expertise to go along with the other grown-up managers recently brought in. (Bonus: That might also help the company dig out of its financial mess and stay in operation.)

The problem is that Charney doesn't inspire only the fashion designs, ad campaigns, and political causes. His cavalier (or worse) personal attitudes toward sex and women have set the tone of the workplace. Most of the complaints are directed at actions he himself—not the company—is said to have taken. As long as he is a physical and psychological presence in that coral-colored factory in downtown Los Angeles, so are the poisons. At the same time, if he has truly built a made-in-the-USA business model that works, not simply a one-man admiration society, it should succeed without him.

CHAPTER 7

The Reality

Perhaps this book could have been written 240 years ago. Arguably, the first time that consumer power was deployed to make a political point was the Boston Tea Party, in 1773.

The consumer movement grew, alongside political populism, union organizing, and the campaign for women's suffrage, in the late nineteenth and early twentieth centuries. That was the era when the Interstate Commerce Act, the Sherman Antitrust Act, the American Federation of Labor, and the Food and Drug Act came into being, while muckrakers at Collier's Weekly and the Ladies' Home Journal investigated phony patent medicines. Corporate management, for its part, recognized a sense of responsibility. The new Harvard Business School's mission statement vowed, "We educate leaders who make a difference in the world"—that is, a nonbusiness difference.

The Depression, World War II, and postwar rebuilding temporarily pushed aside the public's interest in social causes as people made basic survival a priority. Then the second great era of political-consumer activism was ignited by the civil rights movement in the 1960s, antiwar protests in the 1960s and 1970s, and the growing revulsion against South Africa's apartheid in the 1970s and 1980s. Shoppers and investors discovered that their dollars could buy political pressure as well as stuff.

Why should they give their money to bus companies that forced black passengers to give up seats to whites? Why should the universities they attended purchase products from Dow Chemical, which also made the napalm used in Vietnam? Socially responsible investing, for one, is now a $2.7 trillion business. People wanted to feel that they were making a difference for good, and it was so much easier to do it as part of their daily routine, while buying something they needed to buy anyway, rather than seeking out a special activity.

The targets continued to spread. Student groups demanded investigations into the foreign sweatshops that manufactured their official college gear. Advocates for farm workers boycotted California grapes. Gay rights advocates boycotted orange juice.

And increasingly, since the 1990s, business has been responding to this demand.

Frito-Lay plans to make half of its junk food with natural ingredients. International Paper is burning biomass debris to save fuel. The average Climate Counts score has risen nearly 20 points since the website was launched in 2007. Trader Joe's stopped selling orange roughy and other endangered fish and agreed to work with outside groups. Starbucks signed a licensing deal with Ethiopia. Nike has transformed itself from the evil sweatshop abuser to being greener than Timberland in the Amazon. And on and on.

The burgeoning of social-responsibility themes in marketing makes a particularly good yardstick, since ads are the means by which businesses project the image they think will appeal to shoppers. "Companies are trying to move in that direction because it does give them some cachet with the press and customers," said Michael Myers, of the ad agency Palio Communications. "In a few more years, it's going to be expected." As a typical example, Donald Schepers, director of the City University of New York's Robert Zicklin Center for Corporate Integrity, described a recent television commercial for a Honda Civic, a car known for good gas mileage: "It starts out with a car from the seventies. A thin young man gets out, cool looking; he looks like a guy who'd be fun to be with. He walks along, and his T-shirt progresses through the years, but the T-shirts always have eco-friendly things on them. He doesn't age. He's still in his twenties. Now, he's getting into a brand-new Civic. There's a great deal of transference that the company is trying to set up, that being eco-friendly goes along with being cool."

Experts say that certain industries are more susceptible to social-action pressure, whether because their sins seem to stand out, because alternatives are readily available, or because their customer bases are particularly CSR attuned. Among these sectors are clothing, autos, food, and architecture.

"Fashion companies had better be pretty green and socially conscious, because they're very much about image," said Arthur Caplan, the University of Pennsylvania ethicist. "They're selling products that induce guilt. Who needs all that high-end stuff? You'd better do what you can to make it guilt-free." Indeed, while couture designers started slathering on more furs around 2010, they are countered by the growing breed of younger, "ethical" designers like Stella McCartney who offer faux-fur choices. Caplan's logic applies as well to cars: automakers must find trendy and green ways to compensate for their unhip, irresponsible use of fossil fuels, their carbon emissions, and their pollution. (Hello, Prius and Lexus hybrids.) Meanwhile, food is a key sector because "consumers care about something that goes into your body," as Timberland's Gordon Peterson pointed out a little enviously. (If only they cared as much about what goes on their feet!) It may be relatively easier for the food and construction industries to be virtuous, New York University's Russell Winer suggested, since organic food and architectural eco-certifications are becoming widely available.

The businesses that most need a CSR patina are probably those with a client base in the teens to early thirties. They're the Timberland target. They're fine with Trader Joe's limited, prepackaged selection, because they don't have kids and they're too busy with dual careers (and social activism) to cook an old-fashioned meal. And they basically define the Apple and American Apparel communities. Said Jill Kickul, who teaches this age group in New York University's entrepreneurship program, "You have a younger generation in their twenties and thirties that want to see and are expecting business-as-usual to be socially responsible."

Ethical, environmental, political, and other policy concerns are still not—and never will be—the prime reason people buy anything. There are too many other practical factors, like convenience, size, taste, color, fashion, quality, allergies, friends' recommendations, religious requirements, that spark of joy you can get from the right item, and, most of all, price.

Tom Chappell asserted that people will accept a higher price for "natural" goods, and there is some evidence to back him up. Starbucks,

Timberland, and Apple customers obviously pay more, although it's not clear how much they're paying for milieu, gourmet taste, sturdiness, and the Genius Bar and how much for the ethical image. As well, a few weakly supportive surveys are floating around. The Humane Society's Michael Markarian mentioned a January 2005 Ohio State University survey in which 43.1 percent of the respondents said they would fork over a 10 percent premium for humane animal products, and 12.4 percent reported that they would pay as much as 25 percent more. On the other hand, 40.6 percent wouldn't pay extra at all, which comes to a pretty high "unwilling" faction.

Brand strategist Carol Holding cited a different set of analyses, done by Cone, a Boston-based consulting company that specializes in cause branding. This research, she said, found that "an enormous number of people will buy a product that's socially responsible, assuming the price and quality are equal."

Isn't that kind of comparison meaningless, I asked; of course anyone would take a product that came with an extra attribute (ethics) for no extra price. "Consumer-products companies are looking for a hair's difference," Holding replied. That tiny preference for ethics could be enough to outsell a non-CSR rival.

All those calculations go out the window when the economy goes down the tubes. Numerous polls showed that, not surprisingly, outlays on expensive organic food and green products dropped during the 2008–2009 recession. If regular food, clothes, cars, or anything else seemed unaffordable, who is going to pay 10 or 50 percent more to feel virtuous?

To ethicist Arthur Caplan, these surveys are missing the key part of the affordability problem. "It's very much a class issue," he said. "People shopping at Walmart and BJ's [Wholesale Club] and Sam's Club are less interested in being green than people buying Volvos and hybrid cars are. I think the rich have a little more room for it than the poor." In that case, being socially responsible in terms of the environment, working conditions, animal rights, organic and natural ingredients, and other typical standards by definition requires a company to be socially *irresponsible* in terms of bias against working-class and low-income consumers.

Horrified officials at supposedly progressive companies immediately disavow any thought of class prejudice, enumerating all the ways that discounted versions of their goods are available. "There's a range of price points" for Timberland shoes, marketing vice president Jim Davey said, from the $300 boots at Saks Fifth Avenue and Nordstrom to $100 and $120 versions at DSW and the Timberland Factory Outlet. Kate Chappell, of Tom's of Maine, insisted that "there are plenty of low-income people, like students, that buy our products." She cited Tom's outlet stores, and of course, thanks to the Colgate marketing clout, the label is now at Walmart. In the long term, optimists like the University of Virginia's Patricia Werhane say, mass production and economies of scale could bring the price down—if only more of us would pay the few extra pennies now.

So, a lot of consumers are demanding ethics with their Big Macs. How well did the six companies in this book respond, and what do their actions say about business attitudes?

To start, I broke down the basic criteria from the introduction into smaller, measurable chunks, like "reduce energy use" and "reduce or recycle waste" under the broad heading of "climate change and energy." Next, I set up a four-part scoring system: a "good" rating got 3 points, "better than average" got 2, "average" or not applicable got 0, and "bad" got minus 1. Then I scoured the facts, data, interviews, opinions, and analyses in the six chapters to determine how to rate each company. They earned a higher rating if they acted on their own initiative, like Timberland's bringing in outside certification of its overseas factories, versus doing it after a public uproar, as with the environmental campaigns against Apple. Being a pioneer added points, too.

It is, admittedly, an arbitrary and subjective process. Should Timberland's long history of making "Best Companies" lists earn it a "good," or should the fact that it fell off in 2008 drop it to merely "better than average"? Is Tom's of Maine's revamped toothpaste packaging still "good" in the "information" category, or should it be downgraded to "better than average"? Here's what I came up with (omitting the zeroes, to keep it simple):

ENVIRONMENTAL/HUMANE

Reduce energy use: Timberland and Tom's are Good / Starbucks is Better Than Average / Trader Joe's is Bad

Alternative energy: Timberland and Tom's are Good / Starbucks is Better Than Average

Recycle/reduce waste (including packaging): Timberland and Tom's are Good / American Apparel is Better Than Average / Apple, Starbucks, and Trader Joe's are Bad

No animal cruelty: American Apparel and Tom's are Good / Starbucks and Trader Joe's are Better Than Average / Timberland is Bad

Natural/organic/no PVCs, etc.: Timberland and Tom's are Good / Apple, Starbucks, and Trader Joe's are Better Than Average

Local sourcing: Tom's is Good / Trader Joe's is Bad

WORKING CONDITIONS

Unions: All are Bad

Pay and benefits: All but Apple are Good

"Best Companies" lists: Starbucks is Good / Timberland is Better Than Average / Apple is Bad

Overseas sweatshops (absence or monitoring): American Apparel, Starbucks, and Timberland are Good / Apple is Better Than Average

Sexual harassment: American Apparel is Bad

PUBLIC SERVICE

Price: Trader Joe's is Good / Apple and Starbucks are Bad

Community and public service: American Apparel, Starbucks, Timberland, and Tom's are Good

Customer service: Apple, Starbucks, Timberland, and Trader Joe's are Good

Public information: Timberland, Tom's, and Trader Joe's are Good / Apple and Trader Joe's are Bad

(In the category of "public information," Trader Joe's is unusually good in providing consumer information, such as explaining the different types of eggs, yet it is also unusually bad in its corporate secretiveness—which is why it counts twice.)

Putting aside, for the moment, the issue of labor unions, good US working conditions would appear to be the most popular "virtue," with five of the six companies claiming some plaudits for pay, benefits, or "Best Companies." The reason is that it's not just an ethical value. It's an important business practice to treat your workforce well, as Henry Ford discovered nearly a century ago, when he began paying his workers a wage high enough that they could afford to buy his Model Ts. CSR experts say that ethical values can lead to lower turnover, higher morale, and a recruiting edge. At Timberland, Gordon Peterson pointed out, the time off for volunteering was a key attraction for job applicants. When Tom's of Maine employees take their paid volunteer time, Kate Chappell said, "they come back to their jobs reenergized."

But what about unions? Since fewer than 7 percent of private-sector employees are unionized, and collective bargaining among government workers has become a political football, it shouldn't be surprising that a group of six companies would have no unions—except for the fact that these are supposed to be especially socially responsible companies. Wouldn't at least one of them be more open to an organizing drive than the average American manager? Actually, no, say some labor veterans. "I don't think union shops are as much needed at socially responsible workplaces," said Ron Blackwell, the AFL-CIO's chief economist. "A lot of these [CSR] programs are about managing reputational risk, especially about workplace issues." In other words, these companies have already checked off the "working conditions" box by providing long maternity leaves or flextime or whatever nice benefits, so they don't need a union in order to qualify as a good place to work. It's the Tom-and-Kate/Howard Schultz philosophy of the benevolent, socially responsible boss.

The trouble with the benevolent-CEO philosophy is that no CEO lasts forever. Even if generous benefits or community service are supposedly intrinsic to the company's self-definition and have come to be expected by staff and customers alike, expectations erode over time. If the new chief executive doesn't feel as strongly, if rivals aren't providing such benefits, if profit margins are shrinking, if a new generation of workers and customers is less aware of the CSR history—all those factors can make it too easy to snip away at the supposedly sacred corporate mission statement.

The next two most popular categories, with three or four "goods" apiece—which, combined, encompass all six companies—are a set of virtues that usually get ignored by social-responsibility campaigners and investors: community, public, and customer service. The most obvious examples are Timberland's and Tom's of Maine's paid volunteering time and American Apparel's ads, donations, marching, and other support for immigration rights. But these categories also can mean openness and availability to the world at large. Things like Starbucks creating a space where people can sit for hours without being required to buy an overpriced latte. Or Apple Stores staff answering questions at the Genius Bar and letting anyone check e-mail at the display computers.

Why do these two categories rate such high billing? As with wages and benefits, probably because they help basic business operations. Happy customers—especially customers who are encouraged to linger—will buy more. Local organizations that are grateful for a company's donations will spread the word.

After those top categories, the scores drop dramatically. Unfortunately, the cynics are right that many CSR attributes interfere with business operations: low price is hard to achieve if companies pay their workers above-average wages and use expensive organic ingredients. Trying to avoid animal products might limit the kind of fashions American Apparel and Timberland can design. And how can a Starbucks in Manhattan, San Francisco, or Seattle possibly buy local, when the climate in those cities is too wet and cold for growing coffee beans?

Another value that's not usually considered as part of CSR is the corporate structure itself, whether ownership is public or private. Public companies—generally the largest and best known—sell stock to any investors. Private companies are owned by a limited group of people that have committed their own capital—typically, the founders, their friends and relatives, and a few professional investors such as hedge funds. Virtually all companies begin this way, and most, but not all, private companies are small. (Some notable exceptions are Hearst Corporation and Mars Inc., which makes M&Ms.)

The big problem with a public company is that investors are constantly comparing the profit margins, earnings per share of stock, and other data against rival businesses' numbers. So there is tremendous pressure to cut costs here and raise prices there in order to eke out pennies more in returns. Even worse, shareholders tend to focus on the short term—to demand returns *right now*—rather than support investments in, say, solar installations that may pay for themselves over the long run. "Big institutional investors drive companies to increase shareholder values, which often results in oppressive working conditions," said the AFL-CIO's Ron Blackwell. By contrast, privately held companies have the freedom to pay extra for natural ingredients or give their employees time off for community projects. Indeed, that's what Tom Chappell said—before he sold Tom's of Maine to publicly traded Colgate.

All these are powerful points. However, there are stronger arguments in favor of public ownership.

Of course, ordinary stockholders with a few hundred shares don't "own" a company like Apple the way they might own their house and decide whether to put in a solar array. The real power belongs to management, the board of directors, and the large institutions that Blackwell mentioned, such as pension funds, that own millions of shares. Nevertheless, because all shareholders technically own the company, and anyone could become an "owner" in the future, these companies are legally required to provide a wealth of operating and financial information buyers and sellers might need to make informed decisions. The general citizenry can thus learn about top officials' pay and perks, or pending lawsuits over pollution or sexual harassment. "Keeping all of that information private is a problem," said the National Consumers League's Sally Greenberg. "It's really hard for consumers to figure out if you're sharing the price discounts you should. Nobody really knows what you're paying your CEO."

Public companies are also subject to the much more sophisticated and potentially rigorous oversight of the Securities and Exchange Commission. (That oversight may not seem to be doing much to help American Apparel, but the company's ownership structure is really a tangle of private and a veneer of public.) Plus, shareholders have the right to propose changes in corporate policy and ask uncomfortable questions at the annual meeting—exactly what has opened the door to activism by groups like As You Sow and the ICCR. While most resolutions may fail, Domini and Oxfam would have had no influence over Starbucks's policy in Ethiopia without the risk that shareholders would dump the stock.

So far, so good. Businesses have discovered that having a socially responsible reputation is a great way to appeal to the public and to differentiate themselves from competitors. Yet that leads to an obvious risk: when is the CSR claim just a marketing gimmick and when is it real, and how can consumers tell the difference?

"I'm skeptical that you can," Arthur Caplan, the University of Pennsylvania ethicist, said bluntly. Advertising is built on manipulating images and words, after all. "It's simple for a company to create an image that makes them appear to be socially responsible," said Robert Passikoff, the president of the brand-loyalty consulting firm Brand Keys.

With environmental issues, phony marketing is called greenwashing, and the vast majority of companies do it, according to surveys by TerraChoice, an environmental-marketing outfit that's part of Underwriters Laboratories. Common tactics include assertions that aren't backed up by respected certifications, vague claims like "all-natural," and meaningless claims such as touting a product as "CFC-free"—meaningless because all use of chlorofluorocarbons (CFCs), which deplete the Earth's protective ozone layer, has been banned internationally since the 1990s.

Consultant Jacquelyn Ottman has written an entire book telling companies how to eco-pitch themselves, entitled, appropriately, *Green Marketing*. "Use highly illustrative visuals to strengthen the upbeat emotional appeal of environmental advertising," she suggests. And, "Make illustrations big, bright, and beautiful" by showing, for instance, "a close-up shot of a spotted owl looking all feathery and cute or a nest of little owls." To be fair, Ottman isn't simply pushing image; she further advises business readers that there has to be genuine green action behind the owls. Yet, as she admitted to me in an e-mail interview, "Not sure if [consumers] are equipped to catch the fakes."

Food is another area where questionable marketing abounds. Food writer Michael Pollan, in his book *The Omnivore's Dilemma*, described buying a free-range, organic chicken at Whole Foods, sold by a company called Petaluma Poultry, whose packaging boasted that Petaluma's "farming methods strive to create harmonious relationships in nature, sustaining the health of all creatures and the natural world." The label even gave the chicken a name: Rosie. But when Pollan tracked down his chicken, its ostensibly "harmonious" farm "turns out to be more animal factory than farm," he wrote. "She lives in a shed with twenty thousand other Rosies," and her supposed free range is a door that "remains firmly shut until the birds are at least five or six weeks old."

The mass-production chicken giant Perdue Farms ran a TV commercial in 2009 showing company chairman Jim Perdue strolling through a barn with a bunch of happy hens waddling around, while bragging that all Perdue chickens are cage-free. Wow. So Perdue has become, like, organic and stuff? No. All factory-farmed roasters are technically cage-free. The only time that "cage-free" matters is for egg-laying hens.

As for apparel, two University of Missouri researchers published a paper in 2011 asserting that shoppers are willing to pay an extra 15 to 20 percent for clothing manufactured via "sustainable and ethical" practices—but these same shoppers were skeptical when manufacturers claimed to be doing exactly what they sought.

In theory, the kinds of standards cited in the introduction could help consumers find their way through the marketing. But there are far too many labels, and far too little proof behind them. For the environment, the Ecolabel Index has catalogued 365 seals and certifications. Food can be barn roaming, local, natural, vegetarian fed, grass fed, antibiotics-free, preservatives-free, free of added hormones, free of artificial flavors, free of GMOs, minimally treated, family farmed, certified humane raised, sustainable, dolphin safe, trans fat–free, and a lot more. On top of that, add the lists compiled by consumer organizations like PETA, the Monterey Bay Aquarium's Seafood Watch, and Climate Counts.

Only a few terms are actually defined. The US Department of Agriculture has pretty strict standards for organic produce and meat, and much more vague ones for free range and free roaming. Dolphin Safe is a trademark of Earth Island Institute, a nonprofit environmental group, and is supposed to set standards for catching tuna in a way that doesn't harm dolphins. The so-called leaping-bunny logo of the Coalition for Consumer Information on Cosmetics, for personal care and household products, is one way to show that no animal testing was done. However, Tom's of Maine uses a different no-animal-testing bunny from PETA, and Trader Joe's has yet a third bunny. "Fair trade" has—or had—a specific meaning if the label is on coffee, cocoa, rice, sugar, tea, roses, and soccer balls, because an internationally recognized group called the Fairtrade Labelling Organizations International administers those certifications. But the US affiliate, Transfair USA, has now split off. And, in any case, the same term on clothing is meaningless.

How much time does a concerned consumer want to devote to this research? Labor activists suggest checking clothing labels to see where a garment was made. The SEIU's Mark Levinson favors Caribbean factories, because at least they use US-made textiles. Until recently, Jeff Ballinger had been advising shoppers to "go for the countries that are further up the ladder of democracy," on the theory that the workers there have more rights than in dictatorships. "If it's made in Taiwan or South Korea, maybe they don't have a union, but they can vote their governments out," he explained. He's had second thoughts about that tactic ever since a fellow activist pointed out that a lot of sweatshop workers in those countries may be undocumented foreigners who can't vote.

Ah, the Web will save us! And to some degree, that's true. A company that's polluting, using sweatshop labor, or cheating its workers has a tougher time keeping its nefarious deeds secret nowadays. "The guy that was standing by the Dumpster ten years ago watching them pour chemicals, now he can take out his BlackBerry with a camera and have it out to the world within minutes, or videotape it and put it on YouTube," said Palio Communications's Michael Myers.

Yet if social networking can uncover phony greenwashing, it can equally spread phony green attacking. The Body Shop suffered from that in 2006, brand strategist Carol Holding recalled, after it was bought by

French cosmetics giant L'Oréal. While the Body Shop is famous for its policy of not testing on animals, L'Oréal does test, and rumors raced online that the Body Shop would knuckle under to its new owner. Animal rights groups called for a boycott, even as company officials insisted that their policies wouldn't change. Indeed, the Body Shop ultimately retained its policies and its place on PETA's list of nontesting companies.

A positive image "is hard to gain and very easy to lose," warned Northwestern University's Richard Honack. "You can lose it with one bad incident. It goes out viral, and [people begin saying,] 'I'm not using those products anymore.'"

The best way to judge whether to trust a corporate image is to remember that these companies are out to make a buck, and they will be most likely to go green, humane, and squishy if it makes business sense. "It has to be integrated into the business itself," Carol Holding said. "That's when it's authentic." She gave the example of Liz Claiborne Inc.'s long-running campaign, ever since the early 1990s, to raise awareness of domestic abuse. "They do it because their customers are women," Holding explained. "If you have IBM picking up abused women as a cause, it's totally phony. There is no connection to the business."

Fortune's 2004 "Best Places" citation of Timberland noted that employees used their company-paid volunteer time "at the Nashville Rescue Mission this December to fit 217 men with shoes and boots." While those 217 pairs of footwear were presumably donated, the mission employees and any volunteers from other organizations might want to buy shoes someday and would remember Timberland fondly.

CSR ethics can also be reflected in the corporate culture. It shows up in qualities like having an ombudsman or a place where whistle-blowers feel comfortable reporting violations, or quickly recalling faulty products without threats from regulators. In February 2010, Fortune profiled a management consultant, Dov Seidman, who has built an entire business of more than 400 big-name clients on this concept, asserting, as the magazine put it, that "in today's wired and transparent global economy, companies that 'outbehave' their competitors ethically will also tend to outperform them financially." The classic example dates to 1982 but is still evoked frequently: Johnson & Johnson's reaction when seven deaths were traced to its Extra Strength Tylenol. The Food and Drug Administration asked J&J to withdraw the four manufacturing lots that the suspect capsules had come from. Of its own volition, J&J went further, recalling all 31 million containers of the pills—the entire production line.

Certainly, companies have an incentive to be socially responsible if it can save hard cash, and sometimes it does. By now, the corporate world is overflowing with environmental money-saving examples, including CFL and LED lightbulbs, better insulation, and motion-sensor lights. Timberland officials cite the solar panels at the California distribution center, and the reflective white roof and a "new premium-efficiency" heating, air-conditioning, and ventilation system at the New Hampshire headquarters. Moreover, contracting with the most reliable eco-tanneries means less need for oversight, while some of the materials for the ecological Earthkeeper line are less expensive than standard material.

Even if it's only image, by now, CSR has become an integral part of many companies' brands. Timberland would just be a bunch of sturdy boots without it. American Apparel would have no protection against accusations of sleaze. Starbucks would be another chain selling gourmet coffee, perhaps no better than Dunkin' Donuts, certainly less cool than a neighborhood café. Trader Joe's would still be a cute alternative grocer, but it wouldn't be a cuter version of Whole Foods. Tom's wouldn't exist.

Or, in the end, is the whole exercise pointless?

If everyone in the business world from Walmart to Nike to the *Economist* is now touting the virtues of corporate social responsibility—and their own CSR PR, in particular—consumer activists who have been fighting these companies for years might have a moment of doubt. Is that really it? Victory? The worries go deeper than image and marketing, to the basic question of whether CSR is, by definition, a contradiction in terms. Skeptics tend to fall into two camps.

One position is that CSR is meaningless because it's limited and voluntary. No company can survive in today's economy if it ignores fundamentals like globalization, competition, and cost pressures, and those business considerations don't allow for ethics on a company-by-company basis. So LED bulbs save a few pennies and attract a few customers; most CSR efforts are expensive. The network of subcontractors is too long and diffuse to monitor. The few companies that try to be ethical will go bankrupt. And since actions like using recycled ingredients or solar energy are voluntary decisions, the easiest and most logical choice is to stop.

Thus, this camp of skeptics argues, overcoming these powerful, built-in, worldwide, competition-driven pressures requires a counterforce equally powerful, an infrastructure that doesn't depend on a particular CEO's whim and can't be bypassed by a business with cold feet. That's also why a union is so important, with its legally binding contracts, independent voice to counter management, and outside monitoring.

"It was always misguided that, rather than relying on laws, we're going to rely on the conscience, the largesse, of corporations to do the right thing," the SEIU's Mark Levinson scoffed. "It's very easy and comforting. You don't have to have the messy business of passing laws." Former US labor secretary Robert Reich wrote in his 2007 book *Supercapitalism*, "The only way for the citizens in us to trump the consumers and investors in us is through laws and regulations that make our purchases and investments a social choice as well as a personal one." As one example, he endorsed paid leave, going beyond the Family and Medical Leave Act, "so workers can upgrade their skills or take the time to attend to a newborn or sick parent." Maybe there could be harsh penalties for pollution, a tax on carbon emissions, or more subsidies for alternative energy.

Yet even those sorts of rules might not be enough. Just watch a big company declare that unless it's exempted from a particular regulation, it will take its jobs to Bangladesh, China, or some other place with weaker laws.

The other position is that CSR is meaningless because all businesses encourage unnecessary consumption. Everyone needs food, toothpaste, shoes, and clothing. And in the modern world, let's concede that mobile phones and computers are a basic necessity. But how many pairs of shoes, and how many computers? Do we really *need* $3.75 lattes? Or Trader Joe's chicken-sausage calzone with two cheeses and red onions? Or iPods?

Starbucks, Trader Joe's, and Steve Jobs all invented markets that never existed before. Who knew that we could have a device that could easily, cheaply, and legally download our specific taste in music? Who knew that we needed fancy coffee every day? As Howard Schultz said in his second book, "The best innovations sense and fulfill a need before others realize the need even exists."

These invented "needs" do more than waste consumers' money. Trees are cut down, oil is dug up, climate-destroying gases are emitted, and water is siphoned from depleted lakes to create these "natural" and "ethical" products.

Obviously, such criticisms can get carried to ridiculous extremes. If no one ever shopped at Starbucks, Trader Joe's, and all the rest, those businesses would go bankrupt. Their employees would lose their jobs and, therefore, also stop shopping at Starbucks, Trader Joe's, and the rest. Then the companies that supply, ship, advertise, and do the accounting for the first tier of companies would go bankrupt.

"Can you have a transnational corporation that is built on a business model of continuing expansion, selling more things every year, and be sustainable?" Greenpeace's Rolf Skar asked rhetorically. "They are valid questions, but if you answer no, we can't have continual growth, even as the population expands globally."

Well, few people live by absolutes, and activists really would like to believe they can nudge business in the direction of social responsibility—as well as keep drinking their lattes and using iPods. So they find niches of hope.

On the question of globalization, antisweatshop activist Jeff Ballinger noted that brands like Hanes, Russell Athletic, and Timberland own some of the factories that produce their underwear and shoes and therefore can maintain a bit more oversight. In addition to American Apparel's wares, a limited amount of clothing continues to be manufactured in the United States, including about 20 percent of the New Balance label, according to Ballinger, plus the highest-end designer jeans and 20 to 30 percent of what's sold at the youth chain Forever 21. The website StillMadeinUSA.com lists dozens of clothing lines that it says are American sewn, along with stores that sell them.

These are not the greatest solutions. By and large, the StillMadeinUSA.com offerings are frumpy or no-name clothes, without the cachet of the name brands made in sweatshops in Bangladesh, and a lot of the US work is done in a subindustry of microsubcontractors paying wages below the federal minimum, in hidden enclaves in Los Angeles, New York City, and other cities. Nevertheless, presumably the lousy conditions at these shops are easier to uncover than the overseas versions, and in fact lawsuits have ferreted out some of them. At least these ideas are a start.

Although the AFL-CIO's Ron Blackwell considers most codes of conduct too weak, he allowed that having a code, a mission statement, or some other expression of ethics is better than not having one: "If they say they endorse certain practices and you show violations, there is at least a moral force to change that." For similar reasons, he pointed to the way Starbucks brags about its health coverage for part-timers. With so much publicity, it would be a huge PR disaster for Starbucks to renege. "This is a customer-service business, and they want their employees to exude pride in the company," he said. Finally, Blackwell puts some faith in activist shareholders, who can hit publicly traded companies where it hurts.

As for the issue of overconsumption, luckily, more people are worrying about this and tying to limit their resource use, through everything from municipal recycling programs to the consumer-trading website

Freecycle to vintage shops. Economists are rethinking the way gross domestic product is measured, so that the consumption of resources doesn't automatically get counted on the positive side of the ledger. Timberland claims its boots are really ecological because they last forever.

Greenpeace, Rolf Skar said, doesn't try to tackle the basic philosophy of consumerism. That would be too overwhelming. "We're looking at pretty discrete questions," he said, like the deforestation caused by one pulp-and-paper mill or one cattle ranch in the Amazon. One acre of rain forest at a time.

ACKNOWLEDGMENTS

If you want a good conversation starter or pickup line, ask people what companies they consider socially responsible and also hip.

During the past couple of years, when friends and colleagues would question me about the topic of my next book, I'd briefly describe the theme—"I'm writing about six companies that are seen as trendy and ethical"—and immediately, like a good reporter, I'd turn the question around: "Which companies would *you* choose?" Most people love "best" lists, and they also love being asked their opinions, so the suggestions would flood in. Anecdotes, arguments, agreement, sources, head-slapping, eye-rolling, laughter, groans. Someone's friend had worked at Trader Joe's. Someone else knew someone who once was a manager at Apple. Everyone adored Apple. Everyone hated Starbucks, but did they prefer Gorilla Coffee, or Café Regular, or Ozzie's, and was Café Regular du Nord as good as the original Café Regular? I got into discussions at all sorts of places—at my book club and at dinner parties, with my running partners and at my French class, on a charity fund-raising walk and at Jewish funeral *shiva minyans*.

So thank you, Adriana, Ann, Ben, Cara, Dan, Dan, Ed, Elaine, Elizabeth, Erik, Gabriel, Greg, Jan, Jeanne, Jennifer, Jo, Joe, Karen, Kathleen, Les, Lillian, Lisa, Lisa, Mari, Marta, Mary, Michael, Michael, Mike, Mike,

Moira, Mort, Nancy, Nancy, Paola, Patty, Reba, Rick, Scott, Sharon, Sharon, Susana, Theresa, Tom, Trina . . . I won't name you all—I don't even know all your names—but you know who you are.

(Also, thanks to those of you who donated your copies of *Allure*, *Harper's Bazaar*, *InStyle*, *Marie Claire*, *Seventeen*, and *Teen Vogue* for my research.)

In addition, special thanks to my agent, Lauren Abramo, of Dystel & Goderich Literary Management, and my editors at Beacon Press, Allison Trzop and Joanna Green, who had faith in my selections—and one more thanks to Joanna, who was absolutely right about where the excess could be trimmed. Thanks to those who agreed to a formal interview. And finally, as always, thanks to my family for putting up with my frantic intensity in those last (many) months of finishing the manuscript.

NOTES

As a guide for curious readers, these notes indicate the most important books, reports, and newspaper and magazine articles that I consulted for particular points, but no list could possibly encompass all my research. My main source of information was the interviews I conducted between August 2009 and March 2011, plus my direct observations from visits to dozens of stores. In addition, I browsed the six companies' websites along with various consumer, advocacy, and government sites and read voluminous press releases and other official handouts from these companies, most of which are clearly identified in the text. When a news event has been widely reported—such as Apple's problem with the antennas on its iPhones in 2010 or Walmart's green initiatives—I give no specific citation, because I consulted a variety of news sources.

As for the companies themselves, I was able to interview many executives at Timberland and Tom and Kate Chappell at Tom's of Maine, as well as tour both headquarters and Tom's main factory. Trader Joe's rarely grants press interviews and outright declined my request. American Apparel and Starbucks said they would consider my requests but ultimately failed to reply to numerous queries from winter 2010 through spring 2011, though American Apparel did allow me to tour its facility and interview a press spokesperson. Apple failed to respond to any queries.

INTRODUCTION: THE IMAGE

The information about Steve Jobs's wedding is from Jeffrey S. Young and William L. Simon, iCon: Steve Jobs, the Greatest Second Act in the History of Business (Hoboken, NJ: Wiley, 2005), p. 193.

The Bloomberg Businessweek cover story about debt-ridden consumers who splurge on lattes is Devin Leonard, "The New Abnormal," August 2, 2010.

The two articles in the November 2010 issue of Institutional Investor were Imogen Rose-Smith, "No Turning Back," p. 38, and Katie Gilbert, "Money from Trees," p. 42.

The New York Times's Earth Day reference is from Leslie Kaufman, "On 40th Anniversary, Earth Day Is Big Business," April 22, 2010.

The specific quote from the Economist's cover package of January 19, 2008, is on p. 1.

The report from the International Organization for Standardization is "Guidance on Social Responsibility" (final draft, as of summer 2010), ISO/FDIS 26000.

Robert Levering's quote about R. J. Reynolds comes from my book The Overloaded Liberal: Shopping, Investing, Parenting, and Other Daily Dilemmas in an Age of Political Activism (Boston: Beacon Press, 2010), p. 179.

I actually interviewed Calvert's Paul Hilton in July 2008 for The Overloaded Liberal, although I didn't use that particular quote in that book.

John Leland's quote comes from the paperback edition of his book Hip: The History (New York: Harper Perennial, 2005), pp. 69 and 61.

The quotes from No Logo, by Naomi Klein, are from the paperback edition (New York: Picador, 2002), pp. 68, 21, 16, respectively.

Lee Eisenberg's quote is from Shoptimism: Why the American Consumer Will Keep on Buying No Matter What (New York: Free Press, 2009), pp. 186–87.

There are a couple of references from Juliet B. Schor, The Overspent American: Why We Want What We Don't Need (New York: Harper Perennial, 1999). The bulk of the information about how people's role models have become ever more ritzy is found on pp. 3–10, and the direct quote about inner-city tastes is from p. 40.

"Conceptual Consumption" is by Dan Ariely and Michael I. Norton, Annual Review of Psychology 60 (2009): 475–99.

Rob Walker, Buying In: The Secret Dialogue Between What We Buy and Who We Are (New York: Random House, 2008), p. xiii.

The ideas about cult branding come from Matthew W. Ragas and Bolivar J. Bueno, The Power of Cult Branding: How 9 Magnetic Brands Turned Customers into Loyal Followers (and Yours Can, Too!) (New York: Crown Business, 2002).

CHAPTER 1. TOM'S OF MAINE: WOODSTOCK TOOTHPASTE

Tom Chappell's book is *The Soul of a Business: Managing for Profit and the Common Good* (New York: Bantam, 1993), and the quotes (in order) are on pp. 216 and 158, regarding why he wouldn't sell the company; pp. 187–88, for the descriptions of early eco-practices; p. 49, for the history of corporate "tithing"; p. 65, for the chat with the secretary; pp. 111–12, for the description of himself as a young insurance salesman; p. xi, for the explanation of why he enrolled at Harvard Divinity School; pp. x and 24, for what he learned from Harvard; and p. 215, for the later reference about why he wouldn't sell.

Jacquelyn A. Ottman, *Green Marketing: Opportunity for Innovation* (Lincolnwood, IL: NTC Business Books, 1998), describes Tom's of Maine on pp. 196–99; the quote is on p. 196.

The information about the government investigations into triclosan is from Andrew Martin, "Popular Antibacterial Chemical Raises Safety Issues," *New York Times*, August 20, 2011.

The citation from Leo Hickman, ed., *A Good Life: The Guide to Ethical Living* (London: Transworld, 2008), is from p. 159.

Also, Duncan Clark and Richie Unterberger, *The Rough Guide to Shopping with a Conscience* (New York: Rough Guides, 2007), p. 195.

CHAPTER 2. TIMBERLAND: HOW GREEN IS MY LEATHER

Some good sources about Timberland's history, in addition to the timeline on its website, are Steven Flax, "Boot Camp," *Inc.*, September 1, 1987, and the above-cited *Buying In*, pp. 81–84.

A lot has been written about Wyclef Jean, his work in the Haiti hurricane, the financial investigations into his charity, and his campaign for president of Haiti—including an article I wrote for Portfolio.com in January 2010 titled "A Foot Soldier for Haiti (and Timberland)," http://www.portfolio.com/.

I got some great background about leather tanning and chromium from the US Environmental Protection Agency website at "9.15 Leather Tanning," http://www.epa.gov/.

In addition to material found at the Timberland website, there was good information about the company's carbon footprint in a couple of *Wall Street Journal* articles: Jeffrey Ball, "Six Products, Six Carbon Footprints," October 6, 2008, and Jeffrey Ball, "Green Goal of 'Carbon Neutrality' Hits Limit," December 30, 2008.

The reference to my Portfolio.com article is the one cited above, "A Foot Soldier for Haiti (and Timberland)."

CHAPTER 3. STARBUCKS: COFFEE AS A BRAND NAME

Howard Schultz's story of how he created and then returned to Starbucks comes from his two books: *Pour Your Heart Into It: How Starbucks Built a Company One Cup at a Time* (and Dori Jones Yang; New York: Hyperion, 1997) and *Onward: How Starbucks Fought for Its Life without Losing Its Soul* (with Joanne Gordon; New York: Rodale, 2011).

First, the quotes from *Pour Your Heart into It:* The quote at the beginning of the chapter about the front porch is from p. 5, and the one about "the Starbucks experience" is on p. 251. The description of Hammarplast is on p. 22, and the quote about his father is on p. 3. The description of his first taste of Starbucks coffee is on p. 26. The descriptions of "dreadful" and "swill" American coffee pre-Starbucks are on pp. 26 and 30, while the quote about Italy is from p. 52. The description of his goals for Il Giornale is found on p. 77. Schultz's acknowledgement of not quite being the "third place" is on p. 120, and the quote about the Italian cafés is on p. 51. His claim about baristas making eye contact is on pp. 250–51. The quote about Starbucks being targeted is on p. 294. The statistics about the growth of gourmet-coffee consumption are on p. 181, while the quotes are on pp. 278–79. The quote about landlords is on p. 279; the quote about perfume is on p. 252; and the one about treating workers like family is on p. 127. The union decertifications are discussed on pp. 108–9 and 137. The "hot-cup team" quotes are on pp. 303–4. The comparison to Nike is from p. 77.

Now, from *Onward.* The quotes about turning his attention to expanding Starbucks and getting bored with day-to-day operations are from p. 16; the quote about the 15th Avenue and Roy Street shops is on p. 279; the quote about how hard baristas work is on p. 122; the quotes about the "lean" production methods are on pp. 281 and 181; the complaint about four-dollar lattes is on p. 146; and the quote about reducing fat content is on p. 167. The quote denying aspirational motivation is on p. 159.

Bryant Simon, *Everything but the Coffee: Learning About America from Starbucks* (Berkeley: University of California Press, 2009): for the description of old-type coffee, p. 23; Simon's fruitless attempts to start a conversation, p. 100; his complaint about the music, p. 163; his interview with farmers, p. 217; and his comment about yuppies and bobos, p. 11.

The fourth book heavily used for this chapter is Kim Fellner, *Wrestling with Starbucks: Conscience, Capital, Cappuccino* (New Brunswick, NJ: Rutgers University Press, 2008). The description of trying to talk with other customers is on pp. 116–19; the discussions about whether Starbucks is more socially responsible than other cafés are on p. 134; the praise of its environmental work is on p. 102; and the comparison with the stringency of Rainforest Alliance standards is on p. 94. The author's interviews with Starbucks workers are on

p. 111, as is the description of the low pay; the description of her work shift is from p. 151; and the discussion of the unionizing effort at the roasting plant is found on pp. 145–47.

Michael Gates Gill tells his story in *How Starbucks Saved My Life: A Son of Privilege Learns to Live Like Everyone Else* (New York: Gotham Books, 2007). The arcane coffee names are on p. 134; the descriptions of his coworkers and working life are on pp. 51, 217, and 224; the anecdote about working during his break is on p. 139; and the quote about not being able to afford a latte is on p. 13.

Numerous articles have been written about how Starbucks overexpanded, hurt its image, alienated its client base, and faced new competition in the early 2000s. Here are some I used: Ted Botha, "Bean Town," *New York Times*, October 26, 2009; Brad Stone, "Starbucks Plans Return to Its Roots," *New York Times*, March 20, 2008; Barbara Kiviat, "Starbucks Looks for a Fresh Jolt," *Time*, March 27, 2008; Brad Stone, "Original Team Tries to Revive Starbucks," *New York Times*, October 30, 2008; and Sara Kiesler, "Neighbor: Starbucks Stole My Ambience," SeattlePI.com, July 16, 2009; Susan Berfield, "Starbucks: Howard Schultz vs. Howard Schultz," *BusinessWeek*, August 6, 2009; Barbara Kiviat, "Starbucks Can Smell Growth," *Time*, January 21, 2010; Claire Cain Miller, "Now at Starbucks: A Rebound," *New York Times*, January 21, 2010.

The *No Logo* quote about garish decor is found on p. 131, and the anecdote about the Vancouver union is on p. 241.

There are a lot of sources of information about fair trade. I particularly relied on *Rough Guide* (cited above), pp. 23–24, and the website of TransFair USA (http://transfairusa.org). The specifics about price premiums came from Fred Pearce, *Confessions of an Eco-Sinner: Tracking Down the Sources of My Stuff* (Boston: Beacon Press, 2008), p. 22, and Ezra Fieser, "What Price for Good Coffee?" *Time*, October 5, 2009, p. 61. The later quotes from *Eco-Sinner* are from p. 23.

Two *Wall Street Journal* articles in particular discussed the attempt at Japanese-style production: Julie Jargon, "Latest Starbucks Buzzword: 'Lean' Japanese Techniques," August 4, 2009, and Julie Jargon, "At Starbucks, Baristas Told No More Than Two Drinks," October 13, 2010.

The information about loans to small businesses and job-creation partnerships is from "Howard's Way," *Economist*, October 8–14, 2011.

The *Wall Street Journal* article about unionizing efforts in Europe, New Zealand, and Chile is Julie Jargon's "Starbucks Workers Plan Chile Strike," July 11, 2011.

A few examples of Howard Schultz being photographed with paper cups—and I am limiting this to examples from after the publication of his second book, to give him the benefit of a raised eco-consciousness: photos accompanying the articles Julie Jargon, "Coffee Talk: Starbucks Chief on Prices, Mc-

Donald's Rivalry," *Wall Street Journal*, March 7, 2011; John H. Ostdick, "Heart of the Brand," *Success*, April 2011, p. 44; and Howard Schultz, "How Starbucks Got Its Mojo Back," *Newsweek* book excerpt, March 31, 2011, p. 50.

The book by Stacy Mitchell is *Big-Box Swindle: The True Cost of Mega-Retailers* (Boston: Beacon Press, 2006), p. 91.

The *Shoptimism* quote is from p. 178.

The Mayo Clinic reference is from its website (http://www.mayoclinic .com/), particularly the articles "Caffeine Content for Coffee, Tea, Soda, and More" and "Caffeine: How Much Is Too Much?"

The Morgan Stanley data on Starbucks's customers' income is from John Jannarone, "Grounds for Concern at Starbucks," *Wall Street Journal*, May 3, 2011.

The calculations about how much you'd save by skipping a latte are adapted from an online retirement-plan calculator from Fidelity Investments.

CHAPTER 4. APPLE: THE COOLEST OF THEM ALL

The history and general information about Apple and Steve Jobs come mainly from the following books and articles: *iCon* (cited above); Owen W. Linzmayer, *Apple Confidential 2.0: The Definitive History of the World's Most Colorful Company* (San Francisco: No Starch Press, 2004); *Fortune* magazine's cover package "CEO of the Decade," November 23, 2009; Stephen Fry, "On the Mothership: A Confessed Apple Fanboy Gets Finger Time with the iPad—and Face Time with Steve Jobs," *Time*, April 12, 2010, p. 40; Farhad Manjoo, "Invincible Apple: 10 Lessons from the Coolest Company Anywhere," *Fast Company*, July–August 2010; Randall Stross, "What Steve Jobs Learned in the Wilderness," *New York Times*, October 2, 2010; and Leander Kahney, "Being Steve Jobs' Boss," *Bloomberg Businessweek*, October 24, 2010. And for a little insight into Jobs's personality, I read Daniel Lyons, *Options: The Secret Life of Steve Jobs* (Cambridge, MA: Da Capo Press, 2007).

But, of course, I also perused dozens of other articles in my research for this chapter, some of which are cited below in connection with specific topics. News events such as problems with the iPhone antenna, suicides at the Foxconn factory in China, and Steve Jobs's resignation have been widely reported.

The specific quotes from *iCon* are (in the order in which they're quoted) from pp. 235, 282, and 236; and the information about the Jobs family's political activity is on pp. 254–55.

The particular quotes from the Linzmayer book are (also in quote order) from pp. 295 and 298.

The Daniel Lyons quote is from "In iPad We Trust," *Newsweek*, February 8, 2010.

The reference to British prime minister David Cameron is from Catherine Mayer, "Reshaping British Politics from Within," *Time*, November 8, 2010.

The interview with Melinda Gates is Deborah Solomon, "The Donor," *New York Times Magazine*, October 22, 2010.

The iPod is a character in Arthur Phillips, *This Song Is You* (New York: Random House, 2009).

The reference to the branding consultants who studied the brain activity of Apple users is from Martin Lindstrom, "You Love Your iPhone, Literally," *New York Times*, October 1, 2011.

The *Fortune* "Business Person of the Year" ranking was in the issue dated January 10, 2011.

The Steve Jobs accolades come from the following: "The World's Most Influential People," *Time*, May 10, 2010; "27 Brave Thinkers," *Atlantic*, November 2009, "Brave Thinkers 2011," *Atlantic*, November 2011; "The 400 Richest Americans," *Forbes*, September 30, 2009 (although Jobs has made the list in other years as well); and "CEO of the Decade," cited above. And then, when Jobs announced his resignation, the *New York Times* quote is from Andrew Ross Sorkin, "The Mystery of Jobs's Public Giving," August 30, 2011.

The quote about secrecy in the product testing room is from Brad Stone and Ashlee Vance, "Apple Obsessed with Secrecy on Products and Top Executives," *New York Times*, June 23, 2009.

Jeffrey Sonnenfeld's comment is from "The Genius Dilemma," *Newsweek*, January 31, 2011, p. 12.

The article citing Jerome York is Joann S. Lublin and Scott Thurm, "Mum on Succession, Board Got Heat," *Wall Street Journal*, August 25, 2011.

The information about the CalPERS official asking the SEC to require more disclosure about CEO health came from Joann S. Lublin, "Investors Want Right to Know," *Wall Street Journal*, January 24, 2011.

Many, many stories have been written about Apple's obsessive micromanagement and its all-in-one business model. For the specific references to the rejected apps and the new guidelines, I used the following: Ryan Singel, "Now Apple Bans Tiger Woods Satire App. Does Big Media Care?" Wired.com, April 27, 2010; Joshua Brustein, "Apple's Struggle on Political Apps," *New York Times*, May 31, 2010; Jeff Bercovici, "Dirty Apps? How Magazines Are Handling Apple's Erratic Censorship," *Daily Finance*, August 11, 2010; Yukari Iwatani Kane and Thomas Catan, "Apple Blinks in Apps Fight," *Wall Street Journal*, September 10, 2010; and Jenna Wortham, "Apple Plays to App Developers by Revealing Its Policy Guidelines," *New York Times*, September 10, 2010. Also, the quote about the Faustian bargain is from Daniel Lyons, "Think Really Different," *Newsweek*, April 5, 2010, p. 46.

The rare inside look at working at Apple is from Adam Lashinsky, "Inside Apple," *Fortune*, May 23, 2011, p. 124.

The *Wall Street Journal* describes training at the Apple Stores in Yukari Iwatani Kane and Ian Sherr, "Secrets from Genius Bar: Full Loyalty, No Negativity," June 15, 2011.

The interview with the Wintek workers is from David Barboza, "Workers Poisoned at Chinese Factory Wait for Apple to Fulfill a Pledge," *New York Times*, February 23, 2011.

The formation of the Eco-Patent Commons was mentioned in Mary Tripsas, "Everybody in the Pool of Green Innovation," *New York Times*, November 1, 2009.

The interview with Steve Jobs about environmental issues was from Peter Burrows, "Apple Launches Major Green Effort," *BusinessWeek*, October 5, 2009, p. 68.

The *Atlantic* cover story about the global elite is Chrystia Freeland, "The Rise of the New Global Elite," *Atlantic*, January–February 2011, p. 44.

The discussion about Apple taking advantage of bulk discounts on iPad components was in Jenna Wortham, "So Far Rivals Can't Beat iPad's Price," *New York Times*, March 7, 2011.

Of course, numerous articles have been written about the impact of the iPad on publishing, but here are the three examples specifically cited in which experts predicted the tablet could save books and newspapers: David Carr, "A Savior in the Form of a Tablet," *New York Times*, January 4, 2010; Walter Isaacson, "Information Wants to Be Paid For," *Atlantic*, July–August 2010, p. 47; and "'iPads Will Save Newspapers,' Says Unilever CMO," *Marketing*, October 13, 2010.

I read about the accidental social benefits of iPads in two articles: Jennifer Valentino DeVries, "Using the iPad to Connect," *Wall Street Journal*, October 13, 2010; and Winnie Hu, "Math That Moves: Schools Embrace the iPad," *New York Times*, January 5, 2011.

The quote describing Timothy Cook is from Miguel Helft, "The Understudy Takes the Stage," *New York Times*, January 24, 2011.

CHAPTER 5. TRADER JOE'S: ARE WE HAVING FUN YET?

The reference to the Brooklyn shopper is from Anthony Ramirez, "A Tiki Room with Aisles of Discounts Makes Its City Debut," *New York Times*, March 18, 2006.

For the Albany reference, Chriss Churchill, "Trendsetter Shops Bypass Region," (Albany, NY) *Times Union*, May 11, 2008.

All the *Fortune* references are from Beth Kowitt, "Inside the Secret World of Trader Joe's," *Fortune*, September 13, 2010.

Here are the references from Len Lewis, *The Trader Joe's Adventure: Turning a Unique Approach to Business into a Retail and Cultural Phenomenon* (Chicago: Dearborn, 2005): the history of the name, p. 3; the lack of philanthropy, p. 187; Charles Shaw complaint, p. 123; and about labor costs, p. 145. The "Best Companies" claim is made several times, but the specific quote is on p. ix; the starting salaries are on pp. 143–44; and the two demographic descriptions are on pp. 112 and 72, respectively.

From *The Rough Guide to Shopping with a Conscience* (cited above), pp. 156–57.

Theo Albrecht's obituary was written by Patrick Donahue and Holger Elfes in *Bloomberg Businessweek*, August 2, 2010.

The unionizing attempts were mentioned in *Trader Joe's Adventures* (p. 143) and *The Rough Guide to Shopping with a Conscience* (p. 157).

The *Atlantic* article is Don Peck, "Can the Middle Class Be Saved?" September 2011, p. 60.

The description of the tasting-panel members traveling the world is from Julia Moskin, "For Trader Joe's, a New York Taste Test," *New York Times*, March 8, 2006.

CHAPTER 6. AMERICAN APPAREL: SEX AND THE T-SHIRT

Almost any book or article you pick up will cite a different country, year, or methodology for calculating pay rates and weekly hours worked in foreign sweatshops. I took some examples from the following books and newspaper articles: *Confessions of an Eco-Sinner*, cited above (pp. 102–3); my book *The Overloaded Liberal*, cited above (p. 146); Vikas Bajaj, "As Labor Costs Rise in China, Textile Jobs Shift Elsewhere," *New York Times*, July 15, 2010; Steven Greenhouse, "A Factory Defies Stereotypes, but Can It Thrive?" *New York Times*, July 18, 2010; Vikas Bajaj and Julfikar Ali Manik, "Bangladesh Arrests 21 After Rallies," *New York Times*, August 17, 2010; Patrick Barta and Alex Frangos, "Southeast Asia Linking Up to Compete with China," *Wall Street Journal*, August 23, 2010; and Wayne Arnold, "Vietnam Holds Its Own Within China's Vast Economic Shadow," *New York Times*, January 1, 2011.

Regarding Fred Pearce's and Nicholas Kristof's arguments about the relative advantages of sweatshops: Pearce's comments come from his book *Confessions of an Eco-Sinner*. Kristof has written extensively about these topics in the *New York Times*, so I'll cite just one example: "Where Sweatshops Are a Dream," January 15, 2009.

The *BusinessWeek* quote is from Christopher Palmeri, "Living on the Edge at American Apparel," June 27, 2005.

The *Portfolio* quote is from Claire Hoffman, "Barely Legal," November 2008, p. 114.

The particular citations in the ISO report (cited above) begin on p. 31.

The sentiments about moving work offshore are in Allison Abell Schwartz, "American Apparel's Unhip Finances," *BusinessWeek*, August 9, 2010.

Regarding the ICE investigation of American Apparel, the lawyer's explanation and the politicians' comments were reported in several news stories, including Julia Preston, "A New Strategy on Illicit Work by Immigrants," *New York Times*, July 3, 2009, and Julia Preston, "Immigrant Crackdown Leads to 1,800 Pink Slips," *New York Times*, September 20, 2009. The number of layoffs was later recalculated by the company.

Rob Walker discussed the supposed changes in American Apparel's marketing on pp. 223–26 of *Buying In*.

The Eisenberg reference is from p. 52 of the above-cited book *Shoptimism*.

For the specific American Apparel and other ads in the various magazines, here are the dates and page numbers: *Harper's Bazaar*, September 2009, pp. 2 and 213; *Marie Claire*, January 2010, p. 67; *Seventeen*, December 2009–January 2010, p. 21; *Teen Vogue*, March 2010, pp. 4–5, 41, 47, and the Jimmy Choo insert between p. 42 and p. 43. In the case of the *Onion*, it's always the back page: February 25–March 3, March 11–17, March 25–31, April 8–14, April 22–28, and June 3–9, all in 2010. There isn't space to list all the rest of the publications I looked at—and, really, you could probably pick up any issue of the named magazines and find the same thing.

The reference to Abercrombie & Fitch's marketing is from David Carr, "A Naked Calculation Gone Bad," *New York Times*, January 24, 2011.

As the chapter notes, numerous publications have discussed the allegations of sexual harassment and a sexually charged workplace at American Apparel. To name just the ones specifically quoted: Claudine Ko, "Meet Your New Boss," *Jane*, June–July 2004; the *Portfolio* article "Barely Legal," cited above; and the book *Buying In* (pp. 217, 225–26), cited above. As well, I have read the complaints filed by Nikky Yang, Bernhard-Axel Ingo Brake, and Roberto Hernandez.

Again, many of the sources cited above talk about the history of American Apparel and about Dov Charney and his operating style, including "Barely Legal," in *Portfolio*; "Living on the Edge at American Apparel," in *BusinessWeek*; and "Meet Your New Boss," in *Jane*; plus pp. 218–20 of *Buying In*. On the American Apparel website (http://www.americanapparel.net/), go to "About Us," then "Meet Dov Charney," then "My Name Is Dov Charney."

The Gawker.com posting about the employee-grooming memos was reported on *New York* magazine's website (http://www.nymag.com/) on June 18, 2010, under the headline "Revealed in Remarkable Detail: American Apparel's Beauty Guidelines."

The allegations against attorney Keith Fink have been covered in numerous publications, including Saabira Chaudhuri, "American Apparel Aims to Bring Down 'Celebrity Ambulance Chasing' Lawyer," FastCompany.com, December

1, 2008; "The Story Behind American Apparel's Sham Arbitration," *Wall Street Journal* online, November 4, 2008; and James Covert, "Suits Fly at American Apparel," *New York Post*, December 2, 2008.

The *Rough Guide to Shopping with a Conscience* reference is from p. 193.

The company's financial troubles have been discussed in many news articles, but the specific interview with Charney about the 2011 bankruptcy warning is from the online post by Matt Townsend, "American Apparel Glamour Fades Amid Cash Crunch" Bloomberg.com, April 1, 2011. Other good sources: Laura M. Holson, "He's Only Just Begun to Fight," *New York Times*, April 14, 2011; Matt Townsend, "American Apparel Gets Adult Supervision," *Bloomberg Businessweek*, April 18–24, 2011, p. 21; and "American Apparel Gets up to $43M in Rescue Financing, Avoiding Bankruptcy," *New York Post*, April 21, 2011.

Rob Walker's praise of industry veteran Marty Baily is from p. 224 of the above-cited *Buying In.*

Finally, the teenagers named in this article were interviewed with the permission of their parents.

CHAPTER 7. THE REALITY

Frito-Lay's plan for healthier junk food was reported in Mike Esterl, "You Put What in This Chip?" *Wall Street Journal*, March 24, 2011.

The quotes from *Green Marketing* (cited above) are from pp. 119 and 46, respectively.

Michael Pollan's book is *The Omnivore's Dilemma: A Natural History of Four Meals* (New York: Penguin, 2006), pp. 135, 140.

The University of Missouri survey is Jung Ha-Brookshire and Gargi Bhaduri, "Do Transparent Business Practices Pay? Exploration of Transparency and Consumer Purchase Intention," *Clothing and Textile Research Journal* 29, no. 2 (April 2011): 135–49.

The details about the Fairtrade Labelling Organizations International came from *The Rough Guide to Shopping with a Conscience* (cited above), pp. 25–26 and 143.

The "Best Places" citation about Timberland is from Robert Levering and Milton Moskowitz, "The 100 Best Companies to Work For," *Fortune*, January 12, 2004, p. 56.

The article on Dov Seidman is Richard McGill Murphy, "Why Doing Good Is Good for Business," *Fortune*, February 8, 2010, p. 90.

The quotes from Robert B. Reich, *Supercapitalism: The Transformation of Business, Democracy, and Everyday Life* (New York: Knopf, 2007), are on p. 127.

The Howard Schultz quote about fulfilling a need is from p. 251 of *Onward.*

The information about Forever 21 is from Susan Berfield, "Forever 21's Fast (and Loose) Fashion Empire," *Bloomberg Businessweek*, January 24, 2011.